DNS Security

DNS Security
Defending the Domain Name System

Allan Liska

Geoffrey Stowe

Timothy Gallo, Technical Editor

ELSEVIER

AMSTERDAM • BOSTON • HEIDELBERG • LONDON
NEW YORK • OXFORD • PARIS • SAN DIEGO
SAN FRANCISCO • SINGAPORE • SYDNEY • TOKYO
Syngress is an imprint of Elsevier

SYNGRESS.

Syngress is an imprint of Elsevier
50 Hampshire Street, 5th Floor, Cambridge, MA 02139, USA

Notices
Knowledge and best practice in this field are constantly changing. As new research and experience
broaden our understanding, changes in research methods, professional practices, or medical treatment
may become necessary.

Practitioners and researchers must always rely on their own experience and knowledge in evaluating
and using any information, methods, compounds, or experiments described herein. In using such
information or methods they should be mindful of their own safety and the safety of others, including
parties for whom they have a professional responsibility.

To the fullest extent of the law, neither the Publisher nor the authors, contributors, or editors,
assume any liability for any injury and/or damage to persons or property as a matter of products
liability, negligence or otherwise, or from any use or operation of any methods, products, instructions,
or ideas contained in the material herein.

British Library Cataloguing-in-Publication Data
A catalogue record for this book is available from the British Library

Library of Congress Cataloging-in-Publication Data
A catalog record for this book is available from the Library of Congress

ISBN: 978-0-12-803306-7

For Information on all Syngress publications
visit our website at http://www.elsevier.com

Working together
to grow libraries in
developing countries

www.elsevier.com • www.bookaid.org

Publisher: Todd Green
Acquisition Editor: Chris Katsaropoulos
Editorial Project Manager: Anna Valutkevich
Production Project Manager: Punithavathy Govindaradjane
Designer: Matthew Limbert

Typeset by MPS Limited, Chennai, India

Dedication

To Kris and Bruce, as always thank you for your support during the research and writing process, love you both!

Allan Liska

To Katie and Murphy.

Geoffrey Stowe

Contents

About the Authors

Allan Liska is a Consulting Systems Engineer at FireEye Inc. and an "accidental" security expert. While Allan has always been good at breaking things, he got his start professionally working as a customer service representative at GEnie Online Services (a long defunct early competitor to AOL), where he would spend his off hours figuring out how users had gain unauthorized access to the system, booting them off, and letting the developers know what needed to be patched. Unknowingly, this was leading him down the path of becoming a security professional. Since then he has work at companies like UUNET, Symantec, and iSIGHT Partners helping companies better secure their networks. He has also worked at Boeing trying to break into those company networks.

In addition to his time spent on both sides of the security divide Allan has written extensively on security including *The Practice of Network Security* and *Building an Intelligence-Led Security Program*. He was also a contributing author to *Apache Administrator's Handbook*.

Geoffrey Stowe lives in San Francisco and is an Engineering Lead at Palantir Technologies. His network security work has included vulnerability research, reverse engineering, incident response, and anomaly detection. There was a time when he could translate byte code to assembly without looking at a manual. Geoff started Palantir's commercial business in 2010 and built its first platforms for distributed, large-scale data analysis. He graduated from Dartmouth College with a degree in computer science.

Acknowledgments

Allan Liska would like to acknowledge the following people: First and foremost, I have to acknowledge the great work that my coauthor, Geoff Stowe, and our technical editor, Tim Gallo, did to make this book a reality. The idea for this book came to me several years ago and I struggled to bring it into focus. Tim and Geoff were great for bouncing ideas off, calling me out when I missed things and, in general, making this book much better. The book would not have been finished without the two of you. Geoff, I especially appreciate your enthusiasm for the topic and the absolutely fantastic writing you did.

I also need to thank Anna Valutkevich, our project manager at Elsevier. I appreciate you pushing to make this project work, especially as I fell behind. I also appreciate you working with Geoff to bring him onboard and get him up to speed quickly.

Of course, this book also would not have been done without the great support from colleagues from a wide range of companies, who all contributed their thoughts and answered my questions throughout. I want to give special shout out to the analyst teams at iSIGHT Partners and FireEye, JJ Guy and the team at Carbon Black, Arnie Bjorklund and the team at SecurityZones, Sean Blenkhorn and the team at eSentire, and Sean Murphy for your early thoughts on the book.

Finally, I want to thank all of the people who volunteer their time to keep the DNS infrastructure together and protected from everyone who wants to tear it down. People who help write RFCs, contribute to working groups, create tools that others can freely use, and so much more. Thank you for your contributions!

Geoffrey Stowe would like to add his appreciation for Allan Liska pioneering the book and giving me the chance to write about a fascinating topic. Allan, Tim, and Anna are true professionals, and working with them was a wonderful experience. I would also like to thank Drew Dennison, Miles Seiver, and Dane Stuckey from Palantir for providing ideas and feedback. And of course, the support from my wife Katie and son Murphy made everything possible.

Understanding DNS

1

INFORMATION IN THIS CHAPTER

- DNS History
- The Root
- Recursive and Authoritative Services
- Zone Files
- Resource Records

INTRODUCTION

Prior to discussing ways to secure DNS infrastructure, it is important to understand what DNS is, and what needs to be secured. DNS has traditionally been an afterthought at many organizations. Often times initialization and maintenance of an organization's DNS infrastructure falls to the people responsible for the setting up and patching webservers, or configuring and managing the network devices. They are frequently untrained on the intricacies of DNS and are reliant upon information they can glean from various web sources some of which are great and others well, not so much.

From a security perspective, this can be extremely problematic. How can someone be expected to effectively secure a solution they do not understand? Simply put they cannot, without sound understanding of the principles, an administrator cannot be expected to comprehend the nuances associated with securing the system, let alone keeping up with and realizing the risks posed by the volume of vulnerabilities published on this topic alone annually. Given the large number of DNS vulnerabilities published every year and the number of ways an administrator can expose a DNS infrastructure to attack, it is imperative that those who manage DNS installations understand the principles behind DNS, in order to be able to properly secure those installations.

The best place to start is by defining DNS. The acronym DNS stands for Domain Name System, although some use DNS to refer to Domain Name Servers. DNS is a redundant, hierarchical, distributed database that is used to pass information about domain names. The acronym disagreement demonstrates the difficulty anyone would have in documenting DNS. If people cannot even agree

DNS Security. DOI: http://dx.doi.org/10.1016/B978-0-12-803306-7.00001-2

on what the acronym stands for how can they agree on anything else? As you progress through this book, you will note that DNS administrators rarely agree on anything.

The metaphor most often used to describe DNS is a tree. DNS has a root, and the various Top Level Domains (TLDs) are similar to branches that shoot off the root. Each branch has smaller branches, which are Second Level Domains, and the leaves are Fully Qualified Domain Names (FQDNs), sometimes referred to as hostnames. Do not get the idea that this tree is a peaceful Palm Tree or a strong Oak. This is a monstrosity of a tree, planted in cement with roots ensnarling each other and branches spread in every direction, that often feels like it is held together by force of will more than anything else. If DNS is a tree, it is more like the Banyan Tree, in Lahaina, Maui. The Banyan was 8 ft tall when it was first planted in 1873 now it is more than 60 ft tall and it has spread over 2/3 of an acre. Much like DNS, the Banyan Tree has grown so large by dropping new roots from its branches, those roots go on to become new trunks in the Banyan Tree. The complete flow of a DNS query from workstation to response is outlined in Fig. 1.1.

DNS is not only important to the functionality of the Internet, but also important to the functionality of almost any reasonably sized organization. A poorly configured DNS server can impact an entire organization and a poorly secured DNS server or Domain provides an attacker an easy opening into an organization's network. Even if an organization is properly protected, DNS can still be used as an attack vector against an organization.

This chapter covers the basics of DNS—it is designed as a very high level overview of the DNS process and does not get overly bogged down in details. Starting with the beginnings of the DNS it then moves onto the root system, details the different types of DNS servers, and reviews how DNS servers speak to each other, and what type of information is communicated between servers.

DNS HISTORY

When most people think of Internet luminaries Bill Gates, Steve Jobs, Marc Andreessen, and Mark Zuckerberg come to mind. Certainly these people have made great contributions to the progression of the Internet (or its downfall, depending on who you ask), but there are a whole group of people whose impact has been much more profound. These contributions did not necessarily result in multimillion dollar Initial Public Offerings (IPOs), but without them the Internet would not be what it is today.

THE HOSTS.TXT FILE

The Internet is sometimes compared to an organism. Like any organism it evolves over time and also like an organism it leaves traces of its former existence behind.

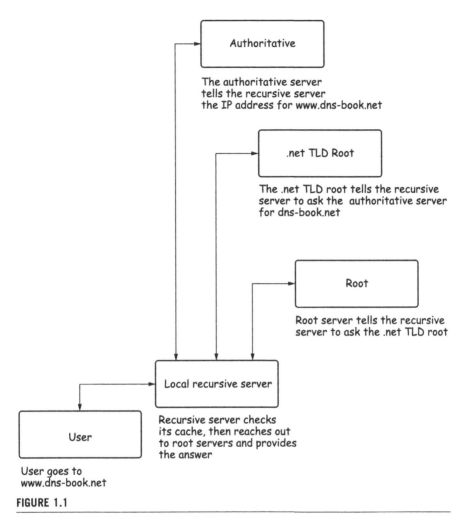

FIGURE 1.1

A stylized version of the traffic flow of a DNS query.

In this case remnant of the precursor to DNS, the hosts.txt file, is still found on many systems.

To understand why DNS became necessary, take a look at the file */etc/hosts* on UNIX systems or *%systemroot%\system32\drivers\etc\hosts.txt* in Microsoft Windows or the *hosts.txt* file on Android devices. The format of all these files is the same:

```
IP Address  Computer Name  Comment
```

These files are used to map IP Addresses to hostnames, in other words they serve the same function that DNS does. These files were the precursor to DNS.

Prior to the introduction of DNS, the host file was used as the primary method of sharing data about hostnames.

Two events helped bring about the birth of the host file. In December of 1973, and outlined in conjunction with RFC 592, an "official" host naming convention was established. Numbers, letters, and dashes were the only characters allowed in hostnames, parentheses were allowed as part of network names.

Once the list of hostnames (all 81 of them!) had been gathered, the next step came with RFC 606 and RFC 608. These RFCs outline the creation of a new centralized file, called HOSTS.TXT, which could be downloaded via FTP so that all administrators connected to the ARPANET would have the same data regarding hostnames.

It is interesting to note that while this idea makes a lot of sense in retrospect, the author of RFC 606, L. Peter Deutsch, felt compelled to add the following disclaimer:

> I realize that there is a time-honored pitfall associated with suggestions such as the present one: it represents a specific solution to a specific problem, and as such may not be compatible with or form a reasonable basis for more general solutions to more general problems. However, (1) this particular problem has been irking me and others I have spoken to for well over a year, and it is really absurd that it should have gone unsolved this Long; (2) no one seems particularly interested in solving any more general problem.

The first hosts.txt file went online March 25, 1974 and was announced by RFC 627. Prior the release of the first hosts.txt file, another DNS institution was introduced. RFC 623 and RFC 625 discussed placing the hosts.txt file on an additional server. If the primary server, OFFICE-1, was unavailable, a host could retrieve the file from the secondary server. Again, this is very similar to the way DNS works today.

MAIL PROBLEMS

ARPANET continued in this manner for more than a decade. As more organizations connected to this Internet, it became obvious that there were some issues with this system, particularly when it came to most commonly used application: Computer Mail.

The problem with computer mail was that too many people were using the system, so it became difficult for postmasters to manage mail messages. The format of mail addresses was based on the addresses in the host file. So, if someone wanted to send a message to Allan Liska at Example Corp, the format would be something along the lines of liska@example or aliska@example. This is fine, as long as there is only one computer to which users at the originating organization are connected. But ARPANET was growing in popularity, and computer users were not isolated to one department or even to one campus. There were ARPANET users spread out across organizations and in multiple locations.

As the popularity of ARPANET increased postmasters we having to add mail servers in multiple locations. Each one would have to be assigned a unique hostname, which would then have to be added to the hosts.txt file. If Allan Liska is located at Example Corp's Virginia office, a hostname for that office would have to be created. Instead of sending mail to liska@example, it would have to be sent to liska@exampleva. On the other hand, if Bruce Liska was in Example Corp's California office, mail would have to be sent to liska@exampleca. This could create a tremendous amount of confusion—if the sender was not sure what office a person was located in, or what the various naming conventions were it was very easy to misaddress mail.

This created a problem that postmasters had to deal with. After all, once a person has been exposed to electronic mail, he cannot be deprived of it. On January 11, 1982 a meeting was held to discuss this mail problem, among others, and to develop a solution. Some of the people in attendance at the meeting included Vint Cerf, Bill Joy, Dave Crocker, Paul Mockapetris, David Mills, and of course Jon Postel.

The results of the meeting were published as RFC 805 "Computer Mail Meeting Notes." The banal title masks the importance that this document had on DNS. The solution proposed during the meeting was a combination of an addition to the current mail format and the incorporation of "Internet Domain Names" proposed by David L. Mills in RFC 799.

The basic proposal was that the format of the electronic mail address system would have to be expanded by adding two levels, called nodes, to the current address scheme. In addition to "address" at "host," the proposal would add the nodes organization and domain to the address. In the example above, if you wanted to send mail to Allan Liska at Example Corp the format would shift to "address" at "hostname" node separator "company" node separator "domain," for example, allan@mailserver.example.in (.in for an Internet Address).

This system would make it a lot easier for geographically dispersed organizations to manage mail for users. Addresses could be broken down geographically. If someone wanted to send mail to Allan Liska at Example Corp's Virginia office, the address could be allan@va.example.in; on the other hand, Bruce Liska in the California office would be something like bruce@ca.example.in. Obviously, this would give organizations a lot more freedom and make life easier for mail administrators. Of course, it also meant having to rewrite mail programs so they could handle multiple nodes.

In March of 1982 the first HOSTNAMES server came online. This server did not support domain queries. It was primarily used to share information about Networks, Gateways, and Hosts, but it used the same format the domain queries would eventually follow.

RFC 819 AND 920

RFC 819 marks a major leap forward in domain evolution; it outlines the domain structure and laid out a foundation for a DNS infrastructure. Jon Postel and

Zaw-Sing Su wrote RFC 819, entitled "The Domain Naming Convention for Internet User Applications" and released it in August of 1982.

The RFC is really a framework for a DNS infrastructure. It does not focus on the specifics, allowing those to be filled in by others. This is one of the great things about the DNS protocol: it has always been less rigid than other protocols, making it very adaptable to change. This flexibility also makes DNS a target for those who develop standards. They often want to create new extensions within DNS or attempt to use the protocol in ways for which it was never intended.

On the surface, the next year was quiet, in terms of DNS—the framework set out in RFC 819 was being refined and molded. In 1983 three RFCS were released in rapid succession. RFC 881, RFC 882, and RFC 883 laid out the framework for the current DNS infrastructure. These RFCs shaped the way DNS works today. RFC 882 and RFC 883, written by Paul Mockapetris, were especially important because they discussed the way DNS lookups would be performed and they provided an overview of delegation, which is the hallmark of DNS and one of the reasons DNS has been so successful.

Once discussion of the DNS design had finished—which took almost another year—RFC 920 was released. RFC 920, released in October 1984, laid out the requirements for actually implementing DNS ARPANET-wide and what steps would have to be taken. RFC 920 also finalized the initial list of TLDs: ARPANET (which was to be a temporary TLD), .GOV, .MIL, .EDU, .COM, .ORG and the two-letter country code domains.

Those involved in initial creation of DNS wanted to get it set up quickly, and RRC 920 outlined a fast pace. From the release of RFC 920 everything was ready to be launched and new domains registered within 6 months. In fact, the first non-TLD domain registered was NORDU.NET on January 1, 1985.[1] The Defense Information Systems Agency, which now controlled ARPANET, awarded the maintenance of the root infrastructure to the Stanford Research Institute and the modern DNS infrastructure was born.

ON TO COMMERCIALIZATION

DNS proceeded pretty much unchanged for the next several years. In October of 1992 the National Science Foundation (NSF)—or more specifically NSFNet, which had taken ownership of ARPANET in 1986—awarded a management services contract to Network Solutions Inc. This was huge change as it moved control of DNS from the, largely, academic community to the private sector.

Up until 1995 anyone who wanted a domain name was able to register one. As more people saw the commercial value in the Internet, some began registering hundreds of domains, thinking that they might be valuable in the future. To stop the spread of this practice, and to recoup some of the costs of maintaining the DNS infrastructure, Network Solutions, with the approval of the NSF, began charging a fee to register domain names. The initial fee was $100 for 2 years, with $30 of that money going to support the Internet infrastructure.

This coincided with the ideas of the US government at the time, which had a mandate to privatize and increase competition on the Internet. The Department of Commerce was especially interested in DNS and had solicited comments from the public about ways to help them fulfill President Clinton's mandate.

In 1998 the government released a paper outlining moving control of DNS from the exclusive domain of Network Solutions to an independent organization that would foster competition and encourage further use of the Internet. From this paper, the Internet Corporation for Assigned Names and Numbers (ICANN) was eventually born.

ICANN took over the management of the root name servers in 1999 and opened up the registration process. Companies meeting a set of requirements are allowed to register domains on behalf of the general public. These domains are entered in the various TLD databases and all ICANN-approved registrars are able to register the Generic TLDs.

THE ROOT

The heart of the DNS is the root, or more appropriately, the multiple roots. The root systems maintain authoritative data about domains and help direct requests to the proper servers. There are two different types of root servers that are used in DNS: the root servers and the TLD roots.

Generally, when people talk about root servers, they are referring to the root servers queried by recursive name servers (discussed in the next section). The 13 root name servers are dispersed around the world, maintained by different organizations and are on different networks.

In addition to the root name servers, each TLD also has its own root server or servers. This root server is authoritative for information about the specific TLD, the root server of a domain is the top node in the domain tree and is represented by a "." which trails the domain name. The trailing "." is generally not displayed outside the realm of DNS, but it is important to remember it is there. So, the domain example.com is properly presented as:

```
example.com.
```

The TLD root servers are not queried directly. Instead, the root servers direct queries to these servers as requests are processed. Obviously, this makes the functioning of the root name servers critical to the continued operation of the Internet. If the root name servers were taken off-line typical Internet communication would eventually stop. This is not to say that all communication on the Internet would stop, routing and other services that do not rely on DNS would continue functioning as expected. But services like mail, FTP, and HTTP would quickly become unusable as they rely so heavily on DNS.

ATTACKS ON THE ROOT NAMESERVERS

In late October of 2002 what was at the time the larger ever recorded Distributed Denial of Service (DDoS) attack was launched against the root name servers, in an attempt to make the Internet unusable. Fortunately, most users were oblivious to this disruption—a sign that DNS is as resilient as it is advertised to be.

In February of 2007 another major DDoS attack was launched against the Root DNS servers, while two of the servers were temporarily crippled, the other Root Servers continued to respond to queries.

Anonymous threatened to take down the Root DNS servers on March 31, 2012. The attack was completely unsuccessful.

One of the primary goals in setting up and maintaining the root servers is availability. DNS needs to be redundant and highly available, so the root servers have to be highly available. To that end, they are dispersed around the world, placed on different backbones, and maintained by different organizations.

The root servers all share the same naming convention: their designated letter followed by the domain root-servers.org. The first is a.root-servers.org, the second is b.root-servers.org, and so on. These servers are among the busiest on the Internet. F.root-servers.org—arguably the busiest—handles more than 270 million queries a day, although it is built to handle significantly more.

A common misconception held is that the A root server is more critical to the DNS infrastructure than the other root servers. That is not the case, all of the root name servers share load equally, and all of the root servers contain the same information about the TLD roots.

```
;     This file holds the information on root name servers needed to
;     initialize cache of Internet domain name servers
;     (e.g. reference this file in the "cache . <file>"
;     configuration file of BIND domain name servers).
;
;     This file is made available by InterNIC
;     under anonymous FTP as
;         file              /domain/named.cache
;         on server         FTP.INTERNIC.NET
;     -OR-                   RS.INTERNIC.NET
;
;     last update:  November 05, 2014
;     related version of root zone:  2014110501
;
; formerly NS.INTERNIC.NET
;
.                           3600000   NS    A.ROOT-SERVERS.NET.
A.ROOT-SERVERS.NET.         3600000   A     198.41.0.4
A.ROOT-SERVERS.NET.         3600000   AAAA  2001:503:ba3e::2:30
;
```

```
; FORMERLY NS1.ISI.EDU
;
.                         3600000    NS     B.ROOT-SERVERS.NET.
B.ROOT-SERVERS.NET.       3600000    A      192.228.79.201
B.ROOT-SERVERS.NET.       3600000    AAAA   2001:500:84::b
;
; FORMERLY C.PSI.NET
;
.                         3600000    NS     C.ROOT-SERVERS.NET.
C.ROOT-SERVERS.NET.       3600000    A      192.33.4.12
C.ROOT-SERVERS.NET.       3600000    AAAA   2001:500:2::c
;
; FORMERLY TERP.UMD.EDU
;
.                         3600000    NS     D.ROOT-SERVERS.NET.
D.ROOT-SERVERS.NET.       3600000    A      199.7.91.13
D.ROOT-SERVERS.NET.       3600000    AAAA   2001:500:2d::d
;
; FORMERLY NS.NASA.GOV
;
.                         3600000    NS     E.ROOT-SERVERS.NET.
E.ROOT-SERVERS.NET.       3600000    A      192.203.230.10
;
; FORMERLY NS.ISC.ORG
;
.                         3600000    NS     F.ROOT-SERVERS.NET.
F.ROOT-SERVERS.NET.       3600000    A      192.5.5.241
F.ROOT-SERVERS.NET.       3600000    AAAA   2001:500:2f::f
;
; FORMERLY NS.NIC.DDN.MIL
;
.                         3600000    NS     G.ROOT-SERVERS.NET.
G.ROOT-SERVERS.NET.       3600000    A      192.112.36.4
;
; FORMERLY AOS.ARL.ARMY.MIL
;
.                         3600000    NS     H.ROOT-SERVERS.NET.
H.ROOT-SERVERS.NET.       3600000    A      128.63.2.53
H.ROOT-SERVERS.NET.       3600000    AAAA   2001:500:1::803f:235
;
; FORMERLY NIC.NORDU.NET
;
.                         3600000    NS     I.ROOT-SERVERS.NET.
I.ROOT-SERVERS.NET.       3600000    A      192.36.148.17
I.ROOT-SERVERS.NET.       3600000    AAAA   2001:7fe::53
;
; OPERATED BY VERISIGN, INC.
;
```

```
.                           3600000   NS    J.ROOT-SERVERS.NET.
J.ROOT-SERVERS.NET.         3600000   A     192.58.128.30
J.ROOT-SERVERS.NET.         3600000   AAAA  2001:503:c27::2:30
;
; OPERATED BY RIPE NCC
;
.                           3600000   NS    K.ROOT-SERVERS.NET.
K.ROOT-SERVERS.NET.         3600000   A     193.0.14.129
K.ROOT-SERVERS.NET.         3600000   AAAA  2001:7fd::1
;
; OPERATED BY ICANN
;
.                           3600000   NS    L.ROOT-SERVERS.NET.
L.ROOT-SERVERS.NET.         3600000   A     199.7.83.42
L.ROOT-SERVERS.NET.         3600000   AAAA  2001:500:3::42
;
; OPERATED BY WIDE
;
.                           3600000   NS    M.ROOT-SERVERS.NET.
M.ROOT-SERVERS.NET.         3600000   A     202.12.27.33
M.ROOT-SERVERS.NET.         3600000   AAAA  2001:dc3::35
; End of file
```

The root servers do not contain information about every TLD available; they only share data from ICANN-approved TLDs. This includes the Generic TLDs, as well as the country-specific TLDs. There are other TLD root servers, which support "alternate" roots. These are less popular than the ICANN-approved TLDs and, because there is no data about them on the root servers, unreachable by most of the Internet.

When a new TLD is approved by ICANN, it is either a sponsored or unsponsored domain (unless it is a country code TLD, such as .us or .ca). Sponsored domains are those TLDs that are used for a specific industry such as .aero (Air Transport) or .museum (Museums). Most TLDs are not sponsored and therefore fall under control of ICANN and adhere to the rules developed through ICANN.

ICANN does not directly manage the TLDs; instead it outsources the maintenance of the TLD to various organizations for a contracted period of time. Different organizations operate different TLDs under their own sets of rules, but within the realm of the rules laid out by ICANN. So, ICANN, with feedback from the Internet community, creates a new TLD, it outsources the maintenance of that TLD to another organization. That organization manages the root server for the specific TLD and updates ICANN as information about the TLD changes.

Country Code TLDs (ccTLDs) are handled slightly different. The ccTLDs are based on the two-character designation assigned to a country by the International Organization for Standardization (ISO). The ISO maintains a document, ISO 3166-1, which lists the countries along with their two-character code.

The Internet Assigned Numbers Authority (IANA) uses that list to determine what the ccTLD for each country will be.

Aside from assigning the ccTLD to each country, IANA has nothing to do with the day-to-day operation of the ccTLDs. Each country is responsible for deciding how their ccTLD will be implemented, or even if it will. Because each country makes up its own rules about its ccTLD, the rules for registering and using ccTLD domains vary widely.

A LIST OF ALL THE CCTLDS

A complete list of the ccTLDs as well as their sponsoring organizations and other important information can be found on the IANA web site: http://www.iana.org/domains/root/db.

The ccTLDs interact with the root servers in the same manner as the Generic TLDs. The organization that maintains the ccTLD shares changes to its database with the root servers, and the root servers direct requests to the ccTLD root as appropriate.

While it is important to understand what the root servers are, and how they work, the reality is that the various root servers will have very little impact on the day-to-day operations of most DNS administrators. The root name servers, and the TLD root servers, are operated with a very high level of security and availability. Although if they were not, there would be very little an individual, or corporation, could do about it.

RECURSIVE AND AUTHORITATIVE SERVERS

Moving from the big picture to the specific, this section covers how organizations find out information about domain names and share information about their own domain names. Two different types of servers are used for these tasks: recursive servers, also called recursive servers, track down information about domains, while authoritative servers contain information about certain domains.

Recursive and authoritative servers can be separate programs, or part of the same program, and they can also be run on the same server or on different servers. This section provides a broad overview of the services.

RECURSIVE NAME SERVERS

Recursive name servers are a blank slate. They do not know anything about domain names; all they know how to do is ask questions. Their work is pretty simple: someone asks the recursive name server about a domain, the recursive name server turns around and asks another server, gets the answer and returns it to the person who originally asked.

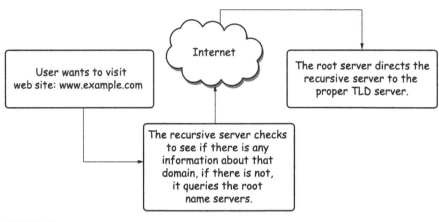

FIGURE 1.2

The recursive server process.

Recursive name servers sit either on the local network or on an Internet Service Provider's network. They can be assigned manually to each desktop, or dynamically through Dynamic Host Configuration Protocol, or a similar protocol. When someone uses an application that requires DNS, their machine sends a message to the locally configured recursive servers, the recursive servers then query root servers for information about the domain, and the root servers direct the recursive server to two or more authoritative name servers. This process is outlined in Fig. 1.2.

The process is amazingly simple, but this simplicity underlies the complexity of the service behind it. As with everything else in DNS availability is important, most network administrators assign at least two recursive DNS servers to each workstation.

A user who wants to visit www.example.com will first query the recursive name server on the workstation, which will look something like this:

```
Domain Name System (query)
    Transaction ID: 0x003e
    Flags: 0x0100 (Standard query)
    0... .... .... .... = Response: Message is a query
    .000 0... .... .... = Opcode: Standard query (0)
    .... ..0. .... .... = Truncated: Message is not truncated
    .... ...1 .... .... = Recursion desired:
    Do query recursively
    .... .... ...0 .... = Non-authenticated data OK: Non-authenticated
data is unacceptable
    Questions: 1
    Answer RRs: 0
    Authority RRs: 0
    Additional RRs: 0
```

```
Queries
www.example.com: type A, class inet
Name: www.example.com
Type: Host address
Class: inet
```

Do not worry too much about the codes, they will be explained shortly. DNS queries are sent over port 53 using the User Datagram Protocol (UDP). The workstation sends a query asking, essentially, "I'd like to know as much about example.com as possible, but I am particularly interested in an A record for www.example.com." The recursive server responds with the following information:

```
Domain Name System (response)
    Transaction ID: 0x003e
    Flags: 0x8580 (Standard query response, No error)
    1... .... .... .... = Response: Message is a response
    .000 0... .... .... = Opcode: Standard query (0)
    .... .1.. .... .... = Authoritative: Server is an authority for domain
    .... ..0. .... .... = Truncated: Message is not truncated
    .... ...1 .... .... = Recursion desired: Do query recursively
    .... .... 1... .... = Recursion available: Server can do recursive queries
    .... .... ..0. .... = Answer authenticated: Answer/authority
    portion was not authenticated by the server
    .... .... .... 0000 = Reply code: No error (0)
    Questions: 1
    Answer RRs: 1
    Authority RRs: 2
    Additional RRs: 2
    Queries
                www.example.com: type A, class inet
                Name: www.example.com
                Type: Host address
                Class: inet
                Answers
                www.example.com: type A, class inet, addr 192.0.34.166
                Name: www.example.com
                Type: Host address
                Class: inet
                Time to live: 2 days
                Data length: 4
                Addr: 192.0.34.166
```

Based on the response, www.example.com resolves to the IP Address 192.0.34.166. Having successfully translated the domain to a usable IP Address, the workstation issues an HTTP request for www.example.com. All of this takes place without any interference from, or the knowledge of, the workstation user.

How does the recursive server make its query? Again, it is a very simple process. The recursive name server runs resolving software, such as BIND, and uses that software to query the root name servers. The resolving software has a hints file, similar to the old hosts.txt file, which contains a list of the root servers. When a query comes into the recursive server, it holds the request and queries one of the root servers. The hints file is available via FTP from the InterNIC FTP server, and its default name is named.root (though different operating systems and different resolvers have different naming conventions).

The named.root file has a very simple format; it is a list of the root servers along with their corresponding IP Addresses. When a query comes into the recursive server it checks to make sure it does not already know something about the domain, if it does not, it then queries the root name servers.

KNOWING WHICH SERVER TO QUERY

How does a recursive server know which name server to query? A recursive name server calculates the Round Trip Time (RTT) for queries to each name server. The RTT is, essentially, a foot race that measures the time—in milliseconds—that it takes to retrieve the zone file. When a recursive server first initiates a query it sets the RTT for all of the authoritative name servers to 0. The recursive server then queries all of the name servers at random; the one with the lowest RTT after they have all been queried will be the preferred name server. After every request the RTT for all servers other than the previously recorded "fastest" name server is decreased. This is done to that other name servers eventually become the servers first queried, which helps to distribute the load between all the name servers. After the initial TTL expires, the RTT process starts over again.

AUTHORITATIVE NAME SERVERS

The final stop in the DNS query process is the authoritative name server. As the name implies, authoritative name servers contain information about a domain name. Recursive servers query authoritative name servers to find specific answers (such as what is the IP Address of www.example.com). These answers are shared with other machines that query the recursive name server.

Authoritative name servers are hosts that are registered with the TLD authority, or authorities, for which the administrator of the name server intends to host domain names. Once the host has been registered it can be assigned to host as many domains as the server can bear.[2]

The process works in the following manner: an organization first registers a domain using their favorite registrar. The organization decides that they will manage DNS in-house; so they create a host record, for instance, ns1.example.com. This record is created through their registrar, and it is a map of the hostname to an IP Address, and it is stored on the TLD root servers. Now, not only can ns1.example.com hold authoritative information for example.com, it can also host authoritative information for other domains. When a domain is registered the organization just tells the registrar to use ns1.example.com as one of the authoritative servers. Alternatively, www.example.com can be registered using third party authoritative servers, as in this example:

```
Domain Name: EXAMPLE.COM
Registrar: RESERVED-INTERNET ASSIGNED NUMBERS AUTHORITY
Whois Server: whois.iana.org
Referral URL: http://res-dom.iana.org
Name Server: A.IANA-SERVERS.NET
Name Server: B.IANA-SERVERS.NET
Status: clientDeleteProhibited
Status: clientTransferProhibited
Status: clientUpdateProhibited
Updated Date: 14-aug-2015
Creation Date: 14-aug-1995
Expiration Date: 13-aug-2016
```

Because information about authoritative name servers is maintained on the TLD root servers it is expected that they will be fairly permanent. It is not advisable to register a hostname changes its IP Address often, especially since it can take up to 3 days for authoritative name server changes to take effect.

A query to the .COM root servers returns both authoritative name servers for the domain example.com. The recursive name server then initiates a foot race between the two authoritative name servers, to see which responds the fastest. Of the two authoritative servers a.iana-servers.net responds the fastest and returns the requested information. This is also outlined in Fig. 1.3.

There are really two types of authoritative name servers: master and slave (also known as primary and secondary, though those terms are depreciated). The master name server maintains authoritative information about a domain and the slave name server, or name servers, pulls the information from the master using a process known as zone transfer.

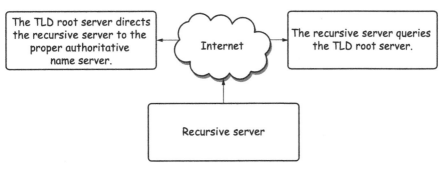

FIGURE 1.3

The TLD root server directs the recursive server to the proper authoritative server.

The master–slave relationship is useful because it means that only a single document has to be maintained. Authoritative information for a domain is automatically replicated from the master to the slave name servers. By automating the process as much as possible there are fewer chances for human error.

As described in the previous section, the recursive server stores the information provided by the authoritative server and provides an answer to the original requestor. The amazing thing is that this all happens in a matter of milliseconds—in fact if it takes more than a second for this transaction to occur it is considered problematic.

ZONE FILES

The zone file is a plain-text file that contains authoritative information about a domain. The original file is stored on the master name server; the slave name server retrieves a copy of the zone file and stores it locally. Recursive servers request information from the file, but do not store local copies; the recursive server simply gathers as much information as the authoritative name servers will share.

A zone file will sometimes look similar to this:

```
1 $ttl 43200
2 example.com.   IN    SOA    ns1.example.com. dns.example.com. (
3    2003040401
4    10800
5    3600
6    432000
7    43200)
8 example.com.    IN  NS  ns1.example.com.
9 ; The servers
10 www      IN    CNAME  example.com.
11 ftp      IN    A    example.com.
12 mail      60    IN    A    10.100.0.10
13 example.com.    IN    A    10.100.0.12
14 ; The name servers
15 example.com.    IN    NS    ns1.foo.com.
16 example.com.    IN    NS    ns2.example.com.
17 ; The mail servers
18 example.com.    IN    MX    10 mail.example.com.
19 example.com.    IN    MX    50 mail.foo.com.
```

This is a pretty basic zone file that includes the most common services: Web, Mail, and FTP. A more extensive zone file might include a list of workstations or additional servers; in fact, some zone files can run thousands of lines long.

The first line in the zone file defines the default Time to Live (TTL)—in seconds—for the zone; this is TTL that will be used for all entries in the zone file, unless another TTL is specified. Line 1 sets the default TTL for this zone to 12 hours.

Line 2 is really the heart of a zone file, and the tool that allows different name servers to speak to each other; it is the Start of Authority (SOA) record. The SOA tells recursive name servers how long a record should be cached and it facilitates communication between master and slave name servers. Line 2 is going to contain the same information for all domains:

```
Domain Name  Class  Resource Record  Origin  Contact
```

The first field in the line is the domain itself, the second field is the class, which is always IN (short for Internet), and the third field is the Resource Record (RR), which is always SOA. The next field is the Origin Server, which is the master server for this domain—the server from where information is drawn. The information in that field is the same on both master and slave servers and it should reference a canonical name, not a CNAME or an IP Address.

The final field is the administrative contact for the domain name. This should be the person, or group, responsible for maintaining the domain name and the zone file. Note the format of the contact information, all three fields are separated by dots, the first dot should be replaced with the "@" sign, so the field really reads as dns@example.com.

CONTACT CONVENTION

The standard convention for the contact field is that the first dot is replaced by the "@", so the address should be kept as simple as possible. Using an address like dns.admin@example.com would translate to dns.admin.example.com and might confuse someone trying to get in touch with the administrator of that domain.

Lines 3 through 6 are designed for use by the slave servers. Line 3 is the serial number; this field should be updated every time a change is made to the master zone file. The standard format is YYYYMMDDNN, but any format is fine as long as every time a change is made, the number is larger.

Line 4 is the refresh time. Expressed in seconds, this field tells slave servers how often they should check back with the master name server to see if there any updates. When the time expires the slaves will query the master server and see if the serial number has increased. If it has not increased the slave server does not do anything, if the serial number has been incremented then the slave server initiates a transfer of the zone file from the master. Generally the refresh field is set low so that the master and slave servers have the same information as much of the time as possible.

Line 5 is the retry field. This is the amount of time—again in seconds—that slave servers will wait after asking for a zone and not receiving it before asking again. Remember, the default DNS transport protocol is UD. UDP is a connectionless protocol, the slave servers send the request and do not know if the master receives it, and the master does not know if the slave servers actually get the information sent to them. The retry field compensates for this lack of stateful communication by forcing a retry if the desired action is not received.

Line 6 is the expire field. The expire time is the time in seconds that a slave should hold onto its data when the master has not responded to queries. After the expire time has run out, the slave server will discard all information it has about the domain name. The purpose of the expire field is to help prevent a plethora of orphaned servers maintaining inaccurate information about domains. It is not uncommon for an administrator to move a domain from one server to another and forget to delete the zone file from the old server—it is certainly not recommended, but it does happen more often than it should.

Line 7 is specifically for recursive servers, it is the default TTL. This should have the same value as the TTL listed in line 1.

The rest of the zone file consists of a series of RRs, which are discussed in detail in the next section.

RESOURCE RECORDS

This chapter has progressed from the general to the specific, and this section is the most specific, it is also the heart of DNS. The primary function of DNS is to share information, to make it very easy—and automated—for someone to get to the web site www.example.com or send mail to user@example.com.

RRs are the entries in a zone file that provide the information that users are looking for. All of the availability built into DNS is there solely so the information contained within the RRs can be transferred from an authoritative server to a recursive server and people can happily visit web sites, share files, and more.

An RR is an entry in the zone file of a domain that serves a specific function. There are many different types of RRs, but really there are only about 10 that are commonly used. One of the common RRs, which we have already reviewed, is the SOA. The SOA is unique in that it is the only common RR that does not follow the standard format.

The standard format for a RR consists of five fields, each containing specific information about the RR:

```
Name    TTL  Class  Type  Data
```

In practice, the format generally looks like this:

```
mail.example.com.    3600    IN    A    10.10.100.102
```

This is where the importance of the trailing dot becomes prominent. If there is no trailing dot after a domain, then DNS software generally interprets that to indicate a hostname and the software will tack on the domain. In the example above, if there were no trailing dot after mail. example.com, the software would think the RR was referring to mail.example.com.example.com.

The Name field is either the hostname or IP Address, depending on the record; it is the object that owns this particular RR. The TTL is only used if a TTL that is different than the one defined in the SLA is required for a particular RR. If no TTL is specified than the default zone TTL is used. Class is always IN (Internet), which is the only class currently supported by DNS. Type defines the purpose the RR serves, in the example above an "A" record is an address record, other records are discussed below. The Data field varies depending on the type of RR; the data is the information the name server is trying to share about that particular RR.

ADDRESS RECORDS

The most common type of RR is the Address, or A, record. An A record maps an FQDN to an IP address, as in the example above. Each host address within a domain must have an A record (hosts in the zone file but not part of the domain do not require A records in that zone file) or a Canonical Name Record:

```
mail.example.com. 3600  IN  A   10.10.100.102
```

Remember, the TTL field is optional, if the RR can use the default TTL for the zone, then there is no need to include it within the RR. The A record is the most basic of RRs, and undoubtedly the one most often used. Even a simple zone file will often have 5 or 6 A records.

If an FQDN point to multiple IP Address the name server will return them in round-robin fashion. The first server requesting the A record will get the first record, the second server will get the second record, the third server will get the third record, etc. Once the name server has returned all the A records, it will start back at the beginning.

There is also an A record designed specifically for IPv6 Addresses. This record is known as an AAAA record, and it follows the same format as an A record, but with an IPv6 Address:

```
ipv6.example.com. 3600  IN  AAAA   2001:468:504:1:210:5aff:fe1a:11e
```

CANONICAL NAME RECORDS

Canonical Name (CNAME) records are aliases that map one FQDN to another FQDN. Rather than mapping an FQDN directly to an IP Address it is often easier to map it to another host. This is especially useful if there are a lot of FQDNs point-ing to the same IP Address, when a change is made to the primary address the other addresses are updated automatically. A CNAME will look similar to this:

```
www.example.com.  3600  IN  CNAME    mail.example.com.
mail.example.com. 3600  IN  A      10.10.100.102
```

In order for the CNAME to work it has to point to FQDN with a valid A record. A CNAME does not have to point to FQDN within the same zone file; it can point to other FQDNs:

```
www.example.com 3600    IN   CNAME   www.foo.com.
```

Again, www.foo.com has to have a valid A record for this CNAME to work. One other important thing about CNAME records is that they cannot be used by other RRs. Neither MX nor NS records can point to CNAME records.

MAIL EXCHANGER RECORDS

The Mail Exchanger (MX) record is used to define the hosts where mail for a domain should be sent. As with CNAME records, MX records do not have to point to FQDNs within the domain, the MX records can point to any host, inside or outside the domain—as long as that host is set up to receive mail for that domain. MX records must point to FQDNs that are represented by A records rather than CNAME records.

Most modern Mail Transport Agents (MTAs) understand CNAME records and can forward mail to them, but some still do not. It also goes against the RFC, so please do not do it.

An MX record will look something like this:

```
example.com.  3600  IN  MX  10 mail.example.com.
example.com.  3600  IN  MX  20 mail.foo.com.
```

There is a field that is unique to MX records called the record weight. The weight used to determine preference for multiple MX records. The lower the weight of a record the greater the preference placed on that record. In the example above, mail.example.com is preferred to mail.foo.com. An MTA trying to send mail to user@example.com will try mail.example.com first, and only try mail.foo.com if mail.example.com times out, or returns the mail.

NAME SERVER RECORDS

In addition to being registered as hosts, name servers must also be defined within a zone file as Name Server (NS) records. As implied, the NS records are used to list the authoritative name servers for a domain. NS records are generally the first RRs after the SOA and are formatted in the following manner:

```
example.com.    IN    NS    ns1.example.com.
example.com.    IN    NS    ns1.foo.com.
example.com.    IN    NS    ns2.example.com.
```

As with MX and CNAME records, NS records do not have to point toward an FQDN that exists within the host file, the NS record can point to any host that has authoritative information about the domain. An NS record does have to be an FQDN, it cannot be an IP Address; it also has to point to an FQDN that is an A record, not a CNAME.

NS records also serve another purpose. For DNS daemons that are capable, the master name server will push updates to zone file to the name servers listed within that zone file. This, of course, is heavily dependent on the DNS infrastructure that is in place.

POINTER RECORDS

Pointer (PTR) records are the opposite of A records. PTR records map IP Addresses to domains names. PTR records are stored in special zone files called *in-addr.arpa* zone files. Information about data for IP Address blocks is distributed through the regional Network Coordination Centers (NCCs).

There are currently five NCCs: The American Registry for Internet Numbers handles information for North America; Latin American and Caribbean Internet Addresses Registry handles the IP space for Latin America and the Carribean; Réseaux IP Européens manages the IP Address space for Europe; The African Network Information Center is the Internet registry for the African continent; and the Asia-Pacific Network Information Center, which is responsible for IP Address space in the Asia Pacific region.

Information about IP Address allocation is handled in pretty much the same manner as domain name information and the DNS structure is identical. The difference is administrators are working with blocks of IP Addresses, not domain names, and the zone files are different in that respect.

The *in-addr.arpa* zone files are named using the IP block in reverse followed by in-addr.arpa. If an organization is allocated the IP block 10.100.50.0/24 (a class "C" net block), the zone file with the information about that net block would be named:

```
50.100.10.IN-ADDR.ARPA
```

The zone files generally only contain three types of RRs: SOA, NS, and PTR records, with PTR records being of primary interest. PTR records follow the same general format as forward zone files, but the hostname is in the data field:

```
102  3600  IN  PTR    mail.example.com.
```

This record states that the IP Address 10.10.100.102 is mapped to mail. example.com. Unlike A records, in which a hostname can be mapped to multiple IP Address, an IP Address can only be mapped to a single hostname.

PTR record information is often used for authentication purposes. Some mail administrators reject mail that does not originate from a server with a reverse record, and some FTP servers reject logins from users who do not have reverse records mapped to their hostname. The advisability of this type of security is debatable, but it does exist and it is something to be aware of.

HOST INFO RECORDS

Host Info (HINFO) records are not used very often these days, but they still pop up occasionally. The HINFO provides operating system and hardware information about a host. The format is the same as other RRs, but the data field contains unstructured host data:

```
mail.example.com.  3600  IN  HINFO  "Dell 1650" "Redhat 9.1"
```

RFC 1035 recommends a format for the HINFO data field, though it is not strictly followed, and other information may be substituted.

SERVER RECORDS

Server (SRV) records were first outlined in RFC 2052. They are a different way of querying name servers for information about a hostname. Normally, when someone wants to access a service for a domain, they need to know the proper hostname. For example, if someone is trying to visit Example Corp's web site that person needs to know that the hostname www.example.com supports HTTP services.

Unfortunately, it is not always possible to know what services are supported by the hosts under a domain. Rather than making haphazard guesses, issuing an SRV helps the requester get to the desired service without knowing the server information. The format of the SRV RR follows:

```
Service.Proto.Name TTL Class SRV Priority Weight Port Target
```

Like MX records, SRV records allow DNS administrators to assign different weights to the various SRV record. A real-world example would be using SRV records to load balance traffic between web servers:

```
http.tcp.www.example.com.  IN  SRV  10 10 80 host1.example.com.
http.tcp.www.example.com.  IN  SRV  10 10 80 host2.example.com.
```

In the example above, the DNS administrator is load balancing HTTP services between two services. There would, of course, have to be A records for both host1.example.com and host2.example.com. In this case, because the administrator wants to spread the load evenly between the two servers, both weight and priority are set the same. If one of the servers needed to take more of the load, its weight would be set lower. Similarly, if one server was the primary server, and the other server simply a failover server, the priority of the primary server would be set lower than that of the failover server.

SRV records are not all that common; they are primarily used by intranetwork services, such a Microsoft's Active Directory.

TEXT RECORDS

Text (TXT) records are another type of RR that is not commonly used. TXT records are free-form text that are used to provide human-readable information about an entry or a domain more generically, they are generally set up similar to this:

```
allan    IN    TXT    "Hello World!"
```

One area where TXT records are still heavily used is in the realm of DNS-based malware. In particular, malware that uses DNS as its exfil path, data and commands are often embedded in DNS queries as TXT records.

CONCLUSIONS

DNS is a complex topic and one that cannot be completely covered in a single chapter. This chapter was intended to serve as a good overview of DNS and some of its complexities. There are many resources available both online and in-print that offer more detailed information about DNS and its complexities. However, the information in this chapter is a good baseline, it contains information that DNS administrators should be familiar with.

NOTES

1. Some people will tell you that the first domain registered was either Symbolics.com or Think.com, you can let them know that those domains were registered in March of 1985 and May of 1985, respectively, at least 3 months after NORDU.NET was registered.
2. This is, of course, assuming the domain associated with the host is also registered.

Issues in DNS security

2

INFORMATION IN THIS CHAPTER

- A Brief History of DNS Security Breaches
- Why is DNS Security Important?
- Common DNS Security Problems
- Developing a DNS Security Plan

INTRODUCTION

DNS is a core component of everyone's daily lives on the Internet, but very few people understand how it works, or how fragile the underlying infrastructure can be. Even security professionals, who are charged with protecting an organization, often do not have a full grasp of the potential security pitfalls in DNS.

Part of this lack of knowledge stems from the fact that DNS is something that is often "set and forget." DNS infrastructure is set up and other than a few zone changes here and there it is rarely considered. DNS is also a long established protocol, many companies registered their domains 20 years or more earlier and the team that set up the original DNS infrastructure has long since moved on to other roles. As long as DNS for the organization is working why make changes? Even worse, there may not be anyone who knows how to make changes.

AN OLD PROBLEM

The "set and forget" DNS problem has been around for years. In the mid-1990s I worked for a major Internet Service Provider (ISP) that had significant turnover within the DNS team. The ISP domain name, which was also used to manage our backbone infrastructure, expired and no one knew. Fortunately, a manager at Verisign knew one of our managers and she called before letting the domain expire. The manager put the $100 renewal on his personal credit card because he knew he could not get an invoice paid in time to keep the domain live and prevent the ISP from effectively shutting down. Lesson one in DNS Security: Make sure domain renewal notices go to an alias, not an individual person.

The fact that DNS is so resilient, combined with domain registrations being done for years at a time and too few security teams that have DNS experience and too few

DNS Security. DOI: http://dx.doi.org/10.1016/B978-0-12-803306-7.00002-4

DNS administrators that have security experience, creates a unique challenge in securing DNS infrastructure. Combine the internal challenges with the external DNS security threats that face an organization: DNS-based Distributed Denial of Service (DDoS) attacks, cache poisoning, malware that uses DNS for command and control purposes, and DNS security is a potential nightmare for any team.

The goal of this chapter is to provide a quick history of the some of the best known attacks against or taking advantage of flaws in DNS. The chapter will also discuss some of the threats and how to put together a plan to better protect an organization from these threats.

A BRIEF HISTORY OF DNS SECURITY BREACHES

A listing of all security breaches that were either attacks against DNS infrastructure or took advantage of flaws in DNS security would fill several books. Rather the purpose of this section is to provide an overview of the different types of breaches that have occurred over the years and to demonstrate how DNS attacks have changed over time.

In 1996 Eugene Kashpureff used a DNS cache poisoning exploit to redirect traffic from the InterNIC's web site to his own web site, AlterNIC, an alternative registry. The exploit went on for several days before Kashpureff returned service to the InterNIC.

In February of 2000 an attacker changed the authoritative name servers listed with the InterNIC for RSA Security's domain. The attacker also set up a spoof RSA Security web site and directed users to that site—giving the mistaken impression that the web site had been compromised.

On January 29, 2001 access to all of Microsoft's sites, including its MSN sites, was disrupted for almost a day because of an attack launched against Microsoft's name servers. Microsoft's DNS administrators made the attack easier by placing all of their name servers on the same network segment, which gave the attacker a single target.

An attack was launched against the root name servers on October 21, 2002. The attack was an ICMP-based DDoS attack that rendered several of the root name servers unreachable. Because of recursiveness and the redundancy in the root servers virtually no one noticed the attack, which lasted about an hour. Had the attack continued for a longer period of time the impact would undoubtedly have been much greater.

In June of 2008 a Turkish hacker group calling itself NetDevilz used social engineering to convince the domain registrar for the Internet Corporation for Assigned Names and Numbers (ICANN) and the Internet Assigned Numbers Authority (IANA) to hand over control the icann.org and iana.org domains to NetDevilz. The record change only lasted 20 minutes or so before it was corrected, but many users were redirected to the wrong web sites for up to 24 hours.

Also in 2008 Dan Kaminsky released details about the "Kaminsky Bug" which would allow an attacker to send authoritative responses to domains for which the server was not authoritative. For example, a user could visit reallyfunwebgames.com and the authoritative name server for reallyfunwebgames.com would also send an authoritative response for americanexpress.com. Thus, every user who relied on the same recursive server as the original user would now be sent to the wrong page when they tried to go to americanexpress.com. Kaminsky was able to engineer this by combining a flaw in which DNS servers managed query IDs with a cache poisoning technique. Unlike other attacks on this list, Kaminsky is a responsible researcher and reported the bug to the appropriate vendors so it could be patched before he released details of the exploit to the general public.

In 2013 web hosting company, CyberBunker, launched what was, at the time the world's largest DDoS attack against the DNS servers of Spamhaus, a volunteer organization that tracks spammers and provides a blacklist other organizations can subscribe to reduce the amount of spam they received, because Spamhaus added CyberBunker's IP address space to the Spamhaus Black List.[1] Other organizations had attempted unsuccessful DDoS attacks against Spamhaus servers before. By targeting the Spamhaus DNS servers, which were hosted by a third party, CyberBunker was able to bypass the DDoS mitigation capabilities that Spamhaus had in place. Those outsourced DNS servers also served other customers around the world, so the DDoS attack not only made Spamhaus servers unreachable it also degraded service for customers around the world.

In 2010 Verisign was the victim of multiple successful attacks by unknown attackers. Verisign manages the .com and the .net root name servers as well as the root name servers for several other Generic Top Level Domains and many Country Code Top Level Domains (ccTLDs). According to Verisign, no data related to the root servers managed by the company was compromised during the attacks.

On March 31, 2012 Anonymous attempted to take the entire Internet off-line with Operation Blackout. The goal with Operation Blackout was to take out the 13 root servers using a DNS Amplification attack (described later in this chapter). DNS Amplification attacks are remarkably easy to launch and have been used effective in a number of DDoS attacks. Fortunately, the crew at Anonymous had very little understanding of the how DNS operates, how the root name servers are configured, how major ISPs deal with the root name servers. Not to mention that they are, for the most part, incompetent. The attack had very little chance of success. In the end the attack either did not happen or simply had no effect on the performance of the root name servers.

A much more effective attack was lunched against Turkey in December of 2015. This DDoS attack was targeted the .tr ccTLD root name servers and effectively isolated Turkey from the rest of the world, Internet-wise. The attack had the side benefit of degrading service throughout Europe because the Reseaux IP Europeens Network Coordination Centre provided secondary authoritative DNS services to the .tr domain.

By attacking the .tr root name servers with a relatively modest 40 Gps DDoS attack the attackers were able to make about 400,000 domains unreachable. Which meant users were not able to reach company web sites or send email to users with the .tr email addresses. In order to block the attack the Turkish government had to temporarily block all Internet traffic originating from outside of Turkey. That allowed people within Turkey to start communicating with .tr domains again, but blocked the rest of the Internet.

These attacks all serve to illustrate a number of points: The first is that in some cases, the attacks may have been prevented if a stronger DNS security policy had been in place. The second point, and in some ways the more important of the two, is that large companies, security savvy companies, and even companies with extensive DNS experience can still be vulnerable to attacks. A third point to note from these examples is the evolution of attacks over time. Were this book written about DNS security 10 years ago, it would have primarily focused on DNS cache poisoning, DNS hijacking, and vulnerabilities in DNS software. Instead, there will be a lot more focus on the protocol itself, and how to take advantage of weaknesses in the protocol to make service unavailable or exfiltrate stolen data.

WHY IS DNS SECURITY IMPORTANT?

Ask any security professional what keeps her awake at night and you will most likely get a response about protecting the organization against phishing attacks.[2] Dive a little deeper and she might express concerns about security challenges with BYOD (bring your own device) or worry over some of the web applications that network users have access to, or that run on the organization's web site. After a few beers she might express concern about the fact that there are more alerts than she can keep up with, or that she does not have a clear picture of everything that is happening on the network.

It is very rare that a discussion about security issues reaches the point where DNS comes up as a topic. That seems like an odd statement to make in a book about DNS security, but it tends to be true. Unless there has been a recent breach in the news involving DNS, generally DNS does not come up as a topic.

DNS is also one of the most outsourced services. Many organizations recognize that they do not have DNS expertise in-house so let their domain registrar or another third party manage the organization's zones and only run recursive DNS services internally (though, often even that is outsourced to the ISP providing connectivity to the organization). With little or no control of the DNS infrastructure residing within the organization it is easy to see how DNS can become an afterthought in security plans.

But, DNS security needs to be at the forefront of every discussion about network security. DNS attacks are more common than most people realize and failures in DNS security can be crippling to an organization. How much money does an organization lose every hour that it is unreachable via email? How about when a fully functioning web site is invisible to the Internet, or worse visitors to a web site are redirected to a malicious web site? A 2014 study done by Vanson Bourne found that 75% of organizations in the United States and the United Kingdom had been impacted by a DNS attack and 49% had uncovered some sort of DNS-based attack in the previous 12 months. So, DNS attacks are prevalent, but they are not necessarily getting the attention they deserve.

DNS falls into a category of "utility protocols" that underpin communications on the Internet. These are robust protocols that help keep traffic flowing and servers talking and that most users do not know exist. Protocols like the Border Gateway Protocol, Network Time Protocol, and of course DNS are critical to keeping the Internet up and running, but generally fall well outside the purview of security teams. The administrators who do configure and manage the systems that run these protocols do not usually think about the security concerns inherent in these protocols.

This lack of security insight combined with the relative obscurity of these protocols makes them ripe for potential exploitation and hackers have figured that out. The result of this perceived utility is that within the black hat community there has been a sizeable increase in exploitation and vulnerability research in these protocols. There has also been a lot of research done by the security community into ways to better protect these protocols. Unfortunately, there is a big gap between the work done by researchers and the people who handle the day-to-day administration of these protocols.

A prime example of this is with DNSSEC (discussed in detail in Chapter 10). RFC 3833, which introduced a way to better secure DNS infrastructure, was first released in 2004. Even in 2016 very few domain names have added DNSSEC signing to their zone file and many domain registrars still do not support it.

In the end DNS security is important because a failure in DNS can render an organization completely unreachable and because attackers are actively looking for new ways to exploit the DNS protocol and the DNS infrastructure itself. Understanding key issues in DNS security is critical to maintaining a strong security posture within an organization.

COMMON DNS SECURITY PROBLEMS

Before a security team can effectively protect an organization's DNS infrastructure they must first determine what the risks to its DNS infrastructure are. When performing a risk assessment of a DNS infrastructure it is important to take a very broad view of what constitutes a security risk. The goal of a DNS security plan is to make sure the DNS infrastructure is available as much as possible and that the proper information is propagated to machines making queries.

Based on the definition above, anything that impacts availability or causes faulty data to be disseminated could be considered a security breach. Some would consider this definition problematic because it expands the definition of security beyond its traditional meaning. However, given the importance of DNS to an organization an expanded definition of security is reasonable and, arguably, essential.

One of the reasons an expanded definition of DNS security is essential is that there are so many points of security failure within a DNS framework. In addition to failures traditionally associated with data security such as hardware failure, unauthorized server access, and DDoS attacks, there are also registrar administrative issues, sleazy marketing, and other types of security breaches unique to DNS. The distributed nature of DNS automatically requires a different set of security concerns and adds a layer of complexity to security plans.

Here is an all-too-common example of the unique problems facing anyone attempting to secure a DNS infrastructure: It is Monday, everyone stumbles into the office and realizes that they cannot check mail, the corporate web site is also unreachable. Internet connectivity is fine, and people are able to send mail and access other web sites. The DNS administrator is asked (usually frantically) to fix the DNS problem. But the DNS servers are working fine. Both the primary and secondary servers are responding as expected, data has not been changed and there is no sign of unauthorized access.

The DNS administrator spends all morning attempting to determine the problem. She checks and rechecks system settings, verifies that DNS information has not been altered with the registrar searches various DNS web sites all to no avail. Finally, she posts a description of the problem to a DNS-related mailing list. Within a few minutes someone replies with output of whois data and points out that the domain name has expired. Shaking her head in disbelief the administrator contacts the accounting department to find out if they received a bill from the registrar and if they did, had the bill been paid? The accounting department says that the bill was never received. Further investigation shows that the billing point of contact that the registrar has on file left the company 8 months ago, so the renewal notice was sent to a nonexistent email account and the domain registrar does not have an effective method to deal with bounced emails.

The example above, while somewhat exaggerated is not too far from the truth. Many a large company has been crippled because someone in the accounting department did not pay the registrar bill on time. The example above also does not advise on the possibility that someone is waiting to squat on the domain is a payment is missed and registration expires. Image the embarrassment a company would have to go through if their domain was purchased out from underneath their noses. Ensuring that bills are paid on time would not normally qualify as a security issue, but in this case it certainly could be considered an aspect of availability: If an organization does not make sure the registrar is paid in a timely fashion the domain can be removed from the root servers and no one will be able to access the domain.

Even after the bill has been paid and the registrar has reinstated the domain, it can take up to 48 hours before the domain is again available to the Internet. In other words, this type of mistake can result in an outage that lasts several days—and there is not anything that can be done to speed up the process. This is why it is important to consider all aspects of availability when developing a DNS security plan.

Taking a broad view of security, a DNS security event is anything that impacts the availability of the DNS service, whether that is an internal or an external event. An internal event is one that is caused by an employee or a contractor of the organization, regardless of whether or not the event is accidental or intentional.

This is important to remember: a security breach does not necessarily have to be intentional. An administrator who enters an incorrect IP Address or accidentally deletes an important file has still created a security situation. These type of events need to planned for with as much concern as hostile events.

Internal nonhostile events can include a mistaken entry in a zone file, misconfigured ACLs, firewall rules which prevent access to DNS or grant more access than desired, deleting zone files, and of course not renewing a domain name in a timely fashion.

Internal events can also be hostile. A disgruntled employee might redirect the organization's web site, might attempt to disrupt mail service by removing entries, may change domain contact information so he is listed as the authority over the domain, or may remove a zone file completely, wreaking havoc within the network. Each of these problems can be prevented if the right checks are put in place. Again, once potential attack vectors are known it is easier to prepare for them, and in the case of internal attacks implementing stronger DNS processes goes a long way toward limiting the problem.

External security breaches are another matter; it is very rare that an external breach will be accidental. Most external attacks against DNS servers are either an instance where an organization is specifically targeted or they are random. A random attack occurs when an attacker is scanning a range of IP Addresses and encounters a DNS server with a known vulnerability. The attacker will launch an attack against that server and attempt to gain access not because the attacker has a particular grudge against the organization, but simply because it is possible. Note, an attack can be targeted and still have collateral damage. For example, in 2012 a hacker going by the name AnonymousOwn3r launched a DDoS attack against Domain Registrar. The DDoS attack not only rendered GoDaddy's web site unreachable it also impacted the ability of GoDaddy's authoritative DNS servers to respond to queries. Degrading the service of GoDaddy's customers—who were not the intended target.

Random attacks are relatively easy to defend against. Most script kiddies do not have the depth of knowledge required to launch a serious attack against a well-protected DNS infrastructure, so they will generally bypass those and focus on DNS infrastructures with weaker security measures in place. In many ways it is the same as car thieves. Someone just looking for a joyride will focus on the easiest car to grab—one that is unlocked or with a weak alarm system. On the other hand, a skilled car thief has a greater knowledge of cars and will know how to defeat the security precautions of the car he wants.

A script kiddie is a lot like a joyriding car thief. Of course as anyone who has had his or her car stolen knows, even a novice car thief can inflict a great deal of damage—especially if it is your car stolen. Likewise, just because a script kiddie is not sophisticated technically does not make the damage inflicted any less painful.

It is important to do everything possible to keep a DNS infrastructure safe from common script kiddie attacks. At the same time DNS administrators must remain watchful for more skilled attackers.

A skilled attacker is more likely to target a specific organization for attack. The attacker may have a grudge against a company, hope to gain access to sensitive data for personal gain, or even be paid by a rival organization.

Two important qualities that good DNS administrators share are vigilance and paranoia; actually, all security administrators share those qualities. As the saying goes, "Just because you are paranoid doesn't mean they are not out to get you." Initially, it is often difficult to distinguish between an attack launched by a skilled attacker and one launched by a novice, an experienced administrator will be able to quickly determine the difference and act appropriately.

A targeted DNS attack can take many forms, depending on the intention of the attacker. If the intention of the attacker is to redirect DNS services away from an organization, then the attacker may not even target that organization's DNS servers directly. In fact, if an attacker wants to take over a domain—also known as domain hijacking—a direct attack against an organization's DNS servers is often the last resort.

A domain hijacker will take advantage of weak DNS security practices within an organization or that organization's registrar to assume ownership of a domain name. Generally, this involves some sort of social engineering. Social engineering is a form of attack that involves manipulating people rather than data. An attacker will take advantage of the willingness of people to share information, even if that information is sensitive.

There are several types of domain hijacking scenarios, and again, these scenarios may not even involve dealing directly with the organization whose domain the hijacker is trying to take over. One way to do hijack a domain is to look for one that was registered using a now-defunct mailing address from a free-mail account. The hijacker reactivates the defunct address and uses it to change the password and contact information for domain. In effect, the hijacker assumes ownership of the domain.

A second type of hijacking revolves around getting information from the domain registrar directly, and this is where social engineering really comes into play. A hijacker calls up a registrar and claims to be the administrator for a domain. The hijacker presents the registrar with a plausible crisis. Perhaps she explains that the company that is hosting her organization's mail servers has abruptly shut down, leaving them without access to their mail. She has signed up with a new company, but she needs to update her domain information and she cannot remember her password to the registrar's control panel.

She would use the password-reset option, but obviously, with her mail unavailable, she will not receive the new password. This is a real problem, and the president of the company is calling her every 5 minutes demanding to know what the status is and even threatening to fire her. Is not there any way the registrar can reset the password over the phone—she will happily fax over a signed request on company letterhead?

At this point many support people will acquiesce and change the password "this one time," over the phone. If the hijacker does encounter resistance at this level, she will escalate it to a manager, sounding increasingly upset. Eventually, she finds someone who is willing to allow her to change the password over the phone and now she has full control over the domain without having to touch the target network.

This ploy does not always work, but remember that the primary role of the customer service person is to help people; therefore, they are naturally inclined to aid a customer in trouble. A registrar that takes security seriously would have other methods of verifying the person's identity. It is important to remember that registrars, like most service companies, depend on happy customers for repeat and new business. If the person on the other end of the phone is really a distraught customer not changing the password may result in a loss of business.

Social engineering attacks are often the most difficult to defend against, especially when an organization has to rely on a vendor to maintain the same level of security. But even within an organization not all staff members will have the same level of urgency when it comes to security, and even the best security plans are useless if people within the organization do not adhere to it.

Other types of attacks involve more traditional, computer-based, methods of aggression. These attacks generally serve to overwhelm a server making it unreachable from the network, exploit weaknesses in the DNS daemon to gain access to the server, or redirect traffic from its intended destination to a server owned by the attacker.

The first type of attack, overwhelming a server with requests making it impossible to serve legitimate requests, is what is commonly referred to as a DoS attack. The requests can be requests for DNS information, but they can also be ICMP requests, or even another service that is housed on the server.

Because DNS uses the UDP as its primary method of communication, it is especially susceptible to attacks. Unlike a Tranmission Control Protocol (TCP) packet, a UDP packet does not require a handshake to ensure that there is good communication between the two hosts. This makes UDP-based protocols especially susceptible to attack, because it is relatively trivial for an attacker to forge UDP packets. More importantly, it is trivial for an attacker to forge hundreds, thousands, or even hundreds of thousands of packets. Forged packets are sent to the target DNS server, they look like legitimate requests, so the DNS server responds to all of them, filling up all available UDP sockets and preventing the server from responding to legitimate requests.

An Internet Control Message Protocol (ICMP) DDoS attack uses the same methodology. An attacker targets a server, but instead of launching DNS packets against the server, he uses ICMP packets. These packets can all be launched from a single server or from multiple servers. Either way, the goal is the same, overwhelm the DNS server and make it unresponsive to valid requests from other hosts.

If a DNS server has other services running on it then focusing on those other services is also an option. It does not matter what service is targeted, the important thing is to use up all of the available connections on the remote server and make it unresponsive.

A second type of attack is one that takes advantage of a weakness in either the DNS daemon or other software running on the server. The attacker exploits the weakness to gain administrative access to the server, once on the server the attacker can either attempt to make further inroads into the network or redirect DNS requests from users on the network to a rogue server controlled by the attacker.

An administrative compromise on a critical server, such as DNS servers, can be especially insidious because it allows an attacker to control parts of the network and redirect traffic away from its intended destination. Security precautions taken throughout the rest of the network become irrelevant, because the attacker has access to everything.

Attacks involving administrative compromise can sometimes go undetected for months. If an attacker is careful to cover her tracks properly and the server is poorly secured or monitored, then there is a good chance no one will notice there is a problem. At least not until long after it is too late.

A third type of attack is not as common as it used to be, but it is still one that can occur and therefore should be protected against. An attacker will load bogus information about a popular domain into a zone transfer, tricking recursive servers into redirecting queries to the wrong location.

For example, an attacker may own the domain foo.com. When DNS servers request information about foo.com, the attacker's server will also send bad data for www.amazon.com. The information is embedded within the legitimate request, so the receiving DNS server just accepts the data and shares it with users.

Note that the attacker's DNS server does not send a full zone transfer for the targeted domain, instead it generally sends a single record, most often an A record. The idea is to redirect traffic to a server owned by the attacker. So, the attacker would set up a web site that mirrored the one at www.amazon.com, send the bad data along with requests for foo.com. Compromised DNS servers would direct users toward the attacker's site and the attacker would be able to gather credit card numbers and account information from users who visit the bogus web site. Because the site would be a mirror of Amazon's web site, users would not know what happened at first, potentially giving the attacker a few weeks to exploit the gathered data.

New exploits against popular DNS daemons are constantly being discovered and reported. In addition to the exploits, new tools are released all the time that automate the process of exploiting security holes in DNS software. The confluence of these two trends creates a difficult situation for DNS administrators. Just about anyone with a computer and the ability to decompress a program can launch an attack against a poorly protected, or updated, DNS server. Because launching an elementary attack against a DNS server is so easy, the need for a strong DNS security policy is critical to any security plan.

In addition to a strong security policy, or more appropriately included as part of a strong security policy, it is important to be aware of the latest DNS exploits and understand how they impact an organization's DNS infrastructure. It is not enough to be aware of the exploit; DNS administrators must understand how the exploit works, and what it does.

Even if an exploit is not known to affect an existing DNS infrastructure—for example, an exploit is listed as being applicable to Linux servers and your DNS servers are BSD based—it cannot hurt to test the exploit against those DNS servers. Oftentimes, initial details of an exploit will be incomplete, so further research is always warranted.

Of course, even when there are no known exploits it is usually a good idea to upgrade DNS servers as soon as possible after a patch is released. Any patch should be thoroughly tested prior to upgrade, but patches generally are released to either protect against a security exploit or in anticipation of a potential new security exploit.

DEVELOPING A DNS SECURITY PLAN

A solid security plan is the key element of any organization's network and data security. A good security plan helps bring into focus the security goals of an organization, it creates policies to which people within the organization must adhere, it outlines responsibilities for different aspects of security, and it creates escalation procedures in the event of a security breach.

A well-developed DNS security plan is not going to exist in a vacuum. Most likely it will exist as a subset of an organization's larger security plan. However, there are organizations that do not have a security plan in place, in such cases, a DNS security plan should be able to stand on its own. However, even if no organizational security plan exists, a DNS security plan will have to function within the realities of the organization.

This is a problem that network and server administrators often fail to realize: The most technically correct solution is not always the most practical for an organization. Developing a security plan is always a tricky balance between security needs and meeting the needs of an organization. It is precisely for this reason that a good security plan will have broad organizational involvement.

Good security plans generally start at the top, getting senior management to approve the development of a security plan generally ensures the cooperation of all departments. Of course, if a general security plan exists for an organization the person or committee who developed the original plan should authorize a DNS offshoot. If an organization has a long-standing security plan there is generally an oversight committee that can sign off on changes to the plan, including adding a plan specifically for DNS.

The first question generally asked when developing a DNS security plan, and one you may be asking now, is "Why is there a need for a separate DNS security plan?" The short answer to that question is that DNS, more so than anything else, impacts all aspects of a network, and a compromised DNS server can have far reaching consequences. The difference between DNS and other network protocols is that DNS underlies and controls those other protocols, so if an organization's DNS infrastructure is compromised it impacts all other services.

For example, if an attacker manages to gain access to an organization's web servers, only web server access is interrupted, the same holds true with the mail server. On the other hand, if a DNS server is compromised, it can prevent access to the web server and the mail server. The unique position that DNS occupies within an organization justifies special security considerations.

Once support for a DNS security plan has been secured from the appropriate party, the next step is to make a list of people who need to be involved. In large organizations putting together a DNS security plan can stretch across multiple departments and involve a large number of people, in smaller organizations it may be as simple as grabbing the person in the next cubicle and hashing out the plan. Generally, the departments involved in implementing a DNS security plan will include those responsible for managing servers, workstations, the network, the firewalls, and possibly even the accounting department (or whoever is responsible for ensuring that bills get paid on time).

In a smaller organization, the same two or three people may fill these roles, so the planning process will be more informal. However, in larger organizations, where different departments fill these roles, with different reporting structures the planning process will have to be more formal. A formal planning process generally needs to be initiated by someone in senior management—which goes back to the previous point. The chain in larger organizations usually works as follows: An administrator feels that it is necessary to develop a DNS security plan. The administrator makes a presentation to her boss; her boss escalates the idea to the appropriate person. That person explains the idea and arranges a meeting between the appropriate groups. Alternatively, senior management may ask the person who originally came up with the idea to make a presentation to all of the department heads, the department heads will then assign someone to the task.

Once the group who will ultimately develop the DNS security plan has been assembled, it is important to set goals and to designate a clear set of responsibilities. This is a particular challenge with DNS, as the protocol crosses a wide range of areas. Some tasks will be relatively simple and involve a one-time adjustment—with periodic review, while others will be more complex and involve ongoing maintenance.

The best way to create a set of goals and define responsibility is to assess the current level of DNS security. Any organization that has given even a passing thought to security will have implemented some basic DNS security measures. Using these measures as a foundation to build a stronger security plan adds focus to the project. Developing a chart can facilitate an initial DNS security assessment. The chart should outline potential threats to DNS security, the results if those threats are exploited, the desired DNS security level, current DNS security practices, and current DNS vulnerabilities within the organization. The chart will look similar to Table 2.1.

The security assessment involves all known threats to DNS security. Each threat should be ranked according to the danger it poses to the organization. The more serious the threat is the higher its rank and the stronger the security measures that must be taken to protect against the threat. For example, a buffer overflow attack that would give the attacker root access is serious vulnerability that could result in DNS servers being taken off-line and provide an attacker with an entry point into the network. Obviously, this is a very serious threat, and one that would need to be addressed immediately, if it was not already being addressed. The assessment for root exploits would look something like Table 2.2.

Table 2.1 DNS Security Assessment

Threats	Threat Results	Security Requirements	Current Practices	Vulnerabilities
Outline known threats to the DNS infrastructure	Worst-case scenario if those threats are exploited	Best practice security policy	Security policy currently in place	Areas in which the organization is vulnerable

Table 2.2 DNS Security Assessment: Root Exploits

Threats	Threat Results	Security Requirements	Current Practices	Vulnerabilities
Root Exploits	Could result in the disabling of all DNS functions and allow an attacker access to the network	DNS servers must be regularly patched and tested against known exploits	No set interval for testing or patching of DNS servers	Too long a period may pass between the release of an exploit or security patch and when the servers are actually patched

This systematic approach to DNS security allows the person or group tasked with securing the DNS infrastructure to prioritize security changes and set goals. Goals are important because it allows the person or group to demonstrate progress in achieving DNS security to senior management. Security costs money, even in cases where no hardware or software purchases are required the time devoted to securing a DNS infrastructure takes away from other projects. Status reports demonstrating progress lead to continued management support. The assessment is all about creating a quantifiable measure of security success.

DNS vulnerabilities can generally be placed into one of three categories. These are vulnerabilities in design, implementation, or configuration. Design vulnerabilities are those vulnerabilities that are inherent in the protocol or application. For instance, some might consider the fact that DNS uses UDP for transport a type of design vulnerability. Weaknesses in DNS software, such as root exploits, are also considered design vulnerabilities. Another vulnerability in design is not monitoring DNS traffic properly, which includes both DNS traffic and monitoring for changes the domain registrar level.

Implementation vulnerabilities are those that occur as a result of the way a solution has been deployed. Running authoritative and recursive DNS services on the same server could be thought of as an implementation threat. Placing two authoritative DNS servers on the same network could be another example. Implementation vulnerabilities do not just have to revolve around the DNS servers or software, not enabling two-factor authentication with the domain registrar could also be considered an implementation vulnerability.

Configuration vulnerabilities are the most common. These vulnerabilities are administrative errors that make a solution less secure. For example, allowing unrestricted access to zone data might be considered a configuration threat. Not assigning the correct permissions to zone files would be another example.

As the DNS security group identifies vulnerabilities, they should be classified into one of the three categories. The response to the vulnerability will depend on the category to which the vulnerability is assigned.

A threat may fall into multiple categories. When threats have been identified and classified, the next step is to determine the course of action. Generally, the response to a threat can fall into one of three categories:

1. Create a new security policy
2. Maintain existing policy
3. Address threat, without changing current policy.

Not addressing a potential threat also falls into the realm of maintaining the existing policy. If the cost to benefit ratio for fixing a problem is simply too great to garner management support it is possible that a solution will not be implemented. Fortunately, in most cases, DNS security is very cost effective.

Once the planning stage has been completed, each proposed solution has to be enabled and the security group has to follow up to ensure newly enacted processes are being followed. This means performing periodic audits of the organization's DNS structure. The audits should be performed at random times, but with regularity.

The DNS security group should determine how often they will perform audits of the DNS infrastructure. The audits should be somewhat random, but still occur regularly. Usually a few months between audits is adequate—though some organizations may require monthly audits.

The process of implementing a strong DNS security plan does not have to be time consuming. A couple of planning sessions can smooth out the whole process and make the initial implementation proceed relatively smoothly and in a coordinated fashion. Regular audits of the system should take less than an hour—again as long as there is a strong process in place.

NOTES

1. CyberBunker has a different version of events, CyberBunker is wrong.
2. Though, it may be phrased more like "How to keep users from clicking on obvious phishing links."

DNS configuration errors

3

INFORMATION IN THIS CHAPTER

- DNS Server Vulnerabilities
- Fingerprinting DNS Servers
- Buffer Overflows, Race Conditions, and Execution with Unnecessary Privileges
- Human Errors

INTRODUCTION

The "sexy" attacks on DNS today tend to be against the DNS protocol itself or against the root servers. Those are the types of attacks that get written up in security publications or are breathlessly, and usually incorrectly, reported on during the nightly news. Do not misunderstand, those are real attacks that pose a real threat to an organization, but often those are attacks that the security team has little or no control over. Sure, if a DNS Distributed Denial of Service (DDoS) attack is launched against an organization there are countermeasures that can be taken, but those countermeasures are almost always reactionary.

There are a number of DNS security threats to an organization that are internal. Security teams have better control over these threats and need to be aware of them. This chapter will review these threats and provide a better understanding of what attackers are looking for when targeting DNS servers inside the network.

DNS SERVER VULNERABILITIES

Internally, one of the biggest threats to an organization's DNS infrastructure is the DNS server itself. DNS server software is complex, with millions of lines of code, and that much code is going to inevitably result in vulnerabilities that an attacker can use to gain access to a network.

This is an especially painful reality for organizations that host their own authoritative DNS servers. Hosting authoritative DNS servers requires that the DNS servers be publicly reachable at all times, usually in a demilitarized zone.

DNS Security. DOI: http://dx.doi.org/10.1016/B978-0-12-803306-7.00003-6

While there are certainly some advantages to this, such as not having to rely on a third party to properly secure their servers, it does introduce additional risk to the organization.

To make matters worse, the most popular DNS servers do not have the best track record when it comes to security. Although, in fairness, both Microsoft DNS and Internet Systems Consortium (ISC)'s BIND have made great strides in security over recent years (discussed in more detail in Chapters 6 and 7), but critical security flaws are still being discovered.

TRACKING NEW VULNERABILITIES

Tracking security flaws within DNS server software (and really all applications running within the network) is extremely important. Fortunately, both ISC and Microsoft make it easy to find out about new security flaws. To find out about security updates in ISC's BIND visit https://www.isc.org/downloads/software-support-policy/security-advisory/ and to find out about the latest in Microsoft DNS server vulnerabilities visit https://technet.microsoft.com/en-us/library/security/. Both Microsoft and ISC also have RSS Feeds and email lists that users can subscribe to in order to find out about new vulnerabilities. There are also a number of excellent services, both free and paid, that catalog new vulnerabilities and present them in a way that can easily be ingested into a Security Information and Event Manager or Governance, Risk, and Compliance server so these announcements can be automatically correlated and prioritized against other alerts.

In addition to flaws within the DNS server software itself, security teams need to worry about flaws within the underlying server itself and other application running on that server. It used to be that too often DNS server software is running on machines that are also hosting other applications. If an attacker manages to exploit a vulnerable application on that server the attacker will potentially have access to everything running on the server, including DNS records. Fortunately with the rise of virtual machines in the data center organizations are more likely to build purpose-built images for different functions, increasing both security and control.

But still, for a DNS security team, that is a nightmare scenario: An attacker gains access to the DNS server and changes the A or CNAME record for the web site and sets a high Time To Live (TTL) for the zone file and suddenly all visitors to that organization's web site are being sent to servers controlled by the attacker. Even if the security quickly identifies and remediates the problem it could still be days before all traffic is flowing to the right location.

The good news is that this specific attack is actually extremely rare. In part because a lot of hackers do not have a good understanding of how DNS works and so do not think about trying to implement a complex attack like this. It is also rare because it is so complex: An attacker has to target an organization, gain access to the DNS server, have a server that she is willing to expose to public traffic, and survive in the network long enough to implement the changes and hope that they go unnoticed for a significant period of time in order to attract enough traffic to make the campaign worthwhile. That is a lot of things that have to go wrong in the target network and go right for the attacker. It is much more likely that an attacker will take advantage of opportunistic vulnerabilities in an organization's DNS authoritative server as a means of gaining access to the network, rather than to specifically create havoc with DNS records. Not that this scenario provides any comfort to already overburdened security teams.

A much more common form of this attack is to simply call the domain registrar or the company that manages DNS records and use social engineering to get them to make changes to the DNS records. This happened to the New York Times, and several other high profile web sites, in 2013 when an attacker called their domain registrar and tricked the registrars into make changes to their respective domain records sending visitors to web sites controlled by the attackers.

How hard is it to conduct a social engineering attack like the one described above? It can be surprisingly easy, depending on what type of security precautions the target company has taken with their domain registration. Let us pick on a very popular web site, reddit, for a minute. To find out what is needed to attempt a social engineering campaign against reddit all that is required is the information contained in the whois output of their domain:

```
Domain Name: reddit.com
Registry Domain ID: 153584275_DOMAIN_COM-VRSN
Registrar WHOIS Server: whois.gandi.net
Registrar URL: http://www.gandi.net
Updated Date: 2014-10-22T02:18:29Z
Creation Date: 2005-04-29T17:59:19Z
Registrar Registration Expiration Date: 2017-04-29T17:59:19Z
Registrar: GANDI SAS
Registrar IANA ID: 81
```

The information above tells an attacker that the domain is registered with gandi.net. Now the attacker knows which registrar to reach out to in order to make the changes. The second part of the whois information provides a DNS contact for reddit:

```
Admin Name: Domain Administrator
Admin Organization: Reddit Inc
Admin Street: 548 Market St., #16093
Admin City: San Francisco
Admin State/Province: California
Admin Postal Code: 94104-5401
Admin Country: US
Admin Phone: +1.4156662330
Admin Phone Ext:
Admin Fax:
Admin Fax Ext:
Admin Email: domainadmin@reddit.com
```

Reddit is smart here because they are using an alias as the domain admin instead of a single point of contact, so the attacker cannot use the "Frank is no longer with the company, I am new DNS administrator" tactic to trick the registrar. No matter, there are plenty of good stories to try. In this case, because reddit is such a high-profile web site an attacker might try to call with a story along the lines of "Reddit is currently experiencing a huge DDoS attack, so we can't get to our email but our DDoS provider needs us to make changes to our DNS records to point to them, can you please do this we are losing millions of dollars every hour the site remains unreachable." Chances are that the employee at the domain registrar does not want to be responsible for keeping the site off-line and may very well comply. Notice, the registrars for reddit are smart and have put in protections to prevent transfers:

```
Domain Status: clientTransferProhibited
http://www.icann.org/epp#clientTransferProhibited
Domain Status:
```

This means an attacker cannot completely take ownership of a domain, but still can do damage in the short term by getting the registrar to make changes on her behalf.

Will this attack work? It depends. Not just on the story the attacker concocts, but also on what types of protection reddit has in place with their domain registrar. Domain registrars usually (though, not always) offer multiple layers of security protection that must be passed before changes can be made to a zone file. However, domain registrars only implement those additional security protections when a customer requests it. Most customers, unsurprisingly, do not make that request.

In addition to the *clientTransferProhibited* protection shown above, there are a number of domain security precautions that domain registrars are required to implement. A whois of NYTimes.com now shows most of these security precautions in place:

```
Domain Status: clientUpdateProhibited
(https://www.icann.org/epp#clientUpdateProhibited)
Domain Status: clientTransferProhibited
(https://www.icann.org/epp#clientTransferProhibited)
Domain Status: clientDeleteProhibited
(https://www.icann.org/epp#clientDeleteProhibited)
Domain Status: serverUpdateProhibited
(https://www.icann.org/epp#serverUpdateProhibited)
Domain Status: serverTransferProhibited
(https://www.icann.org/epp#serverTransferProhibited)
Domain Status: serverDeleteProhibited
(https://www.icann.org/epp#serverDeleteProhibited)
```

These additional status codes are known as Extensible Provisional Protocol (EPP) codes. The Internet Corporation for Assigned Names and Numbers (ICANN) enabled EPP codes and they come in two flavors: client and server. Server EPP codes are set by registries and generally deal with the administration of domain names, such as when a domain is first registered but not yet active, or when it has expired and is going to be deleted (returned to the registration pool). Client EPP statuses are set by the registrar generally by request of their customer, though some registrars will set these by default.

The client EPP statuses of most interest to security teams are *clientDeleteProhibited*, *clientTransferProhibited*, *clientUpdateProhibited*. clientDeleteProhibited prevents a domain from being deleted, even if the request appears to come from an authorized contact. clientTranferProhibited prevents a domain from being transferred from one registrar to another, this is a common tactic among attackers using social engineering to gain control of a domain. Once the domain is under the purview of another registrar it takes significantly longer to undo any damage than it would if the changes were made while the registrar remained in place. The final EPP code, clientUpdateProhibited, is the most severe. clientUpdateProhibited prevents any changes to be made to the domain at all, even from authorized contacts. Every time a legitimate domain administrator wants to make changes to a domain with the clientUpdateProhibited EPP code enabled, he must first have the registrar turn off clientUpdateProhibited code using whatever authentication processes are in place with the registrar, make the changes to the domain, then re-enable clientUpdateProhibited.

Any security professional knows that there is a delicate balance between security and the user experience. If the barriers for security are too high users will find a way to circumvent them and the organization winds up being less secure. EPP codes add an extra layer of security that helps to protect a domain name, but can be a nuisance in an organization that requires a lot of domain changes.

One way around this is to delegate subdomains to a server inside the network. For most organizations, there are relatively few DNS changes made to external-facing infrastructure, such as web servers and mail servers. On the other hand, there may be constant DNS changes being made to internal infrastructure. By consolidating internal infrastructure under a subdomain (eg, corp.dns-book.net) the DNS administration team can now create a subdomain with the registrar and point the NS records for that subdomain to an internal server. This allows the security and administration teams to easily make the changes they need to internal mappings without having to expose a DNS server to the Internet. This topic will be discussed in more detail in Chapter 9.

Stepping back for a second, the last couple of pages really seem to have expanded the definition of "server vulnerabilities." This phenomenon is not unique to the realm of DNS, with more organizations outsourcing key functions to third-party providers, colloquially known as "the cloud," organizations are having to reconsider what falls under the realm of security. Given the critical role that DNS plays in the health of almost every organization it is not enough for security teams to just examine the elements that reside within the network, it is important to have a full understanding of the DNS infrastructure from end-to-end.

DNS server security is even critical to small companies that completely out-source DNS infrastructure. In May of 2015 a group out of Brazil created a simple script that resided on a number of web sites. When the script was accessed, it reached out to the gateway router using default usernames and passwords and changed the DNS settings in the router. The attackers could now redirect their victims to attacker-controlled infrastructure whenever the victims tried to visit certain web sites.

Like home users, most small organizations do not worry too much, if at all, about caching DNS. They will generally purchase a wireless router, connect it to the modem provided by their Internet Service Provider (ISP) and let the ISP populate all of the settings. In 5–10 minutes the network is running and connected to the Internet. After initial setup the router is never touched again.

Like it or not, that wireless router is also a recursive DNS server and needs to maintained as such, because the security on these wireless routers is often very poor. The two most critical steps that need to be taken to secure an organization's wireless router: make sure the web interface is not publicly accessible and change the default password. Both of these steps seem like they are no brainers, however, most users do not make these simple changes.

It happens less often now, but it is used to be commonplace for wireless router manufacturers to make the web interface for the router available on both the public and private IP Address of the router. Most people forget that the outside interface of the router is usually a public IP Address, meaning it can be reached by anyone on the Internet. In other words, anyone who knows your public IP Address (or happens to stumble across it while doing a scan of the ISP's network) has access to the web interface of the router and can make whatever changes they want. It is important to check the configuration of any newly deployed wireless router to ensure that the web interface is only accessible from inside the network.

In order to make life easier for users during setup, most wireless router manufacturers provide a fairly simple username and password combination to access the router and configure it. The combination is something like admin/admin or admin/[No Password]. This is necessary because when a company is selling millions of boxes a year if that company tried to issue unique passwords for each router it would be a logistical and support nightmare to provide unique passwords for each router. However, most people do not change the default password after first use—so, an attacker who gains access to the router web interface has no problem logging into the device.

EASY TO FIND

There are a number of web sites that provide lists of all the default username and password for the most commonly sold wireless routers. Sites like Router Passwords (http://www.routerpasswords.com/) are useful for people who have forgotten the passwords to their routers. They are also extremely helpful to attackers trying to break into networks.

Another problem area for small office wireless routers comes with software updates. Much like DNS in a large organization, wireless routers are "set and forget" appliances. Once a router is set up and working properly, it is rare that anyone goes back to update the software or the configuration, even if the manufacture releases new patches or configuration guidelines, most of their customers are not aware of the changes until it is too late.

Given the number of vulnerabilities that have been announced by wireless router vendors over the last few years, routinely checking the configuration and updating the software and firmware of these routers is critical to the security of small organizations and home users.

FINGERPRINTING DNS SERVERS

Scanning surveys of DNS infrastructure throughout the Internet regularly reveal that a significant portion of DNS servers is vulnerable to attack. There are undoubtedly a couple of reasons behind this. The first, as discussed previously, has to deal with the fact that DNS is often a "set it and forget it" service. A team sets up the DNS server, gets everything running, and moves on to another role or another organization. As long as everything is working, newer teams do not make any changes to the server. Fortunately, this particular scenario happens less frequently as organizations have become more focused on the importance of patch management and regular update cycles across the entire network.

A second scenario, one that is still surprisingly common, is that DNS server software remains unpatched because the server administrators do not realize that it is running on the server. A number of operating system vendors enable DNS services by default. This is expected behavior, especially if the server needs to talk to the rest of the Internet. However, some of these configurations leave the server running as essentially an open recursive server. This is bad for a number of reasons, but specifically in this section it means that if the server is exposed to the Internet it is potentially vulnerable to attack, especially if the server administrator does not know the DNS server is running and is not regularly updating it.

To compound this problem DNS is, by design, relatively easy to fingerprint. Fingerprinting is the act of querying a server to determine what software and version is running on the server. It is a common tactic used by both penetration testers and attackers to quietly test systems to see if there are exploitable vulnerabilities.

DNS server software is relatively easy to fingerprint because there is built-in functionality in some DNS server software to provide this answer through a *dig* query. *Dig* is a command line tool available in every UNIX, BSD, and Linux variant as well as in OS X. Administrators use *dig* to troubleshoot DNS problems and isolate errors in DNS records. You can also use *dig* to find out what version of BIND a DNS server is running. The command to do this is *dig @[IP Address or Domain of Name Server] version.bind chaos txt* and it produces output similar to this:

```
[root@server ~]# dig @127.0.0.1 version.bind chaos txt
; <<>> DiG 9.3.6-P1-RedHat-9.3.6-16.P1.el5_7.1 <<>> @127.0.0.1
version.bind chaos txt
; (1 server found)
;; global options: printcmd
;; Got answer:
;; ->>HEADER<<- opcode: QUERY, status: NOERROR, id: 49112
;; flags: qr aa rd; QUERY: 1, ANSWER: 1, AUTHORITY: 1, ADDITIONAL: 0
;; QUESTION SECTION:
;version.bind.     CH   TXT
;; ANSWER SECTION:
version.bind.  0  CH  TXT  "9.3.6-P1-RedHat-9.3.6-16.P1.el5_7.1"
;; AUTHORITY SECTION:
version.bind.  0  CH  NS  version.bind.
```

The relevant information is in the answer section: "*9.3.6-P1-RedHat-9.3.6-16. P1.el5_7.1.*" This tells the attacker that the server is running BIND version 9.3.6 on RedHat Linux. A quick check shows that this version of BIND is extremely outdated and there is an exploit module available for Metasploit that can take advantage of a known vulnerability.

Not every DNS server software vendor accepts the version.bind command, and DNS administrators can even configure BIND to return a blank response, or even put something misleading in the response field. This will be covered in more detail in Chapter 7.

In cases where version.bind does not work there are purpose-built DNS finger-printing tools, like *fpdns*, which can be used to determine what DNS software is running on a server. For example, Microsoft.com does not use any name servers that run BIND, so none of the name servers will respond to version.bind query. However, running the command *fpdns −D microsoft.com* returns the following:

```
allan@allan-1015E:/$ sudo fpdns -D microsoft.com
fingerprint (microsoft.com, 193.221.113.53): Microsoft Windows DNS 2003
fingerprint (microsoft.com, 2620:0:34:0:0:0:0:53): No match found
fingerprint (microsoft.com, 208.76.45.53): Microsoft Windows DNS 2003
fingerprint (microsoft.com, 2620:0:37:0:0:0:0:53): No match found
fingerprint (microsoft.com, 208.84.0.53): Microsoft Windows DNS 2003
fingerprint (microsoft.com, 2620:0:30:0:0:0:0:53): No match found
```

The tool is not perfect, but because it is open source any user has the ability to update it to ensure that it is returning the right results. Fingerprinting and fpdns will be discussed in more detail in Chapter 5.

> ### DNS SURVEY
>
> The Internet Systems Consortium (ISC) does a biannual survey of hosts on the Internet (latest results are here: https://ftp.isc.org/www/survey/reports/current/). One of the things the survey looks at is the version of DNS software that is running on hosts (current results are here: https://ftp.isc.org/www/survey/reports/current/fpdns.txt). Unsurprisingly, fewer and fewer hosts are returning results, but there are still tens of thousands of hosts that ISC is able to accurately fingerprint, some running surprisingly old versions of DNS software.

BUFFER OVERFLOWS, RACE CONDITIONS, AND EXECUTION WITH UNNECESSARY PRIVILEGES

As with any complex piece of software there are a number of different types of attacks to which DNS server software is susceptible. However, there are three vulnerability types that seem to occur the most frequently: buffer overflow attacks, race conditions, and execution with unnecessary privilege.

Buffer overflow attacks are the most common vulnerabilities reported in DNS server software, not surprising given how broad of a category this is. A buffer overflow attack is any time a user sends more data input than the target program intended to receive at that point. Usually, boundary checking protections are in place to avoid the additional data spilling over to adjacent memory locations. However, when those protections are not in place the data overflow can corrupt adjacent memory and cause the program to crash. At the very least this makes the program unavailable, but in certain circumstances it can also allow an attacker to execute a program after the crash.

A good example of the latter scenario is CVE-2015-6125, which impacted Windows DNS servers running on Windows 2008 and 2012 servers. The vulnerability allowed an attacker to send a specially crafted DNS packet that crashes the server and allows arbitrary code to run as the local system administrator. Often an attacker will bundle a memory-resident loader into the buffer overflow and that is code that will be executed upon successful exploitation of the server. Because the loader is memory-resident only it avoids detection by traditional security systems, and it allows the attacker to survey the system and decide which implant to install to remain persistent on the compromised server.

Windows DNS is not the only platform that is subject to buffer overflows. CVE-2008-0122 documents a buffer overflow in applications that use the libbind BIND library. The vulnerability existed in the inet_network () function and if successful would give the attacker the ability to execute code on the remote system. If unsuccessful the attack would crash the server, making it unavailable.

Another type of vulnerability that can exist within DNS software is a race condition. A race condition occurs in multithreaded software and it occurs when multiple threads try to access shared data simultaneously and those accesses are not properly controlled. When this happens a second thread accesses the same data point and changes the value so that the action of the first thread is now incorrect. A simple example of this is if there is a file with a value in it and the program requires multiplying that value by 10 ($x*10 = y$). A first thread accesses the file and sees that $x = 5$, so processes the calculation to get $5*10 = 50$, but if a second thread access that file while the first thread is processing its equation and changes the value of x to 7, then the result of first equation is incorrect and a race condition occurs.

An example of a race condition in BIND is CVE-2015-8461. The race condition affected BIND 9.9.8 and 9.10 and occurred when there was an INSIST assertion failure in resolver.c. It is a challenging vulnerability for an attacker to execute because the timing has to be spotless, but when successful the attack would cause BIND to crash.

DNS servers, by their very nature, are multithreaded—at any given time a DNS server may be responding to dozens, hundreds, or millions of requests. Not surprisingly, race conditions come up frequently within DNS server software. The good news is that they are usually caught before they rise to the level of remotely exploitable vulnerability. But, reviewing the release notes for various versions of the DNS software shows that race conditions are a persistent problem.

The last type of vulnerability to discuss with regard to DNS servers is execution with unnecessary privilege. Execution with unnecessary privilege is not a vulnerability within the code, instead it is a flaw in the way the program operates. When applications run as the Administrator or root user it is not subject to the same security checks that applications which run as a different user. However, software running as a different user may not have all the accesses the developers would like in order to make the application as efficient as possible.

This creates a constant tug of war: developers want access to as much of the server as possible and the security team wants to restrict the damage that can be caused if an attacker exploits a flaw in the application. If an attacker finds an exploitable vulnerability, like a buffer overflow, that allows them to inject code into memory the attacker now has access to the server at the same administrative level as the user that owned the application process. If Administrator owned the crashed application on a Windows system, the attacker now has Administrator access to the server. Similarly, if the application was running as root on a Linux server the attacker now has root access to the server.

CVE-2015-6125, described above, is an example of this type of vulnerability. The initial vulnerability is a buffer overflow but if the attacker is able to successfully exploit the vulnerability she has administrative access to the server.

BIND developers repeatedly ran into this problem years ago to the point that many Linux distributions now have a BIND user, called *named*, created by default and recommend that this user be dedicated to running the named process. The BIND developers also recommend that BIND be run in a *chroot* environment. A *chroot* environment, usually referred to as a chroot jail, changes the root directory to a specified path. Applications running within that chroot jail cannot access anything outside of the specified path. The goal of the chroot jail is to limit the damage an attacker can do if she gains remote access to the system. Yes, she can potentially damage BIND installation, but she cannot gain access to anything else on the server.

HUMAN ERRORS

For the most part, this discussion has focused on malicious attacks carried out by an attacker in either a targeted or nontargeted fashion. The majority of DNS security problems are external and malicious, but there are mistakes that happen internally that impact the availability of DNS. It is important to examine these errors alongside the malicious errors because both types of action impact the availability of DNS.

How much control over mitigating internal DNS errors is given to the security team will vary from organization to organization, but it is worthwhile to know what to be on the lookout for and the types of steps an organization can take to minimize those errors.

DNS errors are so common, and prolific, that there is an RFC dedicated to documenting the most common. RFC 1912 is entitled *Common DNS Operational and Configuration Errors* and provides a good overview of the types of errors that DNS administrators can expect to run into during the configuration and management process.

Probably the most common DNS error organizations make is one that has been discussed ad nauseam already and is a topic that will be beaten to death throughout this book: ensuring that DNS technical, billing, and administrative contacts are kept up-to-date. Especially within organizations that register their domains for multiple years at a time, it is very easy for individuals to move on from roles and even for internal distribution lists to come and go. When those contacts no longer exist, or those email addresses are no longer valid, making changes with the domain registrar become a lot more difficult and time-consuming. This is especially problematic if a change needs to be made in a hurry, something that is often the case with DNS changes.

The first problem often leads to a second problem: letting a domain name expire because billing information has changed or the domain registrar cannot reach the billing contact they have on file. These two problems are often intertwined, no registrar wants to immediately turn off a domain name when it expires and risk alienating its customer base, so the registrar will reach out to the billing, administrative, and technical contacts multiple times before the domain expires to try to get them to renew. Even when the expiration date occurs, the registrar is required to give their customer a grace period to get the domain renewed. Again, that process is much more difficult if none of the contacts for the domain are still valid.

Beyond the administrative mistakes there are a number of common technical mistakes that DNS administrators make which can dramatically impact the availability of the DNS infrastructure.

Probably the most common technical error is simply fat fingering a change to a DNS record. Depending on whether fat-fingered host is internal only or public facing this can either be a small, easily fixed problem or one with a huge impact. Remember, changing the record and publishing the updated zone file means that any recursive DNS server who has picked up the new record will hold on to it until the TTL expires and it goes out to grab the correct record. To prevent this all-too-common mistake from happening many organizations use a two-tiered submission system. The request is made and confirmed by a second person or team before the change is actually implemented.

Of course, sometimes a change can be made to a zone file and nothing happens because the administrator forgot to update the serial number.

```
aliska-mbpr:~ allan.liska$ dig dns-book.net SOA
;; Got answer:
;; ->>HEADER<<- opcode: QUERY, status: NOERROR, id: 850
;; flags: qr rd ra; QUERY: 1, ANSWER: 1, AUTHORITY: 0, ADDITIONAL: 1
;; QUESTION SECTION:
;dns-book.net.    IN   SOA
;; ANSWER SECTION:
dns-book.net.  3600  IN  SOA  dns1.name-services.com.  info.name-ser-
vices.com. 1447308739 172800 900 1814400 3600
```

Note, the serial number above is 1447308739, if changes are made to the zone file for dns-book.net the zone file must be updated to at least 1447308740. Many DNS administrators make their lives easier by using a date format, so a new zone registered today would start with 20160421 and if a change was made a week from today the new serial number would be 20160428. This helps track when a zone file change was last made and it is easy to keep the numbers moving incrementally.

Serial number updates are usually only important to worry about if authoritative DNS is being managed within the organization. Most third-party DNS providers have web interfaces that manage zone file incremental updates automatically.

Another common mistake is changing the IP Address of an authoritative name server without updating the registration information. Again, this applies to organizations that manage their own authoritative DNS infrastructure. Many Top Level Domain (TLD) registries require that authoritative name servers be registered—it is not enough to just create an A record and an NS record (though, those are required as well) the TLD registry may require that the authoritative server name and its corresponding IP Address must be registered with the registry. Any time the IP Address for that name server is updated the registry entry must be updated not just the zone file for that domain.

This is not something that happens often, but it winds up happening as domains start to age. Ten to fifteen years after a domain is first registered an organization may switch service providers or move infrastructure to a new data center and be forced to re-IP their servers. During this process the zone file may be properly updated, but the registrar will still have old information for the IP to domain mapping (a quick whois check generally confirms this). This results in domain information not being properly propagated across recursive name servers and it can result in an organization's web, email, and other services not being available for up to 72 hours while the registry is updated with the new information.

Another problem, though much less common, with zone file editing is mismanaging CNAME records. CNAME records are great resources for managing DNS information, especially with servers that serve multiple functions. For example, if an organization is hosting HTTP, FTP, and RSS information all on the same server it makes sense to create an A record for the www subdomain and CNAME records for the ftp and rss subdomains. However, using a CNAME for MX or NS records, even if they are all pointing to the same server is frowned upon and many DNS servers will reject those requests. In addition, do not point CNAME records to other records that are themselves CNAME records, doing so has been known to result in wormholes being formed that tear apart the Internet. The result is not quite so severe, but it can create an ugly loop that some recursive DNS servers do not handle well.

Finally, whether DNS records are maintained in-house or outsourced to a DNS provider access control is very important. There should be a limited a number of people who are authorized to make changes to the organization's DNS records. Changes that are made should have to go through a change control/approval process, just as a firewall or router change would. Implementing a change control process, one that involves people who understand the intricacies of DNS, significantly reduces the chances that one of the mistakes outlined in this section will happen.

CONCLUSIONS

DNS is tough to secure, there are a number of different areas that are potentially vulnerable to attack and it requires a security team to examine not just the software, but also the protocol, and the administrative details around maintaining an organization's domain name. The complexity involved in securing an organization's DNS infrastructure may require a new way of thinking about security and what falls into the realm of security.

That being said, it is still important to remember the fundamentals of security. The fundamentals include knowing what services are running within an organization's network, making sure that services that are not needed are disabled, that no service is running at a higher privilege than needed, that server software is kept up-to-date, and that the security team is aware of new vulnerabilities and potential new threats that may impact the organization.

Taking the steps outlined in this chapter will help improve the availability of the DNS service within an organization. Of course, availability is only one aspect of a security program; the next few chapters will cover other aspects of DNS security.

External DNS exploits

4

INFORMATION IN THIS CHAPTER

- Cache Poisoning
- DNS Spoofing
- DDoS Attacks Using DNS
- Using DNS as a Command and Control or Exfil Channel

INTRODUCTION

Chapter 3 focused on attacks against DNS infrastructure, whether that is a locally hosted server or an attack on the infrastructure managed by outsourced providers. This chapter looks at attacks on the protocol itself as well as attacks that take advantage of the way most organizations monitor DNS traffic.

This point has been touched on a number of times already in this book, but it is important to note that the security landscape is constantly evolving. Ten years ago this chapter would have spent a lot of time discussing cache poisoning but after the "Kaminsky bug" in 2008, most DNS server developers have taken steps to ensure that cache poisoning vulnerabilities are extremely rare. That being said, security researchers and hackers are constantly examining protocols looking for new and interesting ways to exploit flaws in commonly used protocols on the Internet. Because of its ubiquitousness DNS is a prime target for those researchers, so it is important to stay current on trends in DNS security.

IN DEFENSE OF SECURITY RESEARCHERS

Security researchers have gotten a bad reputation within some Internet communities. By exposing vulnerabilities in applications on protocols they make the job of the attacker easier. What too few people seem to understand is that these researchers actually perform a very valuable service. Security researchers who practice responsible disclosure help improve the security of everyone connected to the Internet. If a security researcher uncovers a vulnerability, there is a good chance that someone with nefarious intentions has, or will, uncover the same vulnerability. The difference is that the attacker will not disclose that vulnerability; instead the attacker will use it to exploit the vulnerable systems (what security professionals call a 0-day attack). When a security

(Continued)

DNS Security. DOI: http://dx.doi.org/10.1016/B978-0-12-803306-7.00004-8

CACHE POISONING

In a DNS cache poisoning attack an attacker takes advantage of flaws in the DNS protocol to load bad data into a recursive DNS server. That data usually involves passing an incorrect A record to the recursive server in order to redirect traffic to infrastructure owned by the attacker.

The simplest form of this attack is to send additional A records with a request to a malicious domain. Fortunately, this type of cache poisoning attack is no longer effective. To understand how this attack would work, take a look at a traditional DNS request from the user perspective and the DNS recursive server perspective.

This is the user request:

```
[user@workstation ~]# host dns-book.net
dns-book.net has address 8.5.1.36
dns-book.net mail is handled by 10 p.nsm.ctmail.com.
```

This is a part of what the recursive DNS server sees:

```
[root@server data]# tcpdump -n udp port 53 -v
03:05:05.199542 IP (tos 0x0, ttl 64, id 13085, offset 0, flags [none],
proto: UDP (17), length: 73) 192.168.1.15.29092 > 98.124.192.1.domain:
33955 [1au] A? www.dns-book.net. (45)
03:05:05.212049 IP (tos 0x0, ttl 53, id 3897, offset 0, flags [none], pro-
to: UDP (17), length: 201) 98.124.192.1.domain > 192.168.1.15.29092:
33955*- 1/5/1 www.dns-book.net. A 8.5.1.36 (173)
03:05:05.220014 IP (tos 0x0, ttl 64, id 64355, offset 0, flags [none],
proto: UDP (17), length: 73) 192.168.1.15.34388 > 98.124.194.1.domain:
63645 [1au] MX? www.dns-book.net. (45)
03:05:05.232466 IP (tos 0x0, ttl 53, id 13094, offset 0, flags [none],
proto: UDP (17), length: 214) 98.124.194.1.domain > 192.168.1.15.34388:
63645*- 1/5/1 www.dns-book.net. MX[|domain]
```

The recursive DNS server asks for the A record, it also asks for the MX record and stores it in its cache so if other users of this recursive DNS server need that information it will already be available, at least until the Time to Live (TTL) expires.

Up until the bailiwick rule was implemented in 1993 it was relatively trivial to poison a DNS cache. To do so an attacker would set up a bad domain on authoritative name servers that she controls. When users visited that bad domain their recursive DNS server queried the authoritative name servers for the bad domain. The authoritative servers respond with an answer, as shown in the code above, but they also add additional domain mappings. The authoritative server may reply with:

```
03:05:05.212049 IP (tos 0x0, ttl 53, id 3897, offset 0, flags [none],
proto: UDP (17), length: 201) 98.124.192.1.domain > 192.168.1.15.29092:
33955*- 1/5/1 www.google.com A 8.5.1.40 (173)
```

This is an unprompted request, but recursive servers accepted anything that was sent to them, so most of them would cache it. Now, anyone using that recursive server and attempting to visit Google's web site would wind up going to a server owned by the attacker, even though everything would look correct from a DNS perspective.

The bailiwick rule changed that. The bailiwick rule states that a recursive DNS server will not accept responses from an authoritative DNS that fall outside the scope of authority (bailiwick) of the authoritative server. The bailiwick rule is not built into the DNS protocol itself and is not present within an authoritative DNS server; instead the bailiwick logic resides within recursive name servers only. The recursive name server reviews the referral responses given in the response tree to determine whether it should accept an answer given by the authoritative name server. If the response appears to fall outside the scope of the authoritative name server the recursive name server drops it.

While the above type of cache poisoning attack is almost nonexistent at this point, other types of cache poisoning attack still occur. In February of 2015 researchers at RSA uncovered an attack on Boleto transactions that used DNS cache poisoning. Boleto is a common payment method in Brazil. In fact, Boleto is so popular that it accounts for almost 25% of all payment transactions in Brazil. There is actually a malware family, called Bolware, that specifically target Boleto transactions.

This particular attack added a new twist: poisoning the recursive DNS servers of the victims' Internet Service Provider (ISP). The poisoned DNS records pointed toward infrastructure owned by the attacker that mirrored the Boleto web site. Users would supply their credentials to the fake web site and the attackers collected all of the usernames and passwords, while the victims remained unaware—until the attackers drained their bank accounts.

The reason the attackers used the victim machines to launch the attacks is that the Brazilian ISPs smartly restricted who could query their recursive DNS servers. The ISPs prevented hosts from outside of their network from querying their servers, so an external cache poisoning attack would not work.

In order to understand how this type of cache poisoning works, it is first necessary to understand DNS at the packet level. A DNS packet consists of three parts: Header, Question, and Answer (it is actually a little more complex than this, but this provides a good starting point). The header is a fixed size of 12 bytes while the Question and Answer sections vary in size. Because most DNS queries and responses are carried out over UDP, there is a packet size limit on the packet size of 512 bytes. Also, because DNS and responses use UDP there is no handshake between the recursive and authoritative name servers. Instead the DNS server relies on a combination of source port, original destination IP address, and a 16-bit transaction ID in order to validate an incoming response.

To understand how this works, take a look at the following query/response:

```
11:14:20.316430 IP (tos 0x0, ttl 64, id 35386, offset 0, flags [none],
proto: UDP (17), length: 74) 192.168.1.15.16271 > 208.76.58.196.domain:
14324 [1au] A? www.cryptodns.com. (46)
11:14:20.397637 IP (tos 0x0, ttl 54, id 20874, offset 0, flags [none],
proto: UDP (17), length: 196) 208.76.58.196.domain > 192.168.1.15.16271:
14324*- 2/4/1 www.cryptodns.com. CNAME cryptodns.com., cryptodns.com.
(168)
```

The first line is the query from the recursive name server. The query asks for an A record for the domain www.cryptodns.com. The query has a transaction ID of 14324, a source port of 16271 and was sent to IP address 208.76.58.196. The second line, which contains the query response, has the correct originating IP address was sent to the matching port and contains the matching transaction ID, as indicated by the asterisk. In the realm of DNS the fact that these three things match indicated that the response is the correct one.

Forging a DNS packet is relatively simple; in fact there are a number of tools that help attackers create a forged DNS packet and since the protocol is delivered using UDP forging an IP address is trivial. A powerful tool for forging DNS, and other, packets is *hping3*. Using *hping3* an attacker can generate forged DNS packets that look like they come from random addresses:

```
[root@server ~]# hping3 -2 -p 53 --rand-source 8.8.8.8
```

This command tells hping3 to send DNS packets from randomly forged IP addresses to the name server 8.8.8.8. The traffic generated by this command looks like this:

```
11:25:59.915754 IP (tos 0x0, ttl 64, id 50693, offset 0, flags [none],
proto: UDP (17), length: 28) 184.134.243.10.qip-msgd > 8.8.8.8.domain:
[udp sum ok] [|domain]
11:26:00.915799 IP (tos 0x0, ttl 64, id 47876, offset 0, flags [none],
proto: UDP (17), length: 28) 20.110.55.234.mti-tcs-comm > 8.8.8.8.
domain: [udp sum ok] [|domain]
11:26:01.915877 IP (tos 0x0, ttl 64, id 8542, offset 0, flags [none], pro-
to: UDP (17), length: 28) 174.5.167.152.taskman-port > 8.8.8.8.domain:
[udp sum ok] [|domain]
```

Each one of the queries appears to be coming from a different IP address. In order to make this functionality more useful though the traffic needs to appear as if it is coming from the authoritative name server. Using the *cryptodns.com* information from the earlier example *hping3* can create a forged packet that appears to originate from the authoritative DNS server for *cryptodns.com*. The command looks like this:

```
[root@server ~]# hping3 -2 -p 53 --spoof 208.76.58.196 192.168.1.15
```

And the resulting traffic looks like this:

```
11:42:21.136079 IP (tos 0x0, ttl 64, id 45091, offset 0, flags [none],
proto: UDP (17), length: 28) 208.76.58.196.1775 > 196 192.168.1.15.
domain: [|domain]
11:42:22.136132 IP (tos 0x0, ttl 64, id 56073, offset 0, flags [none],
proto: UDP (17), length: 28) 208.76.58.196.femis > 196 192.168.1.15.
domain: [|domain]
11:42:23.136178 IP (tos 0x0, ttl 64, id 30499, offset 0, flags [none],
proto: UDP (17), length: 28) 208.76.58.196.powerguardian > 196
192.168.1.15.domain: [|domain]
```

So, the first part of the job is done: The IP Address is forged. However, the attacker still needs to figure out the random source port and the transaction ID. Before 2008, the first part was easy many DNS resolvers reused the same source port for all DNS transactions; some DNS administrators even set the source port to 53. In fact, there is still a configuration option in BIND to hard code the source port. Thankfully, this feature is rarely used.

In cases where the source port is hard-coded all that is needed is to guess the transaction ID. Because the transaction ID is limited to a 16-bit field, there are only 65535 possible entries in that field. So, for an attacker to successfully poison the cache on a recursive server she needs to wait for a query from that recursive server for the target domain then quickly flood the recursive server with thousands of forged responses, each with a different transaction ID before the actual response is returned by the real authoritative name server and this is without taking into consideration that the source ports have to match as well. This sounds impossible, correct?

Surprisingly, thanks to the Birthday Paradox it is not. The Birthday Paradox states that in a room of 23 people there is a 50% chance that two of the people in that room share a birthday, the percentage jumps to 99.9% in a room of 75 people. The math behind this has to do with combinations and permutations and is beyond the scope of this book.[1] Using the same math, most of the time an attacker will only need to send 700 packets before she matches the source port.

Still, those odds are not very good, but there are ways to improve them even further. One of the most common ways is for the attacker to initiate multiple requests for subdomains that do not exist. For example, if an attacker wants to poison the cache for the domain www.dns-book.net she may create a list of hundreds of random subdomains such as the following:

* xydias.dns-book.net
* f1dzh.dns-book.net
* pazcd.dns-book.net

The attacker will then query the target recursive server with each of these requests one at a time, which will force the recursive to continually reach out to the authoritative server for an answer until it gets match. At the same time, the attacker will send thousands of spoofed packets to a recursive server hoping to beat the response, with a matching transaction ID, from the authoritative server to one of the queries. That is the beauty of the attack: The attacker only needs to get one match. Each of the forged responses contains an additional resource record (RR) response that maps www.dns-book.net to a server controlled by the attacker. Fig. 4.1 shows the Additional RRs field that is part of every DNS response, though not always populated. Any one successful hit will poison the cache for www.dns-book.net and point all traffic to a server controlled by the attacker. This highlights again the importance of not running an open resolver. A cache poisoning attack is much more difficult to carry out if the attacker cannot send requests to the targeted recursive server.

Transaction ID	Flags	
Question count	Answer RR count	12 bytes
Authority RR count	Additional RR count	
Question entries (variable length)		
Answer RRs (variable length)		Variable length
Authority RRs (variable length)		
Additional RRs (variable length)		

FIGURE 4.1

Structure of a DNS packet.

Another type of DNS cache poisoning attack is a local DNS cache poisoning attack. This attack does not impact the victim's recursive DNS server; rather it infects the DNS cache directly on the victim's workstation.

Most people do not know that, by default, Microsoft Windows and Apple OS X workstations maintain a local DNS cache based on responses from the configured recursive server. The local cache speeds up the process of visiting frequently queried domain names. Unfortunately, this is also trivial attack vector to exploit. The command to find out what is in a local cache on a Microsoft Windows workstation is *ipconfig /displaydns*. Below is a snippet of sample output from running the command.

```
C:\Documents and Settings>ipconfig /displaydns
Windows IP Configuration

    fileserver
    - - - - - - - - - - - - - - - - - - - - - - - - - - - - - - - - - - - - -
    Record Name . . . . . : fileserver
    Record Type . . . . . : 1
    Time To Live . . . . : 562795
    Data Length . . . . . : 4
    Section . . . . . . . : Answer
    A (Host) Record . . . : 192.168.1.10
    www.dns-book.net
    - - - - - - - - - - - - - - - - - - - - - - - - - - - - - - - - - - - - -
    Record Name . . . . . : www.cryptodns.com
    Record Type . . . . . : 5
    Time To Live . . . . : 562795
    Data Length . . . . . : 4
    Section . . . . . . . : Answer
    CNAME Record . . . . : cryptodns.com
```

In January of 2016 a group of hackers interested in stealing financial data used this methodology to target banking customers in the United Kingdom. The group used a variant of the Dridex malware family that introduced local DNS cache poisoning. Similar to other types of attacks involving DNS cache poisoning the attackers built mirrors of the targeted banking sites hosted on servers they controlled.

In this particular attack the attackers used Microsoft Office documents to deliver the payload. When the victim opened the trojaned document the malware was downloaded and installed. The malware filled the local cache with DNS records pointing both mail and web domains to the attacker controlled infrastructure.

Because the records were now loaded into the local cache, the victim's workstation would never reach out to the local recursive server when trying to communicate with her bank unless the computer was rebooted or the cache was manually cleared (after the malware was removed, of course). This type of attack is highly effective if the attacker can reach many users, which is also the downside of this type of attack. A DNS cache poisoning attack that targets recursive name servers can impact thousands or even millions of users if it is successful. This type of attack can be much smaller in scope, unless the attacker has access to an expansive delivery system or the attack is a targeted one. Of course, access to an expanded delivery system is easier with Delivery as a Service botnets being readily available and cheap to rent for hours, days, or weeks. Another way to make this attack more effective is through the use of better reconnaissance. If an attacker is specifically targeting an organization she has the time to better understand that organization and its traffic flows and can make these attacks more effective.

POISONING THE LOCAL CACHE

There are a number of ways that an attacker can poison the local cache on a victim machine, but one of the most common methods is to use undocumented DNS Application Programming Interface (APIs) on Microsoft Windows computers. Any application that wants to interact with the underlying Windows operating system has to use API calls to Windows. These APIs allow the application to communicate with the operating system, irrespective of the programming language used. Most Windows API calls are well documented, but there are a lot of different APIs that have no documentation at all. Malware developers will often play with these APIs to determine what changes they can make to the underlying operating system with a specific API call. In the case of DNS cache poisoning on the local host undocumented DNS API calls like DnsAddRecordSet_A allow malware (and legitimate programs) to add A records to the local cache on the victim workstation.

WEB BROWSER CACHING

Another potential area of local caching exploitation is within the web browser. Most web browsers have built-in resolvers that cache DNS responses for a short period of time (anywhere from 30 seconds to 30 minutes, depending on the browser). While this has not been an avenue of attack to this point, it is possible that it will be in the future and should be monitored closely.

On the other hand, an area where DNS caching within browsers has been exploited is in DNS rebinding attacks. A DNS rebinding attack occurs when an attacker takes advantage of web browser DNS caching to launch attacks against other hosts on the network (or outside of the network). The attack works like this: An attacker registers a malicious domain and uses a very short TTL. A victim visits the malicious web site and is told to go to a different host, which is a subdomain of the same domain, where the victim will download a script. The browser then makes another request to the domain, only this time the name server responds to the query with an internal IP address on the victim's network. For example, the attacker could use rebinding to point the domain name to the gateway address of the victim machine, and use the newly downloaded script to access the victim's gateway router and possibly make changes to the configuration.

DNS SPOOFING

A DNS spoofing attack is one in which a victim, or victims, is misdirected via DNS to a host that is not the intended destination. Cache poisoning is one type of DNS spoofing attack, but there are a number of other types of DNS spoofing attacks that do not involve cache poisoning at all.

One example of DNS spoofing is the Trojan known as Win32.QHOST. This malware family has been around since 2005 and variants are still operating in the wild today. The malware itself is not very interesting, but it does use a DNS spoofing technique to avoid detection by security applications.

Built into all versions of the Microsoft Windows operating system is a file called *hosts*. The file sits in the directory *C:\%windir%\system32\drivers\etc \hosts* (Linux, Unix, and Apple OS X systems also have this file, in the case of these operating systems it resides in */etc/hosts*) and is used to map IP addresses to system names or domains. The file is a throwback to days before DNS existed, and it enables communication between machines on a network irrespective of whether or not DNS is configured. A typical *hosts* file looks like this:

```
# Copyright (c) 1993-1999 Microsoft Corp.

#
# This is a sample HOSTS file used by Microsoft TCP/IP for Windows.
# For example:
#
# 102.54.94.97 rhino.acme.com # source server
# 38.25.63.10 x.acme.com # x client host
127.0.0.1 localhost
```

This is a standard *hosts* file, all it does is map the loopback address to localhost, which allows the machine talk to itself. What Win32.QHOST does is modify the *hosts* file so it looks more like this snippet:

```
# Copyright (c) 1993-1999 Microsoft Corp.
#
# This is a sample HOSTS file used by Microsoft TCP/IP for Windows.
# For example:
#
# 102.54.94.97 rhino.acme.com # source server
# 38.25.63.10 x.acme.com # x client host
127.0.0.1 localhost
127.0.0.1 symantec.com
127.0.0.1 f-secure.com
127.0.0.1 kaspersky.com
127.0.0.1 liveupdate.symantec.com
127.0.0.1 mcafee.com
```

The new *hosts* file now points the domains of the most common security vendors to the loopback address preventing these security applications from getting signature updates or reporting on suspicious activity. All-in-all Win32. QHOST creates more than 40 different entries in the *hosts* file and effectively disables all or part of any security application running on the host.

Win32.QHOST is not the only malware that does this, a number of malware families manipulate the *hosts* in order to control communication from the victim box while the attackers get what they need.

Another example of DNS spoofing is the DNSChanger malware created by the group Rove Digital and was widely deployed between 2007 and 2015. The DNSChanger malware would change the recursive DNS servers on the victim machine to hosts that were controlled by the attackers. In the case of DNSChanger the attackers used their recursive DNS servers to display advertising and to redirect victims to sites that paid Rove Digital an advertising fee.

In 2014 a group of attackers tried another variant of this attack. The attack, dubbed "Poisoned Hurricane" by the researchers at FireEye who uncovered it, involved a two-step process. In the first step the attackers discovered that the authoritative DNS servers at data center provider Hurricane Electric would allow users to enter in records for any host, even hosts for which the name server was not authoritative. For example, an attacker was able to enter an A record for www.adobe.com and point the A record to infrastructure owned by the attacker.

The second step in the process was the malware that the attackers used. The malware was a variant of PlugX that was configured with the Hurricane Electric DNS servers as recursive servers. The Hurricane Electric name servers were not recursive servers, but they did respond to queries and would return any host information that was loaded onto the server by the attackers. In all, FireEye analysts uncovered 21 domains that were configured in this manner on the Hurricane Electric DNS servers by the attackers.

Another, less common, method of DNS spoofing is to use a specialized tool sitting on another host on the same network to intercept and respond to DNS queries coming from the target host. This method is a little more complicated because it requires that the attacker already has access to the target network and is able to install a network sniffer on the network without being detected (many security operation centers will receive alerts when an interface goes into promiscuous mode on the network). The attacker listens for DNS requests that match prescribed criteria and sends a forged DNS response back before the recursive DNS server can respond. This is not the same as cache poisoning for two reasons: There is no need to guess the port or transaction ID number; the attacker has the original packet, which provides her with the necessary detail. In addition this attack does not target the local recursive server, instead it is responding to the target host with a pointer toward attacker owned infrastructure.

One of the tools that can be used for this type of attack is *dnsspoof*. The *dnsspoof* tool is part of the *dnsniff* penetration testing toolkit, it is also available as part of the Kali Linux penetration testing distribution. *Dnsspoof* provides a turnkey tool for spoofing DNS traffic. The first step is to edit the *dnsspoof* conf file, located at */etc/dnsspoof.conf*. The format of the file is the same as the format for the */etc/hosts* file. A redirect for Facebook would look something like this:

```
www.facebook.com  [Attacker Controlled IP Address]
```

Once the configuration file has been created the command to run *dnsspoof* is simple:

```
dnsspoof −i [Interface] −f /etc/dnsspoof.conf
```

The above command tells *dnsspoof* to look for any DNS requests for www.facebook.com, and reply with forged queries positing the targets toward the attacker controlled IP space. All the attacker has to do is beat the response from the actual recursive server, a feat that should not be too hard if the two machines are sitting on the same network.

Which, again, is the limitation to this attack, it requires that attacker have a presence inside the target network and on the same network segment as the victim box or boxes.

What distinguishes a DNS spoofing attack from a DNS cache poisoning attack is that a DNS spoofing attack does not cache DNS information either on the victim machine or the victim's recursive DNS server. Instead, the attacker uses a variety of misdirection techniques to send the victim's DNS traffic to the wrong host.

DDoS ATTACKS USING DNS

The category of DNS-based attacks that garner the most press coverage is the Distributed Denial of Service (DDoS) attack. While there are a number of different ways that a DDoS attack can be carried out UDP-based protocols such as DNS and the Network Time Protocol are particularly susceptible to abuse in an attack. Because UDP packets are easy to forge, it is relatively trivial to get a small group of machines to direct a large amount of traffic toward a targeted system in a manner that is difficult to block.

In its simplest form a DNS-based DDoS attack simply means sending more traffic to a target server than the server can process. At that point, the services on the server become unavailable and legitimate users are either completely unable to access them or can only access those services sporadically.

There are a number of tools that can be used to launch this type of straightforward DDoS attack, probably one of the best known is Low Orbit Ion Cannon (LOIC). LOIC was originally developed in 2004 and has been used in a number of successful DDoS campaigns against the Church of Scientology, the Recording Industry Association of America and it played a big part in Operation Payback—in which a number of organizations were attacked because of their opposition to WikiLeaks.

The widespread appeal of LOIC is that it is simple to use and runs on both Windows and Linux platforms. It is also versatile in that it can be used to launch attacks against a variety of services running on a target host.

To make using LOIC even easier to use in 2012 its developers released a variant of the program called LOIC Hive Mind, this allowed an end user to connect to an IRC Channel or RSS Feed to download the latest target set. This version of LOIC was used to great effect during Operation Megaupload in 2012.

Unlike a botnet controlled DDoS attack, users of LOIC are aware of that the tool is installed on their desktop and are intentionally participating in a DDoS attack against an organization with which they have a disagreement.

As mentioned earlier, LOIC is a versatile DDoS tool. As Fig. 4.2 shows, the tool can be used to launch DNS or HTTP attacks or really an attack against any protocol. The interface is simply load the URL or IP Address of the target host, select the protocol and packet type, and the size of the message. Once all that is loaded click the attack button and it will continue sending packets until the attacker stops the attack.

While the tool is easy to use, it is not covert. All of the packets launched from the tool are directly tied to the attacker. However, when used as part of a larger group it is unlikely that any of the attackers will be singled out for prosecution.

Not all DDoS attacks are as simple to carry out many, such as DNS amplification attacks, require some knowledge and are much more difficult to trace. DNS amplification attacks are DNS DDoS attacks that use a series of small DNS queries, which generate large DNS responses. Those responses are directed toward a target host. This type of attack may involve up to three different victims. The first victim could be the host launching the forged query and may be an unwitting member of a botnet, unaware that malware being used in a DDoS attack is installed on her computer. The second victim is the DNS server that is being queried by the victim hosts and the third victim is the target itself.

FIGURE 4.2

Screenshot of LOIC.

To understand how these attacks work, take a look at this dig request:

```
dig @PDNS-PUBLIC-NS1.POWERDNS.COM powerdns.com ANY +dnssec
```

The query is pretty simple; it asks the Power DNS name server to provide all known records for the domain powerdns.com. The query also asks for any DNSSEC information. At 17 bytes the query is a small one, as shown in this tcpdump output:

```
0:41:56.231234 IP (tos 0x0, ttl 53, id 37793, offset 0, flags [+], proto:
UDP (17), length: 1500) 188.166.104.87.domain > 192.168.1.15.49890:
57446*-| q: ANY? powerdns.com. 14/0/1 powerdns.com. Type46[|domain]
```

However, it returns a big response, the dig output shows that the resulting response switched to TCP and returned 2977 bytes.

```
;; Query time: 82 msec
;; SERVER: 188.166.104.87#53(188.166.104.87)
;; WHEN: Mon Feb 1 00:41:56 2016
;; MSG SIZE rcvd: 2977
```

In other words, the response is 175 times larger than the query. An attacker that controls thousands of hosts within a botnet can easily send thousands of queries an hour from the victim botnet members to the DNS server and direct the results of those queries to the target host, easily taking it off-line. The forging of the packets to make it seem like the query is coming from a different host is known as a reflection attack. Using a small query to produce a large amount data is amplification and redirecting that large data to a victim server is reflection. The combination of the two is the most common type of DNS-based DDoS attack.

THE ANY QUERY

Security researchers and DNS admins love the ANY query, especially since almost every DNS administrator restrict full zone transfer (AXFR) queries. However, the ANY query is not an actual query type defined within RFC 1035. Instead, query type 255 is a wildcard query that is designed to provide the information that an ANY query generally provides. There is a strong argument that, much like the AXFR query type, the ANY query type should be restricted. To many DNS administrators and security professionals the potential for DDoS attacks using the results of the ANY query outweigh the benefits of using the ANY query type in troubleshooting or researching DNS issues.

DNS amplification attacks almost always take advantage of open resolvers. A query like the one above that targets the authoritative name server of the domain being used for the attack could easily be shut down by the security team. Instead, attackers will route the attack through a series of open resolvers, making it more difficult to shut the attack down. There are a number of tools that can assist with this type of attack, one of which is the *hping3* tool used earlier. The first step is to change the dig command so it is using an open DNS resolver:

```
[root@server ~]# dig @P50.116.23.211 powerdns.com ANY +dnssec
```

The next step is to capture the actual packet generated by the query using a packet capture tool, such as *tcpdump*, and drop it into a file in this case called query.txt:

```
0x0000: 4500 0045 db59 0000 4011 bb65 c73a d267 E..E.Y..@..e.:.g
0x0010: 3274 17d3 e21d 0035 0031 b2f3 d596 0100 2t.....5.1......
0x0020: 0001 0000 0000 0001 0870 6f77 6572 646e .........powerdn
0x0030: 7303 636f 6d00 00ff 0001 0000 2908 0000 s.com.......)...
0x0040: 0080 0000 00 .....
```

Finally, run the *hping3* command:

```
[root@server ~]# hping3 -2 -p 53 -E /root/query.txt -d 40 --spoof
98.124.192.1
```

The end result in a *tcpdump* output looks like this:

```
10:12:23.246849 IP (tos 0x0, ttl 64, id 20299, offset 0, flags [none],
proto: UDP (17), length: 68) 98.124.192.1.docstor > 50.116.23.211.
domain: [udp sum ok] 30565 zoneInit [b2&3=0x7264] [867a] [28275q]
[28525n] Type256 (Class 41)? [|domain]
```

What the *hping3* command did was take the dig query and run it so that it looked like it was originating from the IP Address 98.124.192.1 (one of the authoritative name servers for dns-book.net). The binary dig request passed through the open resolver, 50.116.23.211, to the authoritative name servers for *powerdns.com* and the large response was sent to 98.124.192.1. To make the attack more complicated an attacker could provide *hping3* with a large list of open resolvers and randomize which one each query passes through. Fig. 4.3 shows the traffic flow of the attack.

Building out a botnet capable of taking down a large server or multiple large servers takes time—if the attacker even has the skills to do it. Fortunately, there are already large botnets that other people have built. Rather than go through the hassle of trying to build and coordinate a large botnet to launch a DDoS attack some attackers opt to rent a botnet. According to one study, a botnet can be rented for less than $40 a month.[2]

Generally, the botnet owner will work with the attacker to craft the appropriate attack, coordinate the time for the attack, and how long the attack should persist. With some botnets, like the ZeroAccess botnet, containing millions of victim hosts being controlled by a single attacker it is easy to see how they can be effectively harnessed to take down even the largest DNS servers.

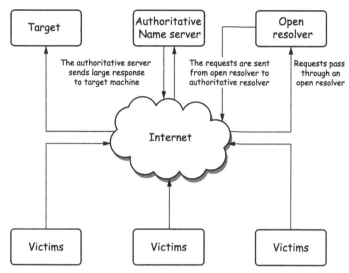

FIGURE 4.3

Traffic flow of a DNS amplification and reflection attack.

USING DNS AS A COMMAND AND CONTROL OR EXFIL CHANNEL

This last section does not really focus on attacks against the DNS protocol; instead it focuses on how organizations treat DNS traffic, especially when it comes to security monitoring. Many organizations ignore DNS traffic completely when it comes to security and those organizations that do pay attention generally focus on DNS blacklists and other types of indicator matching to find potential security problems.

Attackers are aware of the lack of monitoring of DNS traffic and use this to their advantage by using DNS as a communications channel. By using DNS the attackers are usually able to bypass a number of traditional security measures in the network and communicate with installed malware unimpeded.

Why is attacker communication important? It allows the attacker to direct the malware installed on the victim machine to execute commands, send files, grab keystrokes, and take screenshots or dozens of other nefarious activities.

A typical attack starts with a payload of some sort. It may be embedded in a PDF document or Microsoft Office document that the attacker emails to the victim or it could be a malicious Flash or JavaScript file the attacker has embedded on a web site or it could be code that exploits a flaw in the web browser itself. When the victim clicks the link or opens the file (or sometimes just installs a malicious application because the email told him to) a lightweight, often memory resident, loader is executed. That loader will scan the system and send a request to infrastructure owned by the attacker (referred to as command and control—or C&C infrastructure) and more powerful piece of malware will be automatically downloaded and installed. The loader deletes itself and the malware takes over the rest of the attack. But, the attacker needs to be able to talk to the malware installed on the victim's machine. Since most organizations do not allow direct communication to workstations inside their network, the malware needs a way to callback to the attacker's C&C infrastructure.

To understand how this works, let us step back and look at traditional C&C mechanisms for malware. In the early days of malware development any communication channel would do, attackers often used Internet Relay Chat (IRC) because it was easy to script and it did not require standing up a dedicated server or managing infrastructure. The attacker would simply script what she wanted the malware to do when it called in next and the malware would call in every few minutes or hours to deliver the results of the last task and receive new instructions.

As security teams became wise to this activity they would simply block access to IRC at the perimeter, any malware missed by the organization's antivirus vendor would be cut off at the firewall and rendered ineffective.

Just as security teams were able to evolve to respond to the methods of the attackers, attackers were able to find other C&C avenues that were more effective. The most common C&C method used today is to callback over HTTP or HTTPS. This used to require setting up hosting infrastructure and maintaining a permanent presence on the internet, though some attackers have figured out how to use established sites such as Twitter, GitHub, and even Gmail as C&C infrastructure.

Again, security teams have evolved to defeat, though not always successfully, this type of C&C communication. IP Address and domain name black lists, web proxies, SSL inspection, and next-generation firewalls are all useful in identifying and stopping communication from malware to C&C infrastructure over HTTP or HTTPS.

That leads to DNS as a C&C mechanism. There are a number of reasons why using DNS for C&C communication makes a lot of sense. Aside from the fact that DNS is not well monitored, using DNS also means that the victim machine does not interact directly with the C&C infrastructure of the attacker. From a security perspective DNS traffic is often unfettered by firewalls in the network. If recursive DNS is outsourced to a third-party provider then every host in the network needs to be able to talk to the Internet on port 53. Even if DNS is managed in-house, the DNS server itself has to be able to talk out on port 53 and it needs unfettered access to talk to any server in order to do its job properly.

DNS C&C activity, on the surface, looks like standard DNS traffic, as outlined in Fig. 4.4. The malware makes a DNS request, which passes through the recursive server of the victim machine to an authoritative server controlled by the

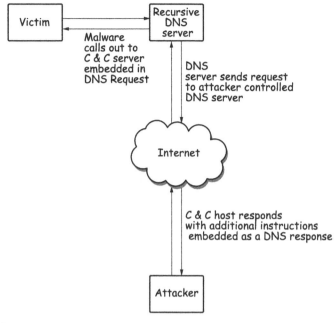

FIGURE 4.4

Traffic flow of DNS C&C communication.

attacker. Embedded in the DNS query is either a check-in request or a status update and embedded in the response is the next instruction set for the malware. The malware intercepts the DNS response when it reaches the victim's machine and carries out the next instruction set.

To demonstrate how this works, let us take a look at the now largely defunct DNSTrojan malware. DNSTrojan was very active in 2010 and 2011, but has largely died down since then. DNSTrojan is a form of malware commonly referred to as "Fake AV." Fake AV are programs that pretend to be security applications, but really engage in malicious activity. They are most often installed because a victim comes across a pop-up window while surfing the web that tells them their machine has a serious infection and they must download this "security tool" to fix it. Of course, rather than downloading a security tool the victim is making the life of the attacker easier by installing the malware for them.

The DNSTrojan malware used the domain *httpdsconfig.com* (which has since been allowed to expire). Once installed, DNSTrojan would call out to one of several subdomains associated with *httpdsconfig.com*. One of the subdomains was *1284726148.httpdsconfig.com*, though there were at least seven different subdomains all numeric based.

The malware on the workstation would make a standard TXT query and the victim workstation would receive a standard TXT response, all using normal DNS channels. A DNS TXT record, as defined in RFC 1035, is a RR that contains free-form descriptive text. Historically, TXT records were used to provide human-readable information about a server, network, or domain, but they are not commonplace today. A TXT query or response can contain up to 255 characters.

In the case of the DNSTrojan malware the TXT query and response were both hashed responses that looked similar to this, from the abuse.ch web site[3]:

```
a0dfe9b34e6c3bc167fc890a20dc283ab8c397eed489f2f737
efceb0064fbba77dc71472b59dde25a2f6f1883ffdc3b1f5ec9
1caf610f02c3b85e8cb831f81e554a83706c8849dd4cfa9ef0c
205c87f5e93f7a5323e71e35d566fe9fc8916717f69304
```

All of this activity generally happens under the nose of the security team because DNS traffic is not being monitored, or it does not look out of place to those who are doing the monitoring.

One way to combat this type of activity is to monitor for TXT queries and responses. Since they are not that common they will stand out as possibly suspicious behavior. This requires a security person or analyst to review each TXT query to determine if it is potentially associated with malware and while legitimate TXT queries are not common, there are still enough of them that it could wind up taking several hours a day to review the queries, on top of other security duties.

Of course, these types of attacks continue to evolve. In late 2015 FireEye researchers uncovered malware, named DUCKWALK, which used CNAME queries and responses as the C&C mechanism. A CNAME record is a canonical name that serves as an alias for a record. For example, *dns-book.net* and www. dns-book.net may both point to same IP Address, rather than creating two A records, the DNS administrator would simply create the A record for *dns-book.net* and a CNAME for www.dns-book.net. This makes life easier because in the future only one record would need to be updated.

In this case, the hashed query and response was part of the RR query itself, not delivered as separate text. In other words the query would look something like this:

```
6IFGEKEAANOPCNRXWRJNPXKPSORORWROOPOVJVIJIRWOROOQSQXORWO.corp.
dns-book.net
```

And the response might contain something like this:

```
4IDZOKFAANOPKVJURIVKLQVKTKOKOQOOOKSSMPMWMWMOOPXLLOQXI.ns.corp.
dns-book.net
```

This type of covert activity is much harder to detect because CNAME and SOA responses are so common. So, while it may seem obvious to the human eye that this query and response combination is suspicious, getting to the point where these particular two queries are reviewed is a bigger challenge.

These same techniques can also be used to exfiltrate data from the network. By stacking multiple TXT or CNAME queries a hashed file or files can be divided up and sent back to the C&C server 512 bytes at a time. Of course, if an organization is not monitoring DNS closely, more data can be added to each query and the recursive DNS server will switch everything over to TCP queries. The danger in using DNS as a channel for exfiltration of data is that it generally takes a lot of queries to accomplish this and it raises the chances of an attacker being discovered.

Sometimes an attacker needs to do more than simply send remote commands and receive exfiltrated data from a victim machine. There are times when the attacker needs to have direct access to the machine. Trying to connect directly to the victim machine through the organization's firewall is not going to work and attempting to launch a shell from the victim box to call directly to a machine controlled by the attacker will also most likely be blocked by the firewall (very few companies allow Telnet or SSH traffic out through firewall).

In cases like this the attacker can use DNS tunneling to create a Telnet or SSH connection through DNS channels. What DNS tunneling allows an attacker to do is to encapsulate another protocol within regular DNS traffic. For example, using DNS tunneling Telnet, which uses TCP packets over port 23, can be sent through DNS. The protocol and port do not change; instead they are encapsulated within the DNS traffic. This is similar to the way traffic is sent over Virtual Private Network (VPN). The big difference between DNS tunneling and VPN traffic is that DNS tunneling does not encrypt the traffic.

The components of a DNS tunneling session are similar to the components involved in DNS C&C communication. The attacker must own a domain or use one obtained from one of the many Dynamic DNS providers and must set up a server as the authoritative name server for that domain. The attacker installs a DNS tunneling server on infrastructure she controls and instructs the malware on the victim box to install the corresponding DNS tunneling client.

Different DNS tunneling servers use different methods of communication, some encapsulate the traffic in TXT record queries others use CNAME queries and so on. Each packet is sent through the DNS infrastructure as the specified query type and the response from the DNS server contains the return packets. Obviously, DNS tunneling creates a lot of DNS traffic in a very short period of time to what is most likely an obscure domain, which can be alerting. However, it does give an attacker keyboard access to the victim machine and can enable her to use that victim machine to jump to other targets on the network.

NOT JUST FOR WORKSTATIONS

DNS tunneling is not just used by attackers to manipulate victim workstations; there are also a number of apps that enabling DNS tunneling on Android phones. In the case of Android phones the reason for DNS tunneling is to bypass paid WiFi Hotspots. Many WiFi Hotspots will allow a user to connect to main web page, but block all other access unless the user pays a fixed price per hour or day. However, these WiFi Hotspots allow DNS queries to pass through unimpeded. By enabling DNS tunneling on an Android device the access restrictions of the WiFi Hotspot can be bypassed and the user can surf or check email freely without paying.

CONCLUSIONS

There are a lot of ways that DNS can be abused and misused to gain entrance into a network, redirect traffic out of a network, or communicate with malware installed inside the network. Because the DNS protocol is so widely used and critical to the day-to-day operation of most organizations it can be hard to protect against all the different threat vectors while still keeping an organization running with minimal impact on the users.

However, there are steps that a security team can take to ensure that they minimize the risk posed by some of the attacks outlined in this chapter.

The next chapter will provide an overview of how an attacker can use DNS to perform reconnaissance on a network and possibly find weaknesses within the organization.

NOTES

1. A great write-up of the Birthday Paradox, with all of the requisite math, is available on the Better Explained web site: http://betterexplained.com/articles/understanding-the-birthday-paradox/.
2. Seebacher, N., 2015. You Can Bring Down a Website for $38. *CMS Wire*. Simpler Media Group, Inc., 9 June 2015. Web. 11 Oct. 2015. <http://www.cmswire.com/information-management/you-can-bring-down-a-website-for-38/>.
3. Bernet, M., 2010. New Dropper Uses DNS to Communicate. *abuse.ch*. abuse.ch, 21 Sept. 2010. Web. 10 Dec. 2015. <https://www.abuse.ch/?p=2740>.

DNS reconnaissance

## 5

INFORMATION IN THIS CHAPTER

- WHOIS
- Mapping DNS Infrastructure
- DNS Fingerprinting
- Reverse DNS
- DNS Cache Snooping
- Passive DNS
- Collection of Query Data

INTRODUCTION

In designing a comprehensive security plan, DNS administrators should think about two types of reconnaissance: data that can be retrieved by anyone on the Internet and data that can be recorded by infrastructure operators. The former is obviously of greater concern, but as stated in RFC 7258, "pervasive monitoring is a technical attack." This chapter will discuss what data is meant to be publicly available, what can be learned in some circumstances from some DNS servers, and what is logged by large operators on the Internet.

WHOIS

When TV shows include a scene of a hacker researching a target, they will often include shots of terminal output from a WHOIS query. That is because at first glance WHOIS provides a surprising amount of information—from a domain name one can learn the name of the person who registered it along with their address, phone number, and email. WHOIS can also reveal when the domain was registered and the last time it was updated. In practice the information is usually incomplete for reasons discussed below.

First a quick recap of terminology. Each Top Level Domain (TLD) is managed by a registry; for example, Verisign operates .com. When a user purchases a domain they often go through a registrar, such as GoDaddy. The registrar will have an agreement in place with the registry to send in domain updates and abide by their policies. The person buying the domain is usually called a registrant.

When purchasing a domain, the registrar will collect contact details for the owner and technical operator of the site. Registrars are generally required by the Internet Corporation for Assigned Names and Numbers (ICANN) to make that information available via the WHOIS service which runs on TCP port 43. The protocol itself is described in RFC 3912. For example, querying for icann. org shows the following output:

```
$ whois -h whois.pir.org icann.org
Domain Name: ICANN.ORG
Domain ID: D2347548-LROR
WHOIS Server:
Referral URL: http://www.godaddy.com
Updated Date: 2015-07-07T17:37:26Z
Creation Date: 1998-09-14T04:00:00Z
Registry Expiry Date: 2017-12-07T17:04:26Z
Sponsoring Registrar: GoDaddy.com, LLC
Sponsoring Registrar IANA ID: 146
Domain Status: clientDeleteProhibited
https://www.icann.org/epp#clientDeleteProhibited
Domain Status: clientRenewProhibited
https://www.icann.org/epp#clientRenewProhibited
Domain Status: clientTransferProhibited
https://www.icann.org/epp#clientTransferProhibited
Domain Status: clientUpdateProhibited
https://www.icann.org/epp#clientUpdateProhibited
Domain Status: serverDeleteProhibited
https://www.icann.org/epp#serverDeleteProhibited
Domain Status: serverRenewProhibited
https://www.icann.org/epp#serverRenewProhibited
Domain Status: serverTransferProhibited
https://www.icann.org/epp#serverTransferProhibited
Domain Status: serverUpdateProhibited
https://www.icann.org/epp#serverUpdateProhibited
Registrant ID: CR12376439
Registrant Name: Domain Administrator
Registrant Organization: ICANN
Registrant Street: 12025 Waterfront Drive
Registrant Street: Suite 300
Registrant City: Los Angeles
Registrant State/Province: California
Registrant Postal Code: 90094-2536
Registrant Country: US
Registrant Phone: <removed>
```

```
Registrant Phone Ext:
Registrant Fax: <removed>
Registrant Fax Ext:
Registrant Email: <removed>
Admin ID: CR12376441
Admin Name: Domain Administrator
Admin Organization: ICANN
<abbreviated>
Tech ID: CR12376440
Tech Name: Domain Administrator
Tech Organization: ICANN
<abbreviated>
Name Server: NS.ICANN.ORG
Name Server: A.IANA-SERVERS.NET
Name Server: B.IANA-SERVERS.NET
Name Server: C.IANA-SERVERS.NET
DNSSEC: signedDelegation
>>> Last update of WHOIS database: 2016-03-09T21:06:11Z <<<
```

Note the authors removed some information from the above output, like names and phone numbers, although it is all publicly available. This provides three categories of information: contact details, name servers, and metadata about the record. From this one can learn its location in Los Angeles, and that it uses the Internet Assigned Numbers Authority (IANA) to run its name servers. The "Domain Status" flags can indicate problems with the registration. Lines labeled "client" statuses are set by the registrar and those labeled "server" statuses by the registry. If the registry is flagging a domain, it is often due to a legal dispute.[1] In this case, since it's a domain affiliated with the registry itself, it is likely to prevent an accidental change.

How does someone know which WHOIS server to query for a given domain? A good place to start is the WHOIS server for the registry of that TLD, which can usually be found by querying for <tld>.whois-servers.net. For example, org.whois-servers.net points to whois.publicinterestregistry.net which is the same server shown in the example above. Some TLDs, including .org, use what is called a thick data model, meaning the registry will store all records. The .com TLD uses a thin data model, meaning the registry may only include a reference to the whois server on the appropriate registrar. For example, querying for icann.org on a different whois server will return a reference to whois.pir.org:

```
$ whois -h whois.iana.org icann.org
% IANA WHOIS server
% for more information on IANA, visit http://www.iana.org
% This query returned 1 object
refer: whois.pir.org
domain: ORG
```

```
organisation: Public Interest Registry (PIR)
address:   1775 Wiehle Avenue
address:   Suite 102A
address:   Reston Virginia 20190
address:   United States
(remainder of the response is not included)
```

Note the organization and address shown here belong to the WHOIS server, not the queried domain. Following the referrer, and querying on whois.pir.org, one would see the full response shown earlier.

Many registrars offer "private registrations," sometimes for an extra fee, where they will list their own contact details instead of the registrant's. An example is from the domain dns-book.net (registered by the authors):

```
Domain Name: DNS-BOOK.NET
Registry Domain ID: 1978779035_DOMAIN_NET-VRSN
Registrar WHOIS Server: whois.dyndns.com
Registrar URL: http://dyn.com
Updated Date: 2016-03-01T06:00:13Z
Creation Date: 2015-11-12T06:12:02Z
Registrar Registration Expiration Date: 2017-11-12T06:12:02Z
Registrar: DYNAMIC NETWORK SERVICES, INC
Registrar IANA ID: 1040
Registrar Abuse Contact Email: <removed>
Registrar Abuse Contact Phone: <removed>
Domain Status: clientDeleteProhibited
Domain Status: clientTransferProhibited
Domain Status: clientUpdateProhibited
Registry Registrant ID:
Registrant Name: dns-book.net, Secret Registration Customer ID 397149
Registrant Organization: Dyn Inc
Registrant Street: c/o dns-book.net, 150 Dow Street, Tower 2
Registrant City: Manchester
Registrant State/Province: NH
Registrant Postal Code: 03101
Registrant Country: US
Registrant Phone: <removed>
Registrant Phone Ext:
Registrant Fax:
Registrant Fax Ext:
```

Note the registrant name in this record includes the phrase "Secret Registration." In other cases it may use the phrase "by proxy" which is also an indication of a private registration. In these cases the address and phone number belong to the registrar, not the registrant. It's rare for a major web site to use a private registration. More often it is a sign of a small business or perhaps a one-person IT shop where the administrator does not want their email address available on the Internet.

Web sites like DomainTools will automate a lot of this research process and also provide historical data. For example, it shows that dns-book.net has had three different whois records since November, 2015 (Fig. 5.1).

WHOIS data can sometimes be used to "connect the dots" between different parts of a cyber-attack. For example, by seeing when malicious domains were registered one can build a more accurate timeline of an incident. DomainTools can show other domains registered by the same email address, which may lead to more of an attacker's infrastructure. A high profile case was Mandiant's APT1 report from 2013, where they used WHOIS records, in part, to connect a large hacking ring to China. The registration information for one of the domains used

Registrant Org	Dyn Inc is associated with ~37,220 other domains
Registrar	DYNAMIC NETWORK SERVICES, INC
Registrar Status	clientDeleteProhibited https://www.icann.org/epp#clientDeleteProhibited, clientTransferProhibited https://www.icann.org/epp#clientTransferProhibited, clientUpdateProhibited https://www.icann.org/epp#clientUpdateProhibited
Dates	Created on 2015-11-12 - Expires on 2017-11-12 - Updated on 2016-03-06
Name Server(s)	DNS1.NAME-SERVICES.COM (has 2,771,741 domains) DNS2.NAME-SERVICES.COM (has 2,771,741 domains) DNS3.NAME-SERVICES.COM (has 2,771,741 domains) DNS4.NAME-SERVICES.COM (has 2,771,741 domains) DNS5.NAME-SERVICES.COM (has 2,771,741 domains)
IP Address	8.5.1.36 - 21,633 other sites hosted on this server
IP Location	- Alaska - Wasilla - Level 3 Communications Inc.
ASN	AS21740 ENOMAS1 - eNom, Incorporated (registered Jun 15, 2001)
Domain Status	Registered And Active Website
Whois History	3 records have been archived since 2015-11-11
IP History	3 changes on 3 unique IP addresses over 1 years
Registrar History	1 registrar
Hosting History	1 change on 2 unique name servers over 1 year
Whois Server	whois.dyndns.com

FIGURE 5.1

A portion of the DomainTools record for dns-book.net.

in an attack included an email address that then led to Internet forum postings and ultimately to an individual. They also looked at aggregate location fields across WHOIS records from all malicious domains they discovered to find common countries.[2]

SOURCES OF WHOIS DATA

To understand what information can be available through WHOIS it's important to first understand what information is collected and shared at each step of the registration process. Most people register a domain through a registrar like GoDaddy or Network Solutions. These companies will have agreements with the operators of each TLD, and ultimately the domain will become live when the registrar sends a database update to the TLD operator. The registrar will generally pay the registry a fee per domain per year. As of 2012, for example, the fee for each .com address was $7.85 annually.[3] The registrar will pass the cost on to the registrant and will need to collect a valid name, address, and credit card number to process the payment. It will also ask for the name, address, and phone number of a technical contact for the domain, although it usually will not verify that information. The registrar also knows the source IP of the connection and may be able to collect the browser fingerprint of the computer used to buy the domain, although this information is usually not shared externally.

When the registrar sends a request to the TLD operator to create a new domain they will need to include whatever information is in their reseller agreement. Verisign's publicly available agreement does not specify what information must be shared, but it does say they may "from time to time use the demographic data collected for statistical analysis."[4] Documentation from ICANN specifies some of the information the registries must collect: "For each registrar, the following data elements shall be given: registrarid, registrar address, registrar telephone number, registrar e-mail address, whois server, referral URL, updated date and the name, telephone number, and e-mail address of all the registrar's administrative, billing, and technical contacts."[5] A backup copy of this data must also be stored under ICANN's Registrar Data Escrow program. Since 2007 the preferred escrow vendor has been Iron Mountain. If a registrar goes out of business, their records will be transferred to a new provider.[6]

Making this data available via WHOIS provides a useful service to the Internet community. For example, if someone discovers spam originating from a domain they can contact its administrators to see if it has been compromised. On the other hand, the WHOIS database itself is a gold mine for spammers because it contains millions of legitimate email addresses. The balance that ICANN imposes is to allow (and in fact mandate) publicly available query-based access to each registrar's WHOIS data, but to prohibit bulk transfers. They also have policies against using the information for any marketing purposes. Despite the policies misuse still occurs, often in the form of unwanted emails or phone calls to the listed contacts.[7] The issue of whether WHOIS data should be made public at all was hotly debated in the early 2000s, including via Congressional hearings.[8] But as of 2016, the same basic policy has remained in place. A best practice for administrators is to use a separate email address for registrations. This account should be regularly monitored but also subjected to additional scrutiny since it will likely be a target of spam.

MAPPING DNS INFRASTRUCTURE

The simplest form of DNS reconnaissance is to query a server and see what records are available. Most domains will have at least an NS record, an MX record, and an A record that give the address of a name server, a mail server, and (usually) a webserver, respectively. This will often show whether a domain hosts its own email and webservers or outsources that infrastructure. For example, in the below case those services are hosted elsewhere.

```
$ dig @8.8.8.8 cryptodns.com ANY
; << >> DiG 9.8.3-P1 << >> @8.8.8.8 cryptodns.com ANY
; (1 server found)
;; global options: +cmd
;; Got answer:
;; ->>HEADER<<- opcode: QUERY, status: NOERROR, id: 13078
;; flags: qr rd ra; QUERY: 1, ANSWER: 8, AUTHORITY: 0, ADDITIONAL: 0
;; QUESTION SECTION:
;cryptodns.com.    IN   ANY
;; ANSWER SECTION:
cryptodns.com.   3594  IN  SOA  dns1.name-services.com. info.name-
services.com. 1446770972 172800 900 1814400 3600
cryptodns.com.   3594  IN  NS  dns4.name-services.com.
cryptodns.com.   3594  IN  NS  dns5.name-services.com.
cryptodns.com.   3594  IN  NS  dns2.name-services.com.
cryptodns.com.   3594  IN  NS  dns1.name-services.com.
cryptodns.com.   3594  IN  NS  dns3.name-services.com.
cryptodns.com.   3594  IN  MX  10 p.nsm.ctmail.com.
cryptodns.com.   3595  IN  A  64.74.223.41
```

These records are generally not considered sensitive in and of themselves, but they may provide more context to an attacker. For example, if a company's email is hosted at an online productivity suite provider like Google Apps or Microsoft Office 360, an attacker may conclude that employees use other services on those sites. This could provide content for a spearphishing attack. Or, an attacker could look for previously leaked credentials from known employees and try them on those services. In general there is not much an administrator can do to protect against the DNS aspects of these attacks, since broadcasting this information is precisely the point of the protocol. It's just important to know what information is publicly available.

With a minor amount of effort, one can also map the DNS resolvers (as opposed to the authoritative servers) operating within an organization. One way to do this is to send an email to a nonexistent user from a domain where the incoming DNS traffic is recorded. If the mail server sends a bounce message, it will look up the domain and the traffic will reveal the source IP of the resolver. If an adversary can get an organization's users to click on a link or otherwise visit a webpage on his domain, they can similarly determine the source IP of the DNS resolver used for outbound web requests. By trying several of these techniques over multiple days or weeks, a more complete picture of all DNS infrastructure could be revealed.

Why would an attacker want to map out DNS infrastructure? Cache poisoning is the most obvious attack vector. If they know where a request will originate, and if they have some control over the query, they could attempt something like the Kaminsky attack described elsewhere in the book. Other potential attacks include cache pollution, where a valid response will include additional, spoofed records. If a network's DNS resolver is publicly accessible, attackers may also attempt Distributed Denial of Service attacks against it directly.

DNS FINGERPRINTING

A more aggressive version of mapping DNS infrastructure is to attempt to "fingerprint" the exact version of the server software used. Some protocols, like SSH and HTTP include the server version in the protocol itself, so fingerprinting is just a matter of connecting to the service and reading the headers. DNS does not, so researchers look for certain features or quirks of the protocol that are only implemented in certain servers (some servers such as BIND optionally provide this information, described below). For example, say a server receives a query in mixed case (www.EXAmple.com). This is perfectly acceptable under the DNS protocol, but some older servers will return an error. Other servers will convert the domain to lowercase in the response packet. BIND will generally match the case in the response. So depending on whether the response has an error, all lower case, or mixed case, an adversary can narrow down the exact version of the server.

With so many different versions of DNS servers, it's generally too time-consuming to write a specific algorithm to identify each one. So fingerprinters will instead develop libraries of unusual queries and then build lists of how each server version responds. An open source program called fpdns has built a large collection of fingerprints and can often identify the server version with three queries.[9] Several web sites also host fingerprinting services, so an administrator can use one of those to determine whether their DNS server version can be determined from the outside.

BIND will optionally provide its version information in a TXT record. This can be viewed with the following query:

```
$ dig @4.2.2.2 -c CH -t txt version.bind
; << >> DiG 9.8.3-P1 << >> @4.2.2.2 -c CH -t txt version.bind
; (1 server found)
;; global options: +cmd
;; Got answer:
;; ->>HEADER<<- opcode: QUERY, status: NOERROR, id: 40753
;; flags: qr rd ra; QUERY: 1, ANSWER: 1, AUTHORITY: 0, ADDITIONAL: 0
;; QUESTION SECTION:
;version.bind.    CH   TXT
;; ANSWER SECTION:
version.bind.    0   CH   TXT   "Version: main/17936"
```

To disable this feature, one can change the "version" option inside the BIND named.conf file. Enabling this feature does make it easier to debug network problems, both for administrators themselves and for people who rely on the infrastructure. And security purists would argue that hiding version information does not add additional protection, it just means an attacker will have to do more work to fingerprint the server. But that same argument can also lead to the conclusion that it adds a marginal improvement in the overall posture.

The most worrisome scenario with DNS fingerprinting is if an adversary discovers a server is vulnerable to a known exploit. The obvious solution (although sometimes difficult to implement in practice) is to keep up to date with patching and not run vulnerable versions of server software. Beyond that, the risks of DNS fingerprinting become more theoretical. It can provide an insight into IT practices within an enterprise. For example, it may reveal that Windows is the server environment of choice, and patching takes place on a predictable quarterly schedule. This information would probably not be extremely sensitive in and of itself, but it could be useful in conjunction with other attack vectors. One potential threat is that attackers could keep lists of what software versions are deployed at which organizations. Then if a vulnerability or exploit is announced, they could quickly apply it to the targets of interest. In busy environments an attacker may be able to utilize a publicly released exploit before an administrator has a chance to schedule downtime and apply a patch.

Preventing DNS fingerprinting is not an area that has been widely developed. Some Intrusion Detection Systems will look for known fingerprinting requests, which is possible because those requests often use unusual combinations of flags. But in general the best practice is to understand the risk, keep servers up to date, and protect against attacks with defense in depth.

REVERSE DNS

In the early days of the Internet, an IP address usually had one and only one hostname. So in addition to looking up a hostname to find the IP, one could look up an IP and find the corresponding hostname. This process is called Reverse DNS. This section will first describe the simpler model originally used on the Internet, then describe the more complicated system currently in use.

It was originally assumed that each Class A on the Internet could be responsible for each of its Class B networks, each Class B for its Class C networks, etc. For example, if a user tried to do a reverse DNS query on 1.2.3.4, the root could point it to the Class A network responsible for "1" which would have an entry for the authoritative servers for each of its Class B servers. When the user was finally routed to the authoritative Class C server for 1.2.3, that service would have an entry for each of the 254 hosts in its IP space. In general, this would be the same server that was authoritative for regular DNS queries for those hostnames. Since the regular DNS server would already have a mapping of hostnames to IPs, it could simply maintain the inverse mapping of IP to hostname.

Reverse DNS queries can be performed with the "-x" option in dig. For example:

```
$ dig @8.8.8.8 www.ripe.net + short
193.0.6.139
$ dig @8.8.8.8 -x 193.0.6.139
; << >> DiG 9.8.3-P1 << >> @8.8.8.8 -x 193.0.6.139
; (1 server found)
;; global options: + cmd
;; Got answer:
;; ->>HEADER<<- opcode: QUERY, status: NOERROR, id: 34402
;; flags: qr rd ra; QUERY: 1, ANSWER: 1, AUTHORITY: 0, ADDITIONAL: 0
;; QUESTION SECTION:
;139.6.0.193.in-addr.arpa.   IN   PTR
;; ANSWER SECTION:
139.6.0.193.in-addr.arpa. 21599   IN   PTR   www.ripe.net.
```

This example first retrieves the IP for www.ripe.net (the + short option limits the output of dig) and then performs a reverse DNS query on that IP. Note the response is returned in a PTR record, which can be thought of as the inverse of an A record. In the simple model, a DNS server could simply look through its A records to find the hostname that matched the reverse DNS query and then dynamically create the PTR response. But for reasons described below, these are generally stored and maintained in the server's configuration as separate lists of PTR records that may or may not match the A records. Also note the format of the question in the above query. To perform a reverse DNS query on 193.0.6.139, the client reverses the order of the octets, then appends "in-addr.arpa" to the end. Using the regular DNS infrastructure, this will route the query to the root responsible for reverse DNS, then find the server that is authoritative for the 193 Class A, then recursively find the server responsible for that IP. There is a convenient symmetry between subdomains separated by a "."and an IP address's octets separated by the same character that lets the same infrastructure parse both types of queries.

Two major developments broke this simple model of how to answer reverse DNS queries. One is that networks wanted to manage and subdivide their IP space in more granular blocks, so having to delegate an entire Class B or C to a single DNS server became impractical. Also virtual hosting on HTTP servers made it much easier to run multiple web sites (each with its own domain) on the same IP address. This broke the general one-to-one mapping of domains to IP addresses. Both of these shifts occurred in the late 1990s, and RFC 2317 was released in 1998 to update the reverse DNS protocol. The RFC specifies that CNAMEs can be used to delegate specific subnets. For example, a CNAME of "1.0/25.2.0.192. in-addr.arpa" (along with an NS record) would indicate that the 192.0.2.0/25 block is administered by a different server.

These days major hosting companies will often run an entire class B or C, but most domains will not have a one-to-one mapping of hostnames to IPs. Larger web sites are often load balanced between multiple IPs, so reverse DNS queries will yield something like "server1. < major domain>.com." Smaller web sites are often run on shared hosting infrastructure, so reverse DNS queries for those will return "server1. < hosting company>.com." In both of these cases, reverse DNS can reveal the organization that administers that block of IP addresses, and it can provide hints to the number of servers that are deployed. Similar to DNS fingerprinting, this information should not be considered sensitive in and of itself, but it's important for administrators to know what can be learned from public research.

DNS CACHE SNOOPING

If an attacker could observe all the DNS requests coming out of an organization they could learn very interesting information: who their customers are, what software is trying to auto-update, even how busy their employees are (by, eg, counting requests to news sites). Unfortunately, many DNS servers can leak exactly this information. A simple way to retrieve it is to query the organization's caching DNS server for a given domain, and see if the answer is returned directly from the cache. If it is, then someone within the organization has recently visited that domain. These techniques are generally called DNS cache snooping. This section will walk through both simple and more sophisticated approaches, then discuss mitigation.

These techniques rely on an adversary being able to query the same caching DNS server used by a target organization, so the examples below will query publicly available DNS servers. What if an organization's cache is only accessible within their corporate firewall? Two attack profiles are still possible: a malicious insider could use these techniques to learn sensitive information, and an external attacker could find an upstream cache provided by the organization's Internet Service Provider (ISP).

The simplest technique is to run the query with the + norecurse option, which turns off the RD flag in the header. For example:

```
$ dig @<server> www.cryptodns.com +norecurse
; (1 server found)
;; global options: +cmd
;; Got answer:
;; ->>HEADER<<- opcode: QUERY, status: SERVFAIL, id: 62318
;; flags: qr ra; QUERY: 1, ANSWER: 0, AUTHORITY: 0, ADDITIONAL: 0
;; QUESTION SECTION:
;www.cryptodns.com.      IN  A
```

The lack of an answer shows that the server does not have that domain in its cache, meaning none of its users have queried the domain recently. To come up with a more specific time window, one could find the Time to Live (TTL) for that record and make a reasonable guess that no users have queried within the TTL number of seconds. There are a few exceptions: the server may not respect TTLs, the server may be busy and therefore ejecting records from the cache before they expire, or the TTL on the authoritative server could have changed right before the snooping query. But in general this provides a reliable indication of whether the cache has recently queried that domain.

What about finding records that do exist in the cache? An attacker has to do this through brute force—by querying for domains they suspect the organization might have visited. Here the TTL will also provide interesting information since it will count down from the time the domain was first cached. In the example below, the TTL is 3563 meaning the domain has been queried on that server in the last 37 seconds (after determining the TTL from the authoritative server).

```
$ dig @server www.cryptodns.com +norecurse
; (1 server found)
;; global options: +cmd
;; Got answer:
;; ->>HEADER<<- opcode: QUERY, status: NOERROR, id: 62127
;; flags: qr ra; QUERY: 1, ANSWER: 1, AUTHORITY: 0, ADDITIONAL: 0
;; QUESTION SECTION:
;www.cryptodns.com.      IN  A
;; ANSWER SECTION:
www.cryptodns.com.  3563  IN  A  64.74.223.41
```

It's very difficult to protect against cache snooping. Normal security hygiene like separating the cache and authoritative portions of the DNS server, or only allowing whitelisted IP space to access the cache, will mitigate most of the external risk. But as long as users are able to query the cache they will have the ability to snoop on other users' requests. One possible defensive layer is for the server to always run a recursive query for noncached records, so the attacker would not receive the telltale blank response. But the TTL on the record will often give this away. For example, if the TTL is the common default value of 86400 or 3600, it was probably freshly queried. Also the latency in the response will be different between cached and recursive queries, since the cache needs time to connect to the authoritative server. So an adversary could measure the response time and guess that faster responses were cached. This could be honed further by measuring the network latency between the client and the server and subtracting that off the response time. In theory the cache could add jitter to all responses and randomly alter the TTLs so new records would show some time having elapsed. One final possibility is to only cache records after they have been queried more than a given number of times. That would enable attackers to learn that a domain had been visited, but makes it impossible to determine a domain had not been visited. But most administrators who are extremely worried about cache snooping instead just disable the caches.

PASSIVE DNS

Large recursive DNS servers, which respond to millions of user queries every day, develop an interesting view of Internet behavior. They can see what web sites are popular, what organizations exchange email with each other, and even when malware infections occur. The main data points they can collect are the time of a query, the source IP, the questions, the authoritative server, and the answers. The source IP may be from an end user, but more often it's from another caching server so the data cannot necessarily be tied to individuals.

In 2005, a practitioner named Florian Weimar proposed aggregating this data in a system known as Passive DNS. It would collect the time, domain, and resulting IP (ie, everything except the source IP of the query). This has many uses in investigating malware outbreaks. For example, a botnet operator may frequently change domains but reuse IP addresses for its command and control infrastructure. With passive DNS, a researcher can start with known bad domains, quickly find associated IPs, and then find all other domains associated with those IPs. Other methods include looking for newly created domains, as many malware sites do not have long histories of usage. There are several large repositories of passive DNS data online, and most provide free search interfaces. Some will allow the entire database to be downloaded for research purposes.

For DNS administrators, these data sets are most useful for detecting cache poisoning attacks. Recall that administrators may have no other visibility into such attacks, since clients will simply receive incorrect data from their own caching DNS servers. Administrators can periodically query passive DNS databases for their own domains and see if any unexpected results ever appear. Of secondary concern, but perhaps still important, is for administrators to know that their authoritative responses may be retained indefinitely in publicly available

rkfk.soman123.com	A	69.64.147.243
cwithington.com	A	69.64.147.243
www.toolification.com	A	69.64.147.243
1f9y.soman123.com	A	69.64.147.243
segpayus.us	A	69.64.147.243
www.di-ve.com	A	69.64.147.243
www.china9986.com	A	69.64.147.243
igq1.soman123.com	A	69.64.147.243
freewso.org	A	69.64.147.243
pqdy.soman123.com	A	69.64.147.243
metcy.meguition.com	A	69.64.147.243

FIGURE 5.2

Unrelated domains hosted on the same IP as dns-book.net.

databases. If there is any sensitive information in the domain names themselves, or in the timing of when domains are utilized, it could be revealed by motivated researchers.

As more of an exercise in curiosity, one can see what other domains share a given IP address. For example, Fig. 5.2 shows several domains using the same IP as dns-book.net.[10]

COLLECTION OF QUERY DATA

DNS queries can be monitored and logged in at least three places besides the client itself: the recursive resolver, the authoritative server, and the network connecting them all. The threat profile is often different for each piece of infrastructure and ultimately will depend on the practices of the organizations running those services. For example, large technology companies may have more robust security practices, but will happily collect and analyze the data themselves for advertising purposes. Small offshore providers may not collect anything, but could be more vulnerable to hacks. In general, an administrator should understand what data is leaving his network, what entities have access to it, and how it could be used in the future.

For administrators who run their own recursive resolvers, they control exactly what data is collected and they set the retention policies. For those who use a public or third-party recursive server, they need to be aware of how their query data is stored and used. One example is Google's Public DNS service, which has a clear policy. They will store detailed records, including the source IP and query, for 24—48 hours in a "temporary log." They then purge the source IP and create a "permanent" log with information like the requested domain, user's region or city, and timing of responses. They also state that they "don't correlate or combine information from our temporary or permanent logs with any personal information that you have provided Google for other services."[11] OpenDNS, another publicly available recursive server, does not provide as much detail on their data handling. But they do say "OpenDNS stores certain DNS, IP address and related information about you to improve the quality of our Service, to provide you with Services and for internal business and analysis purposes."[12] Some competing services advertise that they do not log any data at all. DNS. Watch, a service based out of Germany, is one example. Depending on the sensitivity of an organization's DNS records, some administrators will be fine with recursive providers storing aggregate information but others will want complete anonymity. So with some effort, administrators can usually find recursive DNS providers that will follow the level of privacy they desire.

Authoritative servers, by contrast, should generally be assumed to log and retain all data they receive. Sometimes this is part of their business, as web site visits can be considered "intent" signals, which are used in ad targeting. Often times this data also comes via webserver logs, since DNS queries frequently precede web page requests. Many large hosting providers do not differentiate between DNS data and web data in their privacy policies, but just say that they may collect IP addresses and other online activity. This level of monitoring will come as no surprise to most security professionals, and probably not to most Internet users in general. But one potentially overlooked threat vector is the concentration of DNS providers. As stated in RFC 7626:

> among the Alexa Top 100K, one DNS provider hosts today 10% of the domains. The ten most important DNS providers host together one third of the domains. With the control (or the ability to sniff the traffic) of a few name servers, you can gather a lot of information.

Research from Google and Inria, a French institute, showed that the majority of Internet users could be uniquely identified after visiting four web sites.[13] With large concentrations of DNS from multiple web sites being stored in the same place, the possibility for de-anonymization becomes more likely. As described earlier in this book, authoritative servers will not necessarily see the true source of a query, since it may come through intermediate resolvers. Combined with the effect of caching, authoritative servers will not have nearly as pure a source of data as the researchers worked with. But even small batches of de-anonymized data would present a very sensitive source of information. An oft-cited example is that knowing a specific person has regularly visited a forum for alcoholics support is an extremely personal piece of information.

Network operators theoretically have access to all DNS traffic that passes through their links, but they often have some level of legal or policy restrictions on what they can do with the data. One exception is they almost always have the ability to monitor and collect any traffic in order to run their business and maintain the integrity of the infrastructure. Some of this is definitional; a network operator, of course, needs to view at least some part of a packet in order to perform its business of routing it to the correct place. For example, Time Warner, one of the largest Internet providers in the United States, says in its subscriber privacy notice that "we may collect personally identifiable information (described below) over a cable system without your consent if it is necessary to provide our services to you or to prevent unauthorized access to services or subscriber data." While the policy does not mention DNS specifically, it does differentiate between the content of Internet traffic and aggregate statistics. For example, it says "[i]f you use a web-based email service, we do not collect any information regarding the emails that you send and receive." But they do "have information about how often and how long you use our service, including the amount of bandwidth used; technical information about your computer system, its software and modem; and your geographical location." They may use this information "to make sure you are being billed properly for the services you receive; to send you pertinent information about our services; to maintain or improve the quality of the TWC Equipment...[and] to market Time Warner Cable Services and other products that you may be interested in."[14]

Comcast, another large Internet provider, also says they may "collect and store for a period of time, personally identifiable and non-personally identifiable information about you when you use our high-speed Internet." Examples of an action that could be logged are to "send and receive e-mail, video mail, and instant messages" or "visit websites."[15] In 2014, AT&T generated some news stories when they offered a cheaper version of their fiber Internet service if users would agree to routine data collection.[16]

In the United States, most legal restrictions apply to telephone and video services, but not Internet access. Many other countries have adopted distinctions between content and aggregate information. An example policy from Australia holds that "carriers and carriage service providers are prohibited from using or disclosing any information which comes into their possession in the course of their business and which relates to [among other things] the contents of communications that are being or have been carried by carriers or carriage service providers." Here too they include an exception for "business needs of other carriers or service providers" or "the performance of a person's duties as an employee."[17] As a general rule, specific DNS queries will probably not be viewed by employees operating the Internet infrastructure. But if the queries are so sensitive that no one outside a trusted organization should ever have access, they should never leave the enterprise network unencrypted.

A related form of data collection is how ISPs retain IP assignment records. These tie individual customers to the IP addresses they were using on the Internet. The BitTorrent community is particularly active in tracking these policies because of lawsuits that have been filed over copyright infringement. According to their research, most major US ISPs retain IP records for between 6 and 12 months.[18] For those less concerned about being accused of copyright violations, this data could still be sensitive if combined with DNS logs from another source because it can de-anonymize those queries.

CONCLUSIONS

This chapter has shown that DNS can be a rich source of data. Anyone on the Internet can discover basic infrastructure information about a network, and they may be able to learn contact details for the administrators. They can learn about a domain's history and operation from passive DNS and fingerprinting. Finally, trusted operators of the network like ISPs or large hosting companies can gather a huge amount of information about users and organizations from seeing the flow of DNS data. One future implication is that if more information is stored in DNS it may reveal increasingly sensitive details of people's lives. For example, a public DNS operator can currently discover what web sites users are visiting. If people begin storing email encryption keys in DNS, as has been proposed with DANE, then the same DNS server will see what users are exchanging emails and how often.[19] This plus more capabilities to de-anonymize data will lead to new sensitivities over DNS data.

NOTES

1. https://www.icann.org/resources/pages/epp-status-codes-2014-06-16-en
2. http://intelreport.mandiant.com/Mandiant_APT1_Report.pdf
3. https://www.verisign.com/assets/com-registrar-agreement.doc
4. https://www.verisign.com/assets/com-registrar-agreement.doc
5. https://www.icann.org/en/system/files/files/registry-agmt-app5-22sep05-en.pdf
6. https://www.icann.org/en/system/files/files/rde-specs-09nov07-en.pdf
7. https://whois.icann.org/sites/default/files/files/cmu-misuse-study-26nov13-en.pdf
8. http://jour.sc.edu/news/csj/CSJNov04.html
9. https://miek.nl/2012/January/28/dns-fingerprinting/
10. https://www.bfk.de/bfk_dnslogger.html
11. https://developers.google.com/speed/public-dns/privacy
12. https://www.opendns.com/privacy-policy/
13. https://www.petsymposium.org/2012/papers/hotpets12-4-johnny.pdf
14. http://help.twcable.com/twc_privacy_notice.html
15. http://www.xfinity.com/Corporate/Customers/Policies/CustomerPrivacy.html
16. https://gigaom.com/2014/05/13/atts-gigapower-plans-turn-privacy-into-a-luxury-that-few-would-choose/
17. http://www.acma.gov.au/Industry/Telco/Carriers-and-service-providers/Licensing/service-provider-obligations-licence-fees-and-levies-i-acma
18. https://torrentfreak.com/how-long-does-your-isp-store-ip-address-logs-120629/
19. https://tools.ietf.org/html/rfc7626

DNS network security

6

INFORMATION IN THIS CHAPTER

- Locating DNS Servers
- Public and Private DNS Infrastructure
- Logging and Monitoring DNS Traffic
- Passive DNS
- DNS Firewalls and RPZ
- Blacklists, Whitelists, and Other DNS Threat Intelligence

INTRODUCTION

Most of the book to this point has been about all of the ways an attacker can use DNS servers or the DNS protocol to gain access to a target network, redirect traffic leaving the network, and exfiltrate data out of the network. This chapter is really divided into two parts: the first part is protecting DNS infrastructure in a way that minimizes it as a target and the second part is how an organization can use DNS to better protect the network and even become more predictive in protecting against attacks.

For the longest time, attackers were able to hide in the overwhelming amount of DNS traffic that organizations see every day. Blending in to the point of being invisible, or at the very least being hard to spot. But, that is no longer the case. There are a number of tools that security teams have available to them that allow them to filter out the good traffic and examine the bad, or at least anomalous traffic. By combining smart filters with reliable threat intelligence and trusted security partners it is possible for a security team, even a small one, to get an effective handle on the DNS security threats impacting their organization. No solution is perfect, and even the best solutions are going to miss things, but with a foundational knowledge of how DNS works, what looks like normal DNS traffic, and what looks odd it is possible to continue tightening the control systems so there are fewer false positives and false negatives.

Before doing any of this though, the first step is to ensure that the DNS servers are placed on the network properly, with the proper protections in place and are sending log data to the right place.

DNS Security. DOI: http://dx.doi.org/10.1016/B978-0-12-803306-7.00006-1

LOCATING DNS SERVERS

It seems like placing DNS servers on the network should be a no-brainer. But, it can be a surprisingly complex task, and one that even the most tech-savvy organizations get wrong occasionally.

In January of 2001 *microsoft.com* and many other Microsoft-related domains were off-line for several days. The issue was not a software failure or a successful attack on Microsoft's DNS servers, instead the problem was a router that died. Unfortunately for Microsoft, both its primary and secondary DNS servers were on the same network segment, so when the router went down it rendered all of Microsoft's DNS servers unreachable. As Time to Live (TTL) for *microsoft.com* in recursive servers around the world expired, visitors were unable to reach the domain and many other Microsoft domains (Fig. 6.1).

The outage was a big deal at the time for two reasons. The first is that so many users and systems depend on access to Microsoft's services that users all over the Internet notice an outage. Second, Microsoft is one of the leading technology companies in the world, so if they cannot get DNS right, what hope do other organizations have?

If an organization is going to run their own authoritative DNS servers the first lesson they should learn from Microsoft's mistake is to make sure that those DNS servers are hosted on separate and if possible not only technologically but also geographically diverse networks. If one DNS server is in a local demilitarized

FIGURE 6.1

The outage was very big news at the time.

Comic reprinted with permission.

zone (DMZ) the second should be hosted at a data center. If the primary name server is in the data center the secondary should be live in the disaster recovery site. If none of these options are available, an organization can ask its DNS provider if it will handle secondary services on its DNS infrastructure. The point is that authoritative DNS servers need to be separated so that an attack on a single network segment, or a router configuration error does not render an organization's DNS infrastructure unavailable.

There are ways to achieve this separation behind the scenes, which makes it seem like the name servers are on the same network, but they are actually split up. For example, UUNET used to maintain three name servers: 198.6.1.1, 198.6.1.2, and 198.6.1.3. These look like they are on the same network, but they were routed to different places around world. One way to do this is with Anycast, which will be discussed in greater depth in Chapter 11. Network diversity can also be achieved using global load balancing, which will redirect the traffic sent to a single IP address to multiple different, masked, addresses around the world. Most organizations do not have a large enough DNS infrastructure to have to worry about Anycast or load balancing, maintaining servers on diverse networks in different parts of the country or world is sufficient.

Recursive name services should be separate from authoritative name services. The purpose of authoritative name servers is to be queried by everyone, which means they have to be publicly accessible on port 53. There are very few cases where recursive name servers need to be broadly queried by anyone outside of an organization. Running recursive name services on the same server as the authoritative name server opens an organization to potential security risks, while providing no real benefit to the organization. Given the potential for attacks not just against the organization with the open resolver, but the ability of attackers to use that open resolver to launch attacks against other sites, it is important to follow this rule. Unfortunately, there are many organizations that do not. Even as late as February of 2016 the Measurement Factory was tracking thousands of open resolvers in almost every Autonomous System Number.[1]

Some security teams feel that a recursive server residing within the DMZ is fine, as long as there are good Access Control Lists (ACLs) in place to restrict access to recursive queries. Remember, because DNS queries are UDP by default, they are trivial to spoof and launching thousands of spoofed packets against even a "secured" recursive DNS server is easy on modern hardware. Recursive name servers should be behind the firewall, with no access to the server allowed from outside of the network.

PUBLIC AND PRIVATE DNS INFRASTRUCTURE

In RFC 761, the great Jon Postel famously said, "...be conservative in what you do, be liberal in what you accept from others." This is known as the Robustness

Principle, and it has helped the Internet grow from its infancy into what it is today. At its heart, the Robustness Principle is really about interoperability. It allows different organizations to build products that communicate with each other using the same protocol, even if that protocol is not enabled in exactly the same manner. The Robustness Principle means that Cisco routers speak to Juniper routers so that Ubuntu servers running Apache can deliver HTTP traffic to a Microsoft Windows workstation running Microsoft Edge. Any system that is designed to talk to other systems over the network should be as faithful as possible in the implementation of shared protocols. At the same time, the hosts these systems are talking to should not be so strict in their interpretation of the protocols that they make communication more difficult than it has to be.

Unfortunately, the Internet of today is very different than when RFC 761 was written (in fact, there was an update to the Robustness Principle as early as 1989, in RFC 1122). The fact is that most organizations cannot be too liberal in what they accept. That malformed packet being sent to the DNS server may be the result of a poor implementation of the DNS protocol. But, it is more likely to be specifically designed to launch a Denial of Service attack against the name servers, knocking it off-line for hours and possibly allowing the attacker to gain access to the server.

Organizations who choose to manage their own DNS infrastructure need to keep the reality of today's Internet in mind when building out that infrastructure, especially when it comes to publicly facing DNS servers.

An authoritative DNS server should never share more information than necessary. It should not allow full zone transfers from any server that is not its secondary name server and it should enable some form of two-factor authentication. It is not enough just to enable ACLs within the DNS server configuration; a good second step is to also enable Transaction Signatures (TSIGs). TSIGs, discussed in detail in Chapter 7, enable transactions to be signed. TSIGs use a shared secret combined with a one-way hash algorithm to secure queries from primary and secondary authoritative name servers. This has two effects: It ensures that queries are really coming from the secondary name servers and it also ensures responses are really coming from the primary name server.

Even though a public facing name server is in a DMZ it does not mean that it is not behind a firewall. The DMZ is still part of the network and any public facing DNS servers should sit behind a firewall. Most modern firewalls, such as those by F5 or Palo Alto Networks, have application filtering capabilities. Taking advantage of the capabilities of these firewalls will help ensure that malformed or suspicious packets do not even make to the DNS server in the first place. That being said, because DNS administrators are often disconnected from the security team within an organization they may not be aware of ways in which an application firewall can be enabled to better protect DNS infrastructure. Conversely, the security or network teams may not consider using the application-aware capabilities of these firewalls, especially around the DNS protocol, to protect DNS services. That is why having every team within an organization involved in building out the DNS security planned outlined in Chapter 2 is so important. It helps everyone understand not only what the risks are, but also what capabilities exist within an organization. Any chance to improve security without having to increase budgets should absolutely be explored.

In addition to the physical and network security steps taken to protect DNS servers, it is a good idea to limit the information available on those servers. Queries originating from outside the network are looking for different hosts than those originating from inside the network. No one outside an organization has a legitimate reason to find the canonical name of the color printer inside the break room or the host name of the internal payroll server.

In order to enhance the protection of the organization many DNS administrators implement a split-horizon DNS configuration. This is explained in detail in Chapter 9, but the simple version of this is that users inside the network have access to the full zone file for the domain, allowing them to talk to other hosts inside the network using canonical domain names. On the other hand, those outside of the network have a much smaller zone file that contains only publicly reachable host names. There are a number of ways that this can be implemented including creating one zone file that resides on the public authoritative name servers and a second zone file that resides on an internal authoritative name server. If the information does not exist on the public facing authoritative name server then even if an attacker is able to compromise the server the attacker cannot build a map of the network based on DNS information.

LOGGING AND MONITORING DNS TRAFFIC

To this point in the chapter the discussion has revolved around preventing attackers from gaining access to DNS servers. Protecting DNS servers from attack is important, as is protecting information about the network by limiting who has access to an organization's zone files. But it is also a myopic view of DNS security. There is a treasure trove of information available, with the right analysis, about bad things happening on the network and potential bad things happening on the network. DNS can also provide ways to stop these bad things from happening.

Of course, before any of this can be done DNS logs must be collected and analyzed in a meaningful way. This is a task that too many security teams ignore, which is a shame as DNS is an invaluable tool in incident response (IR) investigations and can be an even more powerful tool in blocking malicious traffic and even in stopping an attack before it starts.

DISABLING LOCAL CACHE

Security has always been about trade-offs. There has to be a balance between security and usability, otherwise users will find a way to circumvent whatever security policies are in place. In order for a security team to be able to effectively monitor DNS requests, local caching should be disabled on Workstations and in the Browser. Local cache poisoning is a potential attack vector, and if security analysts are going to be able to monitor all DNS traffic, there should be no DNS requests that reside solely on the end point. There will undoubtedly be minor performance hits by doing this, but it will increase the security posture of the organization.

FLAGGING BAD DOMAINS

To understand how this can be done, take a look at a truncated sample BIND log:

```
13-Feb-2016 22:54:17.661 queries: info: client 192.168.1.4#47539:
query: www.dns-book.net IN A +
13-Feb-2016 22:54:17.876 queries: info: client 192.168.1.4#58532:
query: www.dns-book.net IN AAAA +
13-Feb-2016 22:54:17.969 queries: info: client 192.168.1.4#46830:
query: www.dns-book.net IN MX +
13-Feb-2016 22:54:23.498 queries: info: client 192.168.1.4#45397:
query: www.google.com IN A +
13-Feb-2016 22:54:25.533 queries: info: client 192.168.1.4#50842:
query: www.google.com IN AAAA +
13-Feb-2016 22:54:25.554 queries: info: client 192.168.1.4#49238:
query: www.google.com IN MX +
13-Feb-2016 22:54:31.852 queries: info: client 192.168.1.4#46170:
query: www.abc.com IN A +
13-Feb-2016 22:54:34.065 queries: info: client 192.168.1.4#33302:
query: abc.com IN AAAA +
13-Feb-2016 22:54:34.133 queries: info: client 192.168.1.4#55908:
query: abc.com IN MX +
13-Feb-2016 22:55:05.827 queries: info: client 192.168.1.4#57957:
query: shibanikashyap.asia IN A +
13-Feb-2016 22:55:05.829 queries: info: client 192.168.1.4#38194:
query: shibanikashyap.asia IN MX +
```

The log contains nothing but standard queries. However, a security analyst has a feeling that the domain name *shibanikashyap.asia* looks strange. A *whois* does not reveal anything interesting, but checking against the VirusTotal passive DNS (pDNS) search, she sees that at least one vendor is suspicious of the site, as shown in Fig. 6.2.

Nine sites out of 66 flagging a site looks like the site could be bad, but what kind of bad is it? Moving on to the next step, she looks up the domain on McAfee's SiteAdvisor and finds out the web site is, or was, pushing out malicious files, as shown in Fig. 6.3.

FIGURE 6.2

VirusTotal search results for *shibanikashyap.asia*.

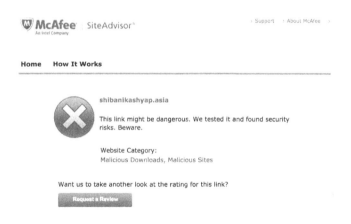

FIGURE 6.3

McAfee SiteAdvisor search results for *shibanikashyap.asia*.

Armed with this information the IR team needs to get to work on investigating the compromised host itself; where, if past sightings of this domain are any indication, they will most likely find the *CryptoWall* ransomware installed (hopefully, they get to it before it has a chance to encrypt the hard drive).

Of course, not everyone is good enough to magically pick bad domains out of the log stream. In fact, with some organizations having millions of DNS transactions an hour, it would seem next to impossible to identify malicious domains in a timely fashion.

Fortunately, there are a number of tricks that can automate the process of highlighting domains that need to be investigated. By implementing these rules within a Security Information and Event Manager (SIEM) or other tool an organization can quickly identify malicious domains that may have been missed by other security tools.

The easiest rule to start with is new domains. According to one report, the vast majority of newly registered domains are used for malicious purposes.[2] A study done in 2013 showed that about 75% of domains found in on Spamhaus Blackhole List had been registered for 15 days on average. The same study found that narrowing to specifically the .com domain (the largest of the TLDs) 50% of .com domains in the URIBL (URI Black List) were registered in the last 60 days.[3] There are really two takeaways from this study: Most newly registered domains are used for malicious activity, that effect is even higher within the newer gTLDs (which explains why the analyst in the earlier example was able to pick out the *.asia* domain so quickly).

Armed with this information, it is easy to create rules that allow security analysts to flag domains that may be associated with malicious activity. Start with something simple, has the domain been registered in the last 24 hours? If a domain has been set up in the last 24 hours and it already has an A record associated with it, there is a good chance that there is something suspicious about. Even as far out as 30 days from initial registration a domain has a chance of being associated with malicious activity. A rule that flags domains registered within the last 24 hours and highlights domains registered within the last 30 days would alert on a great deal of malicious domains. DNS does not exist in a vacuum, there is a good chance that an organization's proxy and mail server contain blacklists. By correlating monitored DNS queries with the information within these blacklists it is possible to actively sinkhole bad domains, rather than simply alert on them.

While a high percentage of malicious domains within the .com space appear on blackhole lists within 30 days, the number is even higher for some of the newer gTLDs. A study at the University of California, San Diego found that newly registered gTLDs were twice as likely as .com domains to appear on the URIBL within the first 30 days.[4] This ties into the previous rule, but when a newly registered domain is a part of a gTLD that is not .com, .net, or .org the alert level should be higher.

DO NOT FORGET ABOUT CCTLDS

This section has focused heavily on gTLDs, but there are some Country Code Top-Level Domains (ccTLDs) that also have a bad reputation, such as the .tk domain. The .tk domain is the country code domain for Tokelau, a territory of New Zealand in the South Pacific. Despite the island's small size it is actually the largest ccTLD, with more than 28 million domains registered. The reason for that is the island has opted to allow anyone to register a .tk domain at no charge. Unfortunately, this means the domain has been overrun with spammers and users with other nefarious intentions. As of the publication of this book, most organizations could sinkhole all DNS queries for .tk domains with no business impact.

There are a few other indicators that are easy to script and may also be point to a domain that is being used to do bad things. In general, one of those things is not having domain privacy enabled. Domain privacy is an important security tool and one that can help protect legitimate organizations from spamming and phishing attacks. One study found that domains with domain privacy enabled are actually less likely to be used for malicious purposes. Which is not surprising, it costs extra to enable domain privacy on a domain and given that spam is often a low margin enterprise the extra $8–$12 is not worth the effort, especially when it is so easy to use fake information during the domain registration process. That same study found that there are some providers that have a significantly higher preponderance of domains involved in malicious activities than one would expect.[5]

For example, more than 16% of domains that use "Information Privacy Protection Services Ltd" were engaged in spamming, phishing, botnet, or malware delivery. That is one out of every six domains using the service. Information Privacy Protection Services Ltd seems to provide domain privacy services for two domain registrars, OurDomains Ltd and Hangzhou Aiming Network Company Ltd. Whichever registrar is being used, the domains all have the email contact whois@privacy-protection-services.com. Again, this is an easy search that will create a list of domains that can be checked or automatically sent to a sinkhole.

This ties directly into another important indicator, the email address of the domain registrant. While it is trivial to create a free email address and use it to register a domain name, many attackers simply do not do that, and there are some free email providers that seem to be used by attackers more than others when registering domains for malicious purposes. The Helming presentation mentioned above uses the example of the *yahoo.co.jp* free email service. In their research 28.70% of domains registered using an address from that provider were engaged in attack activity. Almost one in three domains were bad.

Beyond the study, this is important because it allows the security team in an organization to start building a profile of an attacker. By tying domains, IP addresses, file hashes and tactics, techniques and protocols (TTPs) of an attacker together, the security team has the ability to better protect the organization from these attackers.

For example, a security responder uncovers a variant of the Zeus malware on a user's workstation. The Zeus bot was calling out to *hope-found-now.net* so now the analyst has an IP address, domain name, and associated IP address. She also has the delivery mechanism (phishing, watering hole, USB drive, etc.). Checking *whois* records she sees that the domain is registered by dredskooper@gmail.com. Using a reverse whois tool, like the one offered by DomainTools,[6] she can find out all other domains associated with this registrant, as shown in Fig. 6.4.

Now the analyst has not one but seven domains tied to the same attacker that can be added to monitoring lists or directly sent to a sinkhole. Though, before taking the latter step, it is important to ensure that the domain itself is malicious and not simply a web site that has been compromised and used to redirect attacks. In addition to monitoring the domains, the analyst can check pDNS information

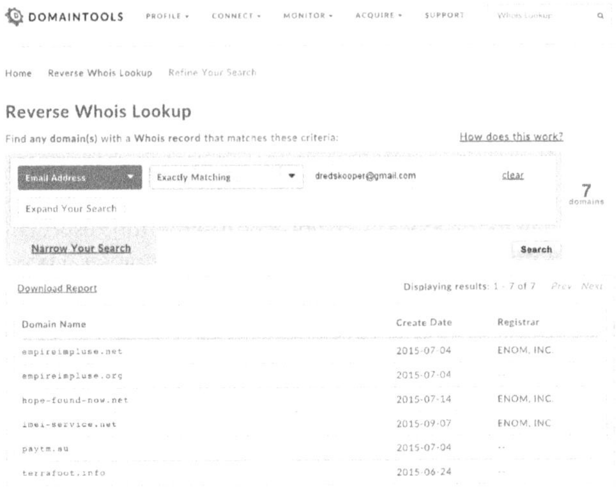

FIGURE 6.4

Finding all domains associated with a domain registrant.

to look for more IP addresses associated with those domains and possibly the file hash used in the attack. This allows the security team to move from protecting against a single attack to protecting against a campaign.

To this point, the focus has been on the registration information, but it is possible to predict the "badness" of a domain based on the domain name itself. It is even possible to do this programmatically, with math.[7] A group of researchers did just that when they developed a system, named EXPOSURE, that has 15 key characteristics, divided into four groups, which can be measured to automatically determine if a domain name is bad.[8] The section on Passive DNS will have more information about the characteristics; in this section there are six domain name based features to focus on. The first set of features to discuss are time-based features, and there are features that involve the number of queries for domain resources over a fixed period of time. There are four features that the EXPOSURE authors tracked for time-based characteristics:

1. Short life
2. Daily similarity
3. Repeating patterns
4. Access ratio

In this case, a domain that has a short life is not a measurement of how long it has been registered; instead security analysts are trying to figure out how long it appears in the DNS logs. Domains used by attackers tend to have a short shelf life, so it is not uncommon to see a flurry of activity out of a network over a few days and then nothing for that domain. The short life trait is one that measures activity to a domain over a relatively short period of time, and then no activity to that domain at all. Daily similarity refers to the pattern of access; are there queries for a domain once or twice a day and then suddenly a few hundred times a day and then back down to a couple of times a day? That type of anomalous query could be indicative of the domain being used for exfiltration or DNS tunneling. Repeating patterns are traits associated with when the domain is accessed. For example, even when an attacker is idle, the malware installed on the end point has to do regular check-ins. If there is a query pattern that seems to occur at regular intervals, it might be a sign of callback activity. In general, repeating patterns of domain activity indicate that an automated process is occurring and may require further investigation. Finally, the access ratio has to deal with how popular a domain is. Is it a domain that is not normally queried or is it a popular domain. A normally quiet domain suddenly engaging in any of the time-based characteristics could be a sign that the domain is suspicious.

The next set of features focused on the construction of the domain name itself. There are two characteristics that security analysts can look at to determine if the domain name is suspicious:

1. Percentage of numerical characters
2. Percentage of the length of the longest meaningful substring (LMS)

Some background is in order before explaining. It is not uncommon for commodity malware to be deployed with a list of domains to use as command and control hosts that do not exist. Instead the malware uses a Domain Generation Algorithm (DGA) to create domains on the fly. There is no chance that the domain is on a blacklist because it is newly created and even if the domain is short lived the attacker will have gotten what she wanted out of the target network and she has other targets doing the same thing.

But, DGA-created domains do not look like human-registered domains. They tend to be much more random than those domains, and that is a potential indicator. The problem is that the randomness is easy for a human to pick out: *5202dlks98.link* does not look right, whereas *937thefan.com* appears to be a perfectly normal domain. What these two rules do is look at the percentage of numbers in a domain. In the first domain 60% of the characters in the domain are numbers that is unusually high. For the second domain only 33% of the characters in the domain are numbers, which is within the norm. However, it is not necessarily a good indicator by itself, suppose the second domain was *1073rock.com*. Now, 50% of the characters in the domain are numbers, which is a statistically high number yet the domain is most likely a valid domain.

That is where the second domain name based feature comes in: the LMS. The notion behind the LMS is that legitimate domain owners want to create a memorable domain. To that end they will generally use words or phrases that are found in a dictionary, where was domains generated using DGA will not have any regard for dictionary-based words. In the previous example of *1073rock.com* while it has a high percentage of numbers in the domain 50% of the characters also form a meaningful string, which is long enough to classify this as most likely a legitimate domain.

How do you put both of these domain name based features together? When a new domain query reaches the recursive name server the first step is to see if this check has been performed before—there is no point in duplicating efforts. If the domain has not been previously checked, then the first step is to check it against a broad whitelist of domains, something like the Alexa top one million domains—there are a lot of popular web sites that do not contain meaningful strings, so this provides a sanity check. The next step is to count how many numbers there are in the domain. If that number reaches a set threshold the domain should be flagged for additional checks. Second, run the domain against a list of dictionary words and see how many appear within the domain. If a domain name fails all three checks it can be flagged for investigation and temporarily sent to a sinkhole.

Like the other checks, this is a process that can be automated in-house and it allows the security team to be proactive in identifying potential malicious domains and protecting the organization.

Of course, even with the best checks in place it is possible to miss bad domains based on the characteristics of the domain itself. This is especially true in situations where an attacker targets a specific organization and builds infrastructure around that organization, including domains names that look legitimate at first glance.

WHAT ABOUT DYNAMIC DNS AND SHORTENED URL SERVICES?

No discussion about blocking domains would be complete without the inclusion of Dynamic DNS and Shortened URL Services. Dynamic DNS providers offer a list of domains to which their users can create subdomains. It is an easy way to get a cheap, and often free, vanity domain to use for testing or to create a home web site. They are called dynamic domains because as the IP address of the home router is updated it populates to the Dynamic DNS provider (usually automatically, though sometimes scripting or manual intervention is involved) and the A record for that subdomain is automatically updated. There is nothing inherently wrong with Dynamic DNS services; unfortunately, a number of malware families have chosen to adopt Dynamic DNS services as their primary mechanism for command and control. This makes the existence of domains belonging to Dynamic DNS providers within an organization suspect at best and possibly malicious. Most organizations that are monitoring DNS maintain a list of the domains used by Dynamic DNS providers (there are a number of lists out there) and either alert when there is a match or automatically sinkhole the traffic.

Shortened URL services are a different story. This is another case where there has to be a trade-off between security and usability. The truth is that shortened URL services, like bit.ly and tr.im, disguise a lot of malicious activity (not specifically calling these two services out) and some attackers use shorted URL services in an attempt to disguise their attack. However, shortened URL services are also relied upon for legitimate purposes. It has happened more than once that security teams have blocked all shortened URL services only to find out that their marketing organization relies heavily on them. Because these services use an HTTP redirect to the longer domain, as opposed to a DNS redirect, this is not strictly a DNS security problem. That being

(Continued)

> **WHAT ABOUT DYNAMIC DNS AND SHORTENED URL SERVICES?—cont'd**
>
> said, depending on an organization's risk profile it probably makes more sense to monitor the HTTP redirects to see if there are particular shortened URL services that are more often associated with malicious activity and block those specific services rather than simply alerting or blocking on all of them. This has the added benefit of simultaneously keeping the network more secure and keeping the organization's users happy.

FLAGGING DNS QUERIES

While not every advanced attacker is going to use DNS queries as a method of communication or exfiltration, it is important to have checks in place to stop attacks that attempt to use DNS as a control mechanism.

The most obvious tool in the security team's DNS protection toolkit is to automatically flag uncommon queries. DNS queries such as TXT and NULL are not widely used, but provide ample unstructured response space to deliver payload or command information. RFC 1035 outlines the different query types and the expected responses and it serves as a useful guide for which fields to flag.

The most common DNS query used by malware for command and control over DNS is the CNAME query. Legitimate sites commonly use CNAME queries so just alerting on CNAME queries will drown the security team in alerts with no real benefit. Instead, there are a couple of techniques that can be used to quickly detect malicious traffic using CNAME queries.

The first technique is to measure the number of CNAME queries to a domain over a given period of time. Most domains are relatively static in terms of host names, so a recursive DNS server may get a large number of queries for *google.com* and its subdomains, but there is not a lot of variety in the hostname requests, as in the snippet of BIND logs for *google.com* below:

```
17-Feb-2016 18:36:06.540 queries: info: client 192.168.1.13#40774:
query: www.google.com IN A +
17-Feb-2016 18:36:06.567 queries: info: client 192.168.1.13#53209:
query: www.google.com IN AAAA +
17-Feb-2016 18:36:06.594 queries: info: client 192.168.1.13#50638:
query: www.google.com IN MX +
17-Feb-2016 18:36:15.373 queries: info: client 192.168.1.13#49980:
query: mail.google.com IN A +
17-Feb-2016 18:36:15.414 queries: info: client 192.168.1.13#40647:
query: googlemail.l.google.com IN AAAA +
17-Feb-2016 18:36:15.435 queries: info: client 192.168.1.13#57577:
query: googlemail.l.google.com IN MX +
```

Even though the recursive name server may see a lot of queries for *google.com* there are not a lot of CNAME queries, so by monitoring CNAME queries for a specific domain, over short bursts of time it is possible to isolate malicious activity. For example, if there are more than 10 CNAME queries from a single host to a domain within 1 minute, that should be flagged as potentially malicious activity. Ten queries in a minute is simply a place to start and not a hard-and-fast rule. Instead, security teams should play with the query to time ratio to find the right balance that will catch malicious traffic, but not generate an overwhelming number of false positives.

The second technique for detecting potentially malicious CNAME queries is to look for DGAs in the CNAME query. This is the same rule that was discussed in the previous section in regard to second-level domains, but now applied to third-level domains. Malware using CNAMEs for tunneling or exfiltration purposes will use domain generating algorithms to create the CNAMEs. Why? Because the malware needs to ensure that each query is unique which forces the recursive server to reach out to the authoritative server to get an answer. Just as with second-level domains, these DGA CNAMEs will not look like normal third-level domains, they will have a preponderance of numbers and a lack of meaningful substrings. By applying the same checks against these CNAME queries that are being applied to the domain names security teams can pick out the CNAME queries that look suspicious and investigate or block access.

IS IT MALWARE OR IS IT CDN?

A big wrinkle in this detection process is growth of Content Delivery Networks (CDNs). CDNs, like Akamai, Amazon, and CloudFlare, are giant load balancing networks that deliver content to popular web sites around the world. These services are very useful to organizations because they can help deliver content faster to web site visitors and they can help deliver localized content more efficiently.

Unfortunately, they also use some of the same techniques as malware developers in order to deliver content as efficiently as possible. Fortunately, most CDNs rank in the Alexa top sites list, so using Alexa as a filter in the analysis will help weed out malware vendors from normal CDN traffic.

One caveat to this is that some of the more sophisticated attack teams have been known to take advantage of CDNs, especially Amazon Web Services. So, while a security team may not want to flag all CDN traffic, it is something to keep an eye on.

Another method of detection for potential malicious activity using DNS is the length of the third or fourth level domain. A typical third or fourth level domain is going to be short, something like www.dns-book.net or *fileserver.corp.dns-book.net*. However, a domain being used for command and control or exifiltration is going to, by definition, be longer. The attacker needs to fit as much data into the 512-byte packet as she can, so it is not uncommon for the third or fourth level domain to be the maximum allowed 253 characters. Generally speaking, any third or fourth level domain that is more than 20 characters should be flagged.

If writing a rule for a specific subdomain is too complex, the rule can be written for the domain as a whole. Start with alerting at 50 characters and adjust depending on the number of false positives.

A WORD ON TCP

There are security experts that tell security analyst that they should flag DNS queries that result in a TCP response. Because most DNS queries and responses operate over UDP, a TCP response is questionable. There may be some merit to this and each organization has to decide what is best for their security team. However, a word of caution with flagging TCP responses: most malware authors using DNS are aware that DNS TCP packets are suspicious and may get flagged by security teams. To that end, these developers do their best to ensure their tools only ever operate over UDP, there is no point in having a piece of malware that took months of development end up on VirusTotal the first week of use.

Second, the Internet is becoming (albeit way too slowly) a world of DNSSEC. Some, but not all, DNSSEC requests will require TCP responses. As DNSSEC is more deployed there will be increased DNS TCP packets, which would result in more false positives for any organization alerting on DNS TCP packets.

These are just a couple of things to think about before implementing alerting on DNS using TCP as a transport mechanism.

DNS AND THE SIEM

A lot of what has been discussed to this point in this section can be done directly on the DNS server or on a Syslog server. However, it is often more effective if it is done on an SIEM platform. Not only does using an SIEM give analysts a way to visually examine the data, it also adds the ability to correlate the DNS information against logs from firewalls, web proxies, and other security devices that contain domain name information.

Always remember, the goal of any security activity should be twofold: Stop the immediate threat and put protections in place to stop the next threat. By using an SIEM to correlate domain information across multiple platforms it is easier to get the big picture of the initial attack and start to collect intelligence about from where the next attack is going to originate.

In a typical attack there are usually at least three callback points, all detected by different security apparatus. An attacker may use a phishing campaign to gain initial access, have a loader that injects into the web browser for initial call back, and use a piece of malware that does regular callbacks to help the attacker expand her presence in the network.

In this scenario the attacker has the potential to be detected (or missed) by the mail security appliance, the web proxy, the end point protection software, and of course the DNS server. By tying logs from all of these sources together within an SIEM and establishing a timeline of events across the network security teams can see what was missed. They can also build a profile of the attacker and her

FIGURE 6.5

DNS Analytics for Splunk showing queries to unregistered domains.

associated indicators, starting with the indicators used in the attack and then using investigative tools, like pDNS and reverse whois, to find associated indicators.

Many SIEM developers have realized the power of DNS queries in identifying malicious activity and have enabled advanced DNS collection. HP's ArcSight has an add-on called DNS Malware Analytics, IBM's QRadar has a big data security extension that enabled DNS forensics, and LogRhythm has special rules just for analyzing DNS traffic.

Splunk also has a number of apps available that will allow security teams to perform advanced analytics on DNS logs. One of the best is DNS Analytics for Splunk, written by AlphaSOC. The DNS Analytics for Splunk app takes a number of the suggested protections listed above and automates them in a way that security analysts can get immediate value from their DNS logs, as shown in Fig. 6.5.

An SIEM can be a powerful tool for analyzing DNS logs and building queries based on the suggestions throughout this chapter. An SIEM also makes it easier to tweak those suggestions to cut down on the false positives and ensure that the rules in place alert on threats the security team needs to worry about.

PASSIVE DNS

pDNS was discussed briefly in Chapter 5 as a tool to analyze the possibility of cache poisoning attacks, but there are a number of uses, especially when it comes to identifying and isolating malicious domains.

FIGURE 6.6

VirusTotal pDNS results for 19bee88.com.

pDNS is a way to track recursive DNS transactions over time. Where a typical recursive DNS server logs the date, time, source IP address, and query that was made a pDNS logging system also logs the response, name server information, and TTL information. The collected queries are stored in a database (or equivalent) and now security analysts have a powerful view of how a domain has changed over time and what those changes look like. Fig. 6.6 demonstrates how this works for the domain *19bee88.com*, a domain associated with the CryptoWall ransomware. Over a period of 5 months the domain *19bee88.com* has been associated with at least different three IP addresses.

If an analyst clicks on the most recent IP address, she will see that there are a number of potentially suspicious domains associated with the same IP address, as shown in Fig. 6.7.

Digging deeper into one of the potentially bad domains, *blocker-cl.info*, the analyst finds that it has the same IP address history as *19bee88.com*, as shown in Fig. 6.8.

Using the collected pDNS information the analyst is now able to correlate a number of bad IP addresses and domains and those indicators to the CryptoWall ransomware. She can put rules in place to sinkhole all of the associated indicators and protect the network before CryptoWall hits the organization. She can also alert network users about the threat and that they should be on alert (hopefully, even more so than usual) for suspicious emails. Finally, because she has information about the domains and infrastructure the attackers behind CryptoWall like to use, she can start to track it and add new IP addresses or domains to the sinkhole as the attackers add them, rather than postattack.

Aside from VirusTotal there are a number of third-party services that provide pDNS capabilities. Most do it by subscription and offer more detailed responses to queries that allow security analysts to look at TTLs, name servers

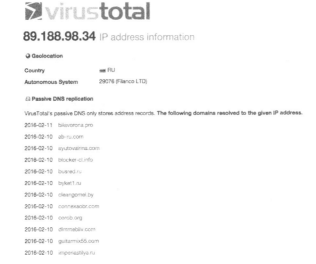

FIGURE 6.7

A number of suspicious domains also associated with this IP address.

FIGURE 6.8

The domain *blocker-cl.info* and *19bee88.com* share an IP address history.

used, and more. OpenDNS, the Computer Incident Response Center of Luxembourg, and, of course, Farsight Security all offer pDNS solutions (Farsight Security is home of the original pDNS database, known as DNSDB). Separately, a number of threat intelligence providers use pDNS on the backend to help improve the efficacy of their offerings. So, while pDNS may not be front and center in all solutions, it is often used to power, in part, the backend of security products.

Third-party pDNS solutions are great for understanding and investigating less targeted threats discovered inside an organization. However, for organizations that are worried about targeted threats (which, quite frankly, should be all organizations), it makes sense to build out an internal pDNS repository that can be queried by the organization's security analysts. There are commercial solutions, offered by companies like Palantir, that can provide dynamic analysis of pDNS data, but it is also possible to quickly build out a pDNS solution without having to invest too much money.

For an in-house pDNS solution to be effective it requires more than standard DNS logs. Standard DNS logs, like those displayed earlier, only show the time of the query, who made the query, what domain was queried, and for which resource record was the query done. What DNS logs do not show are redirects made, TTL values, and the actual responses, information that could be useful in trying to determine if something bad is happening.

To see the difference compare the DNS logs for query for www.google.com to the *tcpdump* output. First the BIND logs:

```
18-Feb-2016  01:08:32.176  queries:  info:  client  192.168.1.4#41780:
query: www.google.com IN A +
18-Feb-2016  01:08:34.440  queries:  info:  client  192.168.1.4#60344:
query: www.google.com IN AAAA +
18-Feb-2016  01:08:34.469  queries:  info:  client  192.168.1.4#33012:
query: www.google.com IN MX +
```

Now, the *tcmpdump* output:

```
01:08:32.179217 IP6 (hlim 64, next-header: UDP (17), length: 51) ::1.29195
> 2001:503:231d::2:30.domain: 24072 [1au] A? www.google.com. (43)
01:08:34.179167 IP (tos 0x0, ttl 64, id 57330, offset 0, flags [none],
proto: UDP (17), length: 71) 192.168.1.4.12422 > 192.48.79.30.domain:
12718 [1au] A? www.google.com. (43)
01:08:34.419433 IP (tos 0x0, ttl 50, id 30710, offset 0, flags [none],
proto: UDP (17), length: 692) 192.48.79.30.domain > 192.168.1.4.12422:
12718- 0/8/5 (664)
01:08:34.419803 IP (tos 0x0, ttl 64, id 42075, offset 0, flags [none],
proto: UDP (17), length: 71) 192.168.1.4.54064 > 216.239.36.10.domain:
5847 [1au] A? www.google.com. (43)
01:08:34.440282 IP (tos 0x0, ttl 43, id 14987, offset 0, flags [none],
proto: UDP (17), length: 156) 216.239.36.10.domain > 192.168.1.4.54064:
5847*- 6/0/0 www.google.com. A 74.125.29.105, www.google.com.[|domain]
01:08:34.441109 IP (tos 0x0, ttl 64, id 2779, offset 0, flags [none], proto:
UDP (17), length: 71) 192.168.1.4.8838 > 216.239.34.10.domain: 19649
[1au] AAAA? www.google.com. (43)
```

```
01:08:34.468735 IP (tos 0x0, ttl 40, id 24789, offset 0, flags [none],
proto: UDP (17), length: 88) 216.239.34.10.domain > 192.168.1.4.8838:
19649*- 1/0/0 www.google.com. AAAA[|domain]
01:08:34.469563 IP (tos 0x0, ttl 64, id 45957, offset 0, flags [none],
proto: UDP (17), length: 71) 192.168.1.4.41887 > 216.239.38.10.domain:
2196 [1au] MX? www.google.com. (43)
01:08:34.493793 IP (tos 0x0, ttl 43, id 26352, offset 0, flags [none],
proto: UDP (17), length: 110) 216.239.38.10.domain > 192.168.1.4.41887:
2196*- 0/1/0 (82)
```

The *tcpdump* output provides all of the information needed to maintain a pDNS database:

1. The queries, including the source IP address of the query
2. The name servers that responded to the query at the time
3. Whether the query and response were UDP or TCP
4. The TTLs that were provided by the authoritative name server
5. The response, including IP address and any other information the authoritative name server sent

While *tcpdump* is a great tool for demonstration purposes, it is not a good long-term solution for collecting pDNS data. On the other hand, the Bro Network Security Monitor is a popular tool for monitoring and forwarding DNS packets from a caching name server. In fact, bro even has a pDNS module called *bro-pdns* that will send the data into a MySQL database. Though, for collection from larger recursive name servers, or from clusters of recursive name servers, HADOOP might be a better solution.

There are also commercial solutions that can feed pDNS data into whatever solution is developed, some take more work than others, but security companies like Palo Alto and Carbon Black collect pDNS data as part of their collection process. Importing that data into in a database or into a SIEM will help correlate what the end point and edge are seeing with what the recursive DNS server is seeing. This process will, among other things, help security administrators determine if there are gaps in their DNS security plan, such as rogue hosts configured to use other recursive DNS servers or acting as their own recursive DNS server.

Whichever method is used to collect and analyze pDNS data there is a great deal of information that can be gleaned by mining internetwork pDNS data looking for patterns and identifying suspicious domains within the organization. Even if those domains are not currently identified by other sources.

For example, the last section talked about the EXPOSURE paper and the 15 traits the authors developed for identifying suspicious domains. Six of the 15 traits could be identified by reviewing recursive DNS logs. However, nine of the traits require pDNS in order to run the proper algorithms. The first set of traits that require pDNS are the DNS answer based features, which include the following characteristics:

1. Number of distinct IP addresses
2. Number of distinct countries

3. Reverse DNS query results
4. Number of domains that use the same IP address

Each one of these traits is not inherently bad. For example, most small businesses host their web site on a shared hosting server. That server is likely hosting hundreds of other web sites as well, all pointing the same IP address. That does not mean that each of those sites is bad. Similarly, the PTR of that IP address most likely resolved to the hostname of the server itself, not any of the domains hosted on that server. On the other hand, most small businesses do not change frequently the IP addresses associated with A records in their domains, nor do they serve up query responses from a wide range of countries. By mining pDNS data for all four characteristics of the DNS answer features and measuring a domain against all four combined, a security analyst can get a better picture of how suspect a domain is.

The same is true with the third feature of bad domains: TTL-based features. There are five characteristics of a potentially bad domain that revolve around TTL length. Those five characteristics are:

1. Average TTL
2. TTL standard deviation
3. Number of distinct TTL values
4. Number of changes in TTL
5. Percentage of specific TTL ranges

Depending on the purpose of a domain in an attack it may have a very low TTL (often, TTL for malicious domains is set to 0). But there are also valid domains that use low TTLs, especially those that use a CDN to serve web content. However, the low TTLs for legitimate sites using CDNs remain relatively static, whereas the TTL for dubious domains can fluctuate wildly, depending on the purpose of the domain at a given time. Attackers tend to use specific TTL values, more so than are traditionally used. TTL ranges for legitimate domains tend to have values like (in seconds) 300, 600, 3600, 14,440, and 86,400. Malicious domains tend to have values like 1 or 100. In addition to having lower TTLs, on average, than most domains malicious domains also use nonstandard TTL values and vary those TTL values more often than legitimate domains. Again, all of the TTL information is available in the DNS query response, which is stored as part of pDNS data collection.

FAST-FLUX DOMAINS

One of the reasons that malicious domains tend to have lower TTLs is the widespread use of fast-flux domains. Fast-flux domains are used by attackers a means of obscuring and protecting their real infrastructure. In a fast-flux attack, the attacker compromises a number of easy targets, such as unprotected computers or insecure home routers. These routers are then used as tunnels to redirect command and control messages and exfiltrated data to and from the real infrastructure.

Using a combination of DNS round robin and low TTLs, the attacker will constantly update the A records for the subdomains in the domain. Every time the malware on the host has a new request the DNS query response returns a new IP address. The captured data or command response is sent to the compromised host and forwarded on to the real infrastructure, which also sends out commands redirected through the same set of compromised hosts.

In addition to fast-flux domains, there are also double-flux domains. Double-flux domains also use the same fast-flux technique on the authoritative name servers for the domain. In a double-flux scenario, name servers for the domain are also compromised hosts. When a query comes into the name server it is forward through the compromised hosts and to the real authoritative name server. Again, this allows the attacker to protect her authoritative DNS infrastructure and continue to manage her fast-flux hosts without interruption. If the IP addresses for the fake authoritative name servers are blocked, she simply changes to new compromised hosts.

DNS FIREWALLS AND RPZ

So far there has been a lot of discussion around identifying potentially malicious domains, but the question becomes what should be done with those domains? The most common answer is to use whitelists and blacklists on the recursive DNS server as a method of restricting access to potentially bad domains. This technique will be discussed in more detail in the next chapter, but there is actually a more effective solution: DNS firewalls.

There are two types of DNS firewalls, on premise and in the cloud. On-premise DNS firewalls are installed directly on the recursive server and stop network users from reaching suspect domains. Companies like Infoblox and ThreatSTOP make these types of firewalls, which usually use Response Policy Zones (RPZs) or blacklists to enable enforcement of bad domains. There are also cloud-based solutions. Rather than manage enforcement on-premise, with solutions like the one offered by OpenDNS, recursive DNS functions are outsourced to the DNS provider who monitors the DNS traffic originating from the organization and look for known bad domains as well as anomalous activity.

Another version of cloud delivery is the "as a service" model that is offered by companies like eSentire. These services offer a wide range of capabilities for a monthly subscription. In addition to powering the service with their own intelligence, these "as a service delivery" providers give clients the chance to maintain some level of control of the DNS Firewall by including the ability to create custom whitelists and blacklists as well as closely monitor their DNS activity, as shown in Fig. 6.9. The "as a service" model also has the benefit of being significantly more scalable than an on-premise solution.

FIGURE 6.9

eSentire DNS firewall alert dashboard.

DNS firewalls make sense because almost all attackers rely on DNS at some point during incursion and exfiltration. Since DNS requests have to traverse the recursive DNS server, why not stop them there? Using blacklists to sinkhole domains has been a common practice for a while. Real-time black holes, like those from Spamhaus and DNSBL, have been used by mail server administrators for years to drop spam before it has a chance to hit the mail server.

Analysis of DNS log and pDNS data, as outlined in this chapter, combined with a DNS firewall allows security administrators to be proactive in blocking domains and doing more than just stopping spam. This analysis allows security teams to proactively stop some of the worst threats that face an organization, threats coming from organized and advanced attackers. The thing to remember is that no matter how advanced they are, in order to gain access to an organization and successfully get data out of that organization they not only need to use DNS, but they need to use many of the same DNS tricks that other attackers use and that are outlined throughout this book.

The big problem with blacklists is that they are difficult to manage and they very quickly become unwieldy. That is why the team at the Internet Systems Consortium, led by Paul Vixie, introduced RPZs in 2010.[9] RPZs are specially constructed zone files that reside on recursive DNS servers that turn the DNS server into a firewall of sorts, but one focused entirely on domain activity.

Because RPZs are merely zone files, they act like other zone files do. Which means they can be transferred, updated, have an SOA, TTL and can be sourced from multiple places. This means that an organization can create their own RPZ based on intelligence gathered by the security team and still maintain a different set of RPZs from partners and security vendors. RPZs allow flexibility in coordinating information from bad domains from multiple sources, and automating the process of updating that information, all within the caching DNS server. On top of all that, each hit against an RPZ file can be logged, so security teams can determine over time the efficacy of each RPZ, in addition they can determine the number of false positives that each RPZ generates.

While, an RPZ is essentially a zone file, it has the ability to intercept a DNS request and send one of four answers. Really, what RPZs do is take advantage of the fact that a recursive DNS server can respond with an authoritative reply to a query, even if the recursive server is not really authoritative.

The four policy responses that can be returned are as follows:

1. NXDOMAIN
2. NODATA
3. NO-OP
4. Local Data

NXDOMAIN and NODATA function as they do in normal DNS query responses. NXDOMAIN means that there are no records at all associated with the domain whereas a NODATA response means that there are records for the domain, but none that match the query. NO-OP, also referred to as PASSTHRU, allows a specific query to receive the correct response—even if the rest of the domain is blocked by another rule. A DNS firewall administrator may want to allow users to visit www.dns-book.net but does not want to allow traffic to any other subdomains. The fourth policy response is Local Data, which redirects the user to a local server, or at least a local IP address. This response is very common for security administrators who want to let users know that they have attempted to reach a domain that is malicious. Especially common as a response to a domain used in a phishing campaign these local pages can be used as an educational moment letting the user know that they were potentially compromising the organization by clicking on that link.

Configuration and set up of RPZs are discussed in more detail in Chapter 7.

BLACKLISTS, WHITELISTS, AND OTHER DNS THREAT INTELLIGENCE

As more security teams have realized the importance of monitoring and analyzing DNS traffic, DNS-based "threat intelligence" lists have become more common. There are a number of services that provide excellent threat intelligence around DNS, but most are simply providing lists of bad domains, with no context and often those can be less effective than having no intelligence.

Any third-party list is going to be prone to false positives, and lists that provide thousands or even hundreds of thousands of new bad domains every day can be especially problematic when it comes to false positives. False positives mean more work for the security teams as they try to track down alleged bad domains and possibly miss real threats.

That does not mean that blacklists are bad, but they should be taken for what they are: lists of domains with little or no context of how they wound up on that list. That is why any blacklist that an organization uses should be compared to collected DNS logs and pDNS traffic before using it to block access to domains. There is a lot of value in learning what third-party vendors see as bad in the wild, and seeing how that matches up with what is seen within the organization. This allows the security team to provide proper context around the domains that the blacklist providers are delivering. For example, if a domain on a blacklist has been seen inside the organization and is exhibiting behavior indicative of a malicious domain, there are now two data points indicating that the domain is malicious and can be sinkholed. Conversely, if a domain on the blacklist has been seen in the network, but does not appear to be suspicious it could require further investigation.

The same logic can be applied to DNS whitelists as well. There are a number of organizations that have DNS whitelists, like DNSWL and the Spamhaus Whitelist, that provide lists of good domains that should not be blocked. In addition, many DNS administrators make use of the Alexa top 1 million domains list to create whitelists for their DNS server.

Even good domains can fall victim to malicious activity or have compromised subdomains. So, while whitelists can help speed up DNS response times, they should be used with caution to ensure they are not giving attackers easy access to the organization.

As stated previously, there is a difference between a blacklist and real threat intelligence. Where a blacklist is simply a list of bad domains with no context, real threat intelligence is both actionable and it provides context around the threat.

This is an important distinction because where blacklists can make the job of the security team harder, threat intelligence can actually make it easier. Real DNS threat intelligence will tie domains together with a threat and associated indicators all of which helps the security analyst respond and remediate the threat faster. For example, a report that shows a domain tied to a particular variant of the Zeus bot, along with the file hash for that variant and other domains and IP addresses associated with the campaign. Now, the security team knows what to look for and has steps to remove the bot if it is installed on any workstations in the network. To take it a step further, if a threat report ties a domain to the use of ModPOS (malware designed specifically to steal bulk credit card information) not only does the security team have the domains and file hashes it needs, it also knows it is dealing with a group attempting to steal credit card data. That is a different profile than a group who is trying to steal company secrets. Again, this type of reporting allows security analysts to take meaningful action to remove the threat and be more confident in preventing its return.

CONCLUSIONS

There are multiple aspects to DNS security. Not only are there physical concerns about where to place DNS servers, but there is also upkeep of the DNS software itself. Making sure that the software remains fully patched and that security teams are keeping up with the latest security announcements from the DNS vendors can be a full time job in and of itself.

But, beyond the DNS infrastructure there is great value in the DNS logs themselves. Because most attackers use some sort of DNS-based protocol to carry out attacks, DNS traffic can be a great source of data if security teams understand how to properly mine it. That means more than just viewing DNS logs, it also means diving into the actual DNS traffic, both queries and responses. Within DNS traffic there are a number of patterns that can be found which point to a domain having the potential to be bad. When security teams mine DNS traffic looking for these patterns they can often identify previously unknown malicious domains and, using third-party sources, can often tie those domains to more domains and even to specific pieces of malware.

As powerful as DNS can be as a detection mechanism, too few organizations take advantage of the capabilities inherent within DNS to identify and stop threats inside the organization.

NOTES

1. Measurement Factory, 2016. DNS Survey: Open Resolvers. Measurement Factory, 10 Feb. 2016. Web. 11 Feb. 2016. <http://dns.measurement-factory.com/surveys/openre-solvers/ASN-reports/latest.html>.
2. Jayan, J., 2015. Easy Creation of Domain Names by Hackers Leaves SMBs Dangerously Exposed. Third Certainty, 21 Sept. 2015. Web. 15 Feb. 2016. <http://thirdcertainty.com/featured-story/easy-creation-of-domain-names-by-hackers-leaves-smbs-dangerously-exposed/>.
3. Hao, S., Thomas, M., Paxson, V., Feamster, N., Kreibich, C., Grier, C., et al., 2015. Understanding the Domain Registration Behavior of Spammers. The ICSI Networking and Security Group. 23 Oct. 2013. Web. 15 Feb. 2016. <http://www.icir.org/>.
4. Halvorson, T., Der, N., Foster, I., Savage, S., Saul, L., Voelker, G., 2015. From .academy to .zone: An Analysis of the New TLD Land Rush. Internet Measurement Conference (2015). 28 Oct. 2015. Web. 15 Feb. 2016. <http://conferences2.sigcomm.org/imc/2015/papers/p381.pdf>.
5. Helming, T., 2015. Where Badness Lurks: A New Threat Cartography. FireEye Cyber Defense Summit 2015.
6. DomainTools did not provide free services to the authors, we are simply fans of the service.
7. Math is outside the scope of this book.

8. Bilge, L., Sen, S., Balzarotti, D., Kirda, E., Kruegel, C., 2014. EXPOSURE: A Passive DNS Analysis Service to Detect and Report Malicious Domains. ACM Transactions on Information and System Security (TISSEC) 16.4 (2014). June 2014. Web. 16 Feb. 2016. <http://seclab.nu/static/publications/tissec14_exposure.pdf>.
9. You can watch the original presentation here: https://www.youtube.com/watch?v=0S-SWxSYhNc.

BIND security

7

INFORMATION IN THIS CHAPTER

- Running BIND in a *chroot* Jail
- Fingerprint Evasion Techniques
- Response Rate Limiting
- Queries and Transfers
- Response Policy Zones
- Logging

INTRODUCTION

BIND is, by far, the most popular DNS server deployed today. According to one survey BIND accounted for almost 54% of publicly facing DNS servers. BIND is so popular that, in the same survey, second place, at 34%, was "no match."[1] BIND was designed, and is still maintained, as a reference implementation of the DNS protocol. That means BIND supports any current DNS standards, even those standards that are less secure. So, it becomes important for DNS administrators using BIND to understand what the risks are and restrict access to services that are not needed.

BIND also has a reputation for being insecure. According to Mitre's Common Vulnerabilities and Exposures database there have been more than 60 BIND vulnerabilities reported since 1999. The Internet Systems Consortium (ISC), the organization behind BIND, reports more than 70 vulnerabilities over all versions of BIND.

However, in recent years, the team at ISC has gotten more serious about the security of BIND. BIND 9, the current version of BIND, wound up being a complete code-rewrite of BIND 8 with a particular emphasis on security. There are still security vulnerabilities that surface in BIND, but it happens a lot less frequently.

That being said, because of BIND's popularity, and the fact that is deployed on public facing servers all over the Internet, it remains a target for security researchers, both the white hat and the black hat kind. Because of this it is important to maintain the security of a BIND installation, not just the server itself but it is important to secure the files BIND uses and secure all BIND transactions to the extent possible. As has been discussed throughout the book, DNS security is not just about securing hardware and software it also means securing the protocol, irrespective of the chosen DNS software.

Before getting to the rest of the chapter, there are two things that every DNS administrator and security team responsible for maintaining a BIND installation must do:

1. Ensure that the BIND server has been upgraded to the latest version of BIND. Given the large number of vulnerabilities in older versions of BIND, and the ease with which a BIND version can be fingerprinted, it is important to maintain a current version of BIND. The latest version of BIND can be found on the ISC web site at: https://www.isc.org/downloads/bind/.
2. Be aware of any BIND security advisories. ISC publishes all BIND 9 security advisories at: https://kb.isc.org/category/74/0/10/Software-Products/BIND9/Security-Advisories/. ISC allows users to subscribe to an RSS feed or a mailing list to receive notification when new security advisories are published.

Staying on top of these two items will vastly improve the security of an organization's BIND installation versus most installs of BIND. There are some additional steps that a security team can take to improve the security of a BIND server. These have nothing to do with BIND itself, instead they are general guidelines for good server security:

1. Do not run unnecessary services on a public facing BIND server. Make sure httpd, ftpd, telnetd, and other services are disabled, or ideally, removed.
2. SSH access should be restricted to certain networks and ideally access should be restricted to a different interface than the interface answering DNS queries.
3. NEVER run BIND as root. Use an unprivileged account to run BIND, preferably an account that is only used to run BIND.
4. Ensure that whichever unprivileged account is used to run BIND does not have remote access privileges to the BIND server.
5. Any files associated with BIND, especially the *named.conf* file and any associated zone files should be owned by the unprivileged BIND user and should have only the permissions necessary for BIND to function (eg, read/write by the BIND user only).

Again, these rules are not just applicable to BIND; they also apply to any public facing server that an organization may operate.

RUNNING BIND IN A *CHROOT* JAIL

Securing a BIND server starts with the installation of BIND. The reality is that a security and DNS administration team can do everything correctly when it comes to the security of the BIND installation and their BIND server could still be compromised. A hacker group in Russia might find a 0-day vulnerability in BIND and develop an exploit to take advantage of that vulnerability against the organization's BIND server. A vulnerability could be announced and exploited on the network before the team has a chance to put the patch in place. Even the best-run security teams have to plan for a security process to fail and the organization's systems to be compromised, in fact the best-run security teams do plan for that. In the case of a compromise of the BIND server, the goal is to minimize the damage an attacker can do, and that starts by running BIND in a *chroot jail*.

Chroot is a native UNIX/Linux tools that allow server administrators to run a program in a modified root directory known as a jail. The jail contains everything the program needs to run and the user that owns the process running in the jails sees the modified root directory as the server root. In practical terms, this means that if an attacker is able to exploit a vulnerability in a program and that vulnerability allows the attacker to gain command-line access to the server, because the attacker will be running at the same privilege level as the user that owns the compromised application, the attacker will not be able to access anything outside of the jailed directory.

For example, an administrator can implement a *chroot jail* so that BIND resides in */var/named/chroot/var/named* instead of residing in */var/named*. Now, if an attacker compromises the BIND daemon and gains access to the server she would only be able to access everything below the *chroot/* directory, essentially *chroot/* would look like */* to the attacker.

Creating a *chroot jail* should not be the beginning and end of a security strategy when it comes to BIND. In fact, relying on *chroot* as the only security mechanism may make a BIND installation less secure. However, a *chroot jail* can be part of a comprehensive security strategy as long as the files that are included in the jail are limited to only those that are needed to run BIND and as long as BIND is not run as root. If BIND is run as root in a *chroot jail* it means there is, essentially, no jail. The root user on a server can quickly escape out of a *chroot jail* and access other parts of the server.

There are a couple of ways to install BIND in a *chroot jail*. The first, and most common, is to download the BIND install package and walk through one of the many tutorials available on the Internet, the one delivered by Team Cymru is excellent.[2] This works for organizations that have a dedicated DNS administrator who can devote the time to ensure that patches are installed in a timely manner and can ensure that each update does not have significant impact on the organization's DNS infrastructure.

The second way to install BIND in a *chroot jail* is to see if the package manager of the underlying operating system has a package available, for example, using the yum package manager on CentOS:

```
[root@server ~]# yum list bind-chroot
Available Packages
bind-chroot.x86_64     30:9.3.6-25.P1.el5_11.8     updates
```

Using a package manager has the advantage of allowing BIND to follow the same upgrade path as all of the other services running on that server. It is easier for an administrator to schedule routine updates across all platforms and not have to perform special updates for BIND, which also means that BIND is more likely to be kept patched.

The downside is that this puts the security of the BIND *chroot* installation in the hands of a third party, and it requires hoping that the third party stays current with patching and updated the package—especially when critical security vulnerabilities are reported.

Before deciding which method of installation to choose it is important for an organization to make an honest assessment of its ability to maintain a BIND installation and keep it current.

FINGERPRINT EVASION TECHNIQUES

Chapter 5 provided an overview of reconnaissance methods for determining the version of BIND an organization is running. There are some steps that an organization can take that will minimize their exposure to these fingerprinting attempts. This section will provide an overview of some of these techniques. However, it should be noted that no evasion technique is going to be perfect. Given enough query responses, an attacker will be able to figure out what version of BIND, or any other DNS server, an organization is running. The reason for this is that while the DNS protocol is supposed to be implemented the same way across all implementations, the reality is that is not. Based on the responses a DNS server gives to legitimate queries, an attacker will be able to determine what that DNS software is running on the server.

One of the simplest things a DNS administrator can do to deter attackers is to disable the version information in the options section of the *named.conf* file. An attacker can determine which version of a BIND server is running by issuing the following command:

```
dig @192.168.1.15 version.bind chaos txt
```

Which, on an unedited BIND configuration returns something like this:

```
;; ANSWER SECTION:
version.bind. 0  CH  TXT "9.9.5-3ubuntu0.8-Ubuntu"
```

Not only does it provide the version of BIND running on the server, it also provides the underlying operating system. The query response can be changed by editing the *named.conf* file to add the following line in the options section:

```
version "Unknown";
```

Which will now return the following:

```
;; ANSWER SECTION:
version.bind. 0 CH TXT "Unknown"
```

Of course, the data between the quotations marks can be replaced with any text. A lot of DNS administrators prefer to use versions of other DNS servers, such as Microsoft's, in an attempt to throw would-be attackers off the trail. Again, this really only dissuades the most novice of attacker, it is a good idea to make the change, but security teams should not expect real security benefit from it.

ANY RESPONSE TO A VERSION.BIND QUERY

Because the version.bind query is not implemented in many popular DNS servers any response provided by the query is potentially revealing. While BIND does not give DNS administrators the ability to disable the version.bind query other DNS vendors such as Knot and Microsoft DNS do. Whenever possible, it is better to disable this feature entirely.

To really protect a server from being effectively fingerprinted, it is first necessary to understand how fingerprinting software works. Take this snippet of code from *fpdns*, one of the most popular DNS fingerprinting applications:

```
{
  fingerprint = > $iq[3],
  header = > $qy[2],
  query = > $nct[2],
  ruleset = > [
    {
      fingerprint = > $iq[4],
      result = > {
      vendor = > "ISC",
      product = > "BIND",
      version = > "9.3.0 -- 9.3.6-P1"
    },
```

fpdns is looking at "borderline query responses," in other words responses that are unique to a particular DNS server. By cataloging those responses the tools are able to narrow down the DNS server. In the case of the code snippet above, iq[3], qy[2], and nct[2] indicate that it is a version of BIND, those query responses look like this:

```
"1,QUERY,0,0,0,1,0,0,NOERROR,.+,.+,.+,.+", #iq3
"0,$NOTIFY,0,1,1,0,1,1,NOTIMP,0,0,0,0", #qy2a
". IN A",    #nct2
```

It is then the final line, iq[4] that narrows the version down to a more specific version of BIND, the query response iq[4] looks like this:

```
"1,$NOTIFY,0,0,1,1,0,1,FORMERR,1,0,0,0",  #iq4
```

Most, if not all, DNS fingerprinting scanners are simply big if/then statements. If the query responses match one of the predefined strings then the program is able to identify the target DNS server. Unfortunately, that requires a lot of work on the part of the developers. As new versions of the DNS server are released the response behavior often changes, which means that unless the fingerprint scanner is continually updated (and the developers have access to all of the latest versions of DNS software) it quickly falls out of date.

One way to keep ahead of attackers using DNS scanners is simply to stay updated with the latest version, after proper testing of course. In addition to making sense from a patching perspective, it also could mean foiling attackers attempting to scan for vulnerable DNS servers.

Depending on the size of an organization's DNS infrastructure, there is another option to consider. Placing an authoritative DNS server behind an application-aware firewall or load balancer will alter the query response and aid in obscuring what DNS server software is running on the server. The obvious question to ask is: Is it worth rearchitecting an entire network for a minor improvement in security? For some organizations the answer may be yes, but for many it probably will not be.

RESPONSE RATE LIMITING

No organization wants their authoritative DNS server to be used in a Distributed Denial of Service (DDoS) amplification attack, but the fact is that any is a potential target for attackers. To that end, BIND introduced the concept of Response Rate Limiting (RRL) in version 9.10. RRL limits the number of queries from a host that the authoritative name server will respond to over a given period of time.

RRL in BIND requires at least version 9.10 and BIND must be compiled with *-enable-rrl* during the configure phase of the install. Once BIND has been compiled with RRL support enabled activating it is as simple as adding a statement to the options section of the *named.conf* file:

```
rate-limit{ responses-per-second 5;};
```

This code snipped limits the number of responses per second to 5 to a specific host. Remember, from Chapter 4, the way a DNS amplification attack works is that the attacker launches millions of small forged queries that appear to be originating from the target of the attack. The authoritative server has a much larger response and all of those responses are directed at the target. By limiting the number of queries per host that the authoritative server will respond to the DNS Amplification attack becomes muted.

There is a danger in limiting the number of responses in that it may create false negatives, in other words the DNS server may drop legitimate traffic.

To that end BIND provides the ability to test the configuration by enabling log-only mode, to see if legitimate traffic is dropped using the new configuration:

```
rate-limit {
        responses-per-second 5;
        log-only yes;
        };
```

That snipped will implement the same rule, but it will only log the results, not drop any traffic.

BIND also provides the option to make exemptions to this rule for certain hosts. For example, the secondary name server or the organization's mail server may need to make frequent queries to the DNS server. In cases like that DNS administrators can add an exemption statement, such as the following:

```
rate-limit {
responses-per-second 5;
exempt-clients {10.100.50.8;};
};
```

This will allow the DNS server to respond to any query made by 10.100.50.8, no matter how many queries are made per second.

QUERIES AND TRANSFERS

This section primarily focuses on securing queries and transfers to an authoritative name server. It has been stressed throughout this book (and will continue to be), but it bears repeating, a public-facing authoritative server should not also function as a recursive server. Those two services should be separate and almost no organization needs a public-facing recursive server.

Given the above paragraph, one of the first things a DNS administrator should do while reading this section is ensure that the following lines are in place in the *named.conf* in the options section:

```
options {
// Do not allow queries to the cache
    allow-query-cache { none; };
// Disable recursive queries
    recursion no;
};
```

The first line prevents any hosts from querying the cache on the server. The second line, *recursion no*, prevents the recursive service from running on that installation. Disabling recursion not only prevents the potential for cache poisoning attacks, it also prevents the server from being used as a man in the middle host in a DDoS attack.

BIND offers other ways to restrict the access to DNS queries, most notably the use of Access Control Lists (ACLs) to control traffic. ACLs in BIND are not designed to work in the same manner as ACLs in firewalls. If there is a need to completely restrict access to a BIND server from an IP address or network block that should be done on the firewall, though it technically can be done with the following entry on BIND:

```
acl blacklist { 10.10.50.3; 192.168.10.0/24; };
options {
    blackhole { blacklist; };
};
```

This set of commands creates an ACL called *blacklist* that consists of the singe IP address 10.10.50.3 and the network block of 192.168.10.0-255, it then uses the *blackhole* options command to ignore all queries to and from those IP addresses. Note that the *blackhole* option is the most extreme method for doing this, not only will the BIND server not accept queries from these IP addresses, it will not query them either. That means it is important to ensure there are no hosts in the set of blackholed IP addresses with which the BIND server will need to communicate in the future.

To this point the discussion has been about how to restrict access to the authoritative DNS server, but the point of an authoritative server is to provide information to a wide range of hosts who are requesting it. The next area of focus needs to be on how to ensure that the BIND server does not share more information than necessary.

This process starts with restricting zone transfers (AXFR queries) to only those servers that need to see the full zone. To do this, add the following line to the global options section of the *named.conf* file:

```
allow-transfer { none; };
```

Any command in the global options section of the *named.conf* file becomes the default behavior for BIND, so this statement prevents any response to an AXFR query. The next step is to use ACLs to create rules that allow secondary name servers to conduct zone transfers. For example, if an organization has a domain cryptodns.com with the primary name server 192.168.1.15 (ns1.cryptodns.com) and the secondary name server 10.100.50.8 (ns2.cryptondns.com). The DNS administrator can edit the *named.conf* file to allow that DNS server to conduct zone transfers. Start by creating an ACL:

```
acl "cryptodns" {
            192.168.1.15; // ns1.cryptodns.com
            10.100.50.8; // ns2.cryptodns.com
        };
```

Then allow transfers specifically within that domain:

```
zone "cryptodns.com" {
    type master;
    file "file "/var/named/cryptodns.com";
    allow-transfer { localhost; cryptodns; };
};
```

The snippet above allows, for the domain cryptodns.com only, zone transfers from all of the hosts listed in the cryptodns ACL. Of course, the ACL does not need to be limited to just secondary name servers, it also makes sense to allow requests from the organization's gateway for troubleshooting purposes and there may be other hosts that have legitimate need for making AXFR queries (such as a monitoring service).

USING TSIG TO SIGN ZONE TRANSFERS

To further enhance the security of zone transfers BIND allows the use of Transaction SIGnatures (TSIG) for transaction-level authentication. TSIG enforcement can be used for queries, transfers, and updates. This section will examine how to enforce TSIG for zone transfers.

TSIGs use a combination of shared secrets and one-way hashing to confirm that the host making the request is authorized to access the data. DNS queries are trivial to spoof, enabling TSIGs between primary and secondary authoritative name servers helps to provide a second form of authentication (the first being that the requesting IP address is one that is allowed to request transfers, based on enabled ACLs).

In order for a TSIG transaction to work, the first step is to generate a shared secret key. They key can be created manually (as long as it is properly base-64 encoded) or generated any number of ways including using the built-in functionality of the BIND server:

```
dnssec-keygen -a hmac-sha512 -b 256 -n HOST cryptodns-key
```

This command generates a HOST key using the HMAC-SHA512 message authentication code that is 256 bits in length and stored in a file called cryptodns-key. The command, in this case, generated a shared secret key that looks like this:

```
KYe4aOU6oG7NdaOzhWAlO213jF + ocn9ftTSonVrQmvA =
```

The next step is to add the key to the *named.conf* file of both the primary and the secondary name servers:

```
key cryptodns {
 algorithm hmac-sha512;
 secret "KYe4aOU6oG7NdaOzhWAlO213jF + ocn9ftTSonVrQmvA = ";
 };
```

Obviously, publishing a shared secret key like this in an insecure *named.conf* file defeats the purpose of securing the transactions in the first place. It is important to ensure that access to the *named.conf* file is restricted and only the BIND user has access to read/write to the file. If that is not possible, because multiple users need to make edits to the *named.conf* file, it is possible to store the key in a separate, more restricted, file. DNS administrators can then just add the key file through an include statement in the *named.conf* file:

```
include "/var/named/cryptodns.key";
```

The next step is to get the two hosts to use the newly generated key when making rests. Using the example above of ns1.cryptodns.com being assigned IP address 192.168.1.15 and ns2.cryptodns.com being assigned IP address 10.100.50.8, there are two statements needed. On ns1.cryptodns.com, the statement would look like this:

```
server 10.100.50.8 {
keys { cryptodns ;};
};
```

On ns2.cryptodns.com, the statement would be the opposite:

```
server 192.168.1.15 {
  keys { cryptodns ;};
};
```

Now all DNS queries between the two hosts will include the TSIG hash from the shared secret (the shared secret is never passed between the two hosts).

Finally, in order to prevent transfers to hosts that do not have the proper key information the following line can be added to the options section of *named.conf*:

```
allow-transfer { key cryptodns ;};
```

Now, all transfer requests require the proper hash before they will be responded to, and since that hash is only allowed from a specific IP address, the request must have the right hash and originate from the correct IP address.

RESPONSE POLICY ZONES

Chapter 6 introduced the concept of Response Policy Zones (RPZs) as a way to easily manipulate blacklists and whitelists directly on the DNS server. RPZs also provide an easy way to subscribe to third-party threat intelligence, preventing users from visiting potentially malicious sites.

Unlike the rest of the chapter, this section is focused on a configuration option for a BIND recursive server. RPZs are available starting with version 9.8 of BIND. One of the really nice things about using RPZs in BIND is that it allows for real-time updating of potentially malicious domain names without having to continually restart the BIND service.

Setting up an RPZ, or multiple RPZs, within BIND is relatively easy. It starts with adding a command in the options section of *named.conf*:

```
response-policy {
        zone "rpz.blacklist";
        zone "rpz.mw.surbl.org";
        zone "rpz.ph.surbl.org";
        zone "rpz.spamhaus.org";
};
```

The lines above show four different zones. The first one is a local zone created by the security team and the DNS administrators. The other two are subscription services available from SURBL` and Spamhaus. Both of these organizations, along with other companies, such as Farsight Security, and Internet Identity offer subscription-based RPZ access. These companies all take advantage of their unique views of malicious activity happening on the Internet to compile lists of bad domains and deliver them on a regular basis, in the form of RPZ updates, to their clients. Some of these companies, like SURBL, offer the option to subscribe to different RPZs such as a malware and a phishing RPZ or have everything self-contained. Of course, one size does not fit all when it comes to security. Some organizations need to be more aggressive about blocking potentially bad domains; others are more concerned about false positives. To that end, a number of RPZ providers do offer customized RPZ feeds, SURBL, Spamhaus, and Farsight Security are examples of companies that do, but it is a good question to ask any RPZ vendor an organization is considering using.

CONFUSION

A lot of organizations are interested in a service like outsourced RPZ data feeds, but are not sure how to approach it or how to choose the right vendor or vendors. Organizations looking for help often turn to a security broker. A security broker is a company that has relationships with a number of vendors and can help an organization refine their requires, answer the all-powerful, "what problem are you trying to solve?" and then help the organization find the right fit. There are even companies, like SecurityZones, that specialize in RPZ and DNS in general that can answer very specific questions.

Starting from the bottom, the next step is to make zone file entries in the *named.conf* file for each of the response policy listed zones. Both the SURBL and the Spamhaus RPZs are slave zones to the master, which resides on an authoritative name server controlled by SURBL and Spamhaus, respectively. Creating the zone file entries would look like this:

```
zone "rpz.surbl.org";
  type slave;
  masters { [IP Address of Master Nameserver]; };
  file "slave/rpz.mw.surbl.org";
  allow-query { localhost; };
  allow-transfer { none; };
};
zone "rpz.spamhaus.org";
  type slave;
  masters { [IP Address of Master Nameserver]; };
  file "slave/ rpz.spamhaus.org";
  allow-query { localhost; };
  allow-transfer { none; };
};
```

After the first RPZ files are pulled down from the respective vendors, they will update automatically, based on the Time To Live information contained in the zone file. It works in the same manner as any other zone transfer.

Once the third-party RPZs are enabled, when a user makes a request for a domain in that zone file the query will be redirected to a nonexistent host, and the user will not be able to access the domain. On the server side, the request will look similar to this:

```
;; OPT PSEUDOSECTION:
; EDNS: version: 0, flags:; udp: 4096
;; QUESTION SECTION:
;alamman.com.  IN A
;; AUTHORITY SECTION:
rpz.mw.surbl.org. 180 IN SOA dev.null.  zone.surbl.org.  1459306070  180
180 604800 180
```

WORKING WITH THIRD PARTIES

There are a lot of benefits to bringing in third-party subscription data to enhance the security of an organization. The primary benefit is that DNS RPZ providers see a lot more DNS traffic than any single organization and they have a larger and more diverse view of attack traffic streaming across the Internet. Ultimately, an organization's security team is responsible for not only protecting the organization, but also ensuring that security measures do not cause too much disruption to the users. To that end, it is important to closely monitor the efficacy of any third-party RPZ subscriptions and work with the provider if there are too many false positives or false negatives generated by the zones.

The top entry, rpz.blacklist, is the local RPZ file that is populated based on intelligence gathered by security teams and again is added the same as a standard zone file by adding a statement similar to this in the *named.conf* file:

```
zone "rpz.blacklist" {
  type master;
  file "master/rpz.blacklist";
  allow-query { localhost; };
};
```

This tells BIND to look in the file master/rpz.blacklist for information about the zone and it also prevents the BIND server from responding to any queries that do not originate from localhost.

The last step is to put the zone file together, remember from Chapter 6 that there are four possible responses to a domain name in an RPZ: NXDOMAIN, NODATA, NO-OP, and Local Data. Here is what sample zone file entries would look like in BIND. Start with NXDOMAIN and NODATA:

```
mgm88tv.com CNAME .   ; Locky
jeansowghsqq.com CNAME .   ; TeslaCrypt
9hrds.wolfcrap.at CNAME *  ; TeslaCrypt
```

The first two entries are NXDOMAIN entries; an NXDOMAIN response denies the existence of the domain entirely. Each of these records are turned into a CNAME that points to the root domain "." and will return the proper response. The third entry, wolfcrap.at, returns an NODATA response, which acknowledges the existence of the domain, but says there is no data for that domain. The result to the end user is the same: He cannot access any of the domains.

Sometimes not returning an answer is enough. For either education purposes or to cut down on support calls it might be necessary to send users to a redirect page. That redirect page can be used to explain to users why they received this page and perhaps advice on next steps. This redirect page is often called a walled-garden, or Local Data in BIND parlance. The entries for Local Data domains look similar to this:

```
isityoureqq.com  A 192.168.1.4  ; TeslaCrypt
*.jambola.com CNAME *.wall.cryptodns.com. ; CryptoWall
```

The first entry is a straight up A record that points isityoureqq.com to local IP address 192.168.1.4, where there is a web site set up to let the user know that there was a potential problem with the web site he tried to visit. The second entry does the same thing but uses a CNAME record as well as a wildcard record. In this case the entry will redirect any subdomain of jambola.com to the same subdomain at wall.cryptodns.com where, again, there will be a web site that tell the user there was a potential problem with a domain he attempted to visit.

Finally, there are sometimes domains critical to the business that security teams do not want to see accidentally blocked. These domains can be added as NO-OP domains, which, essentially, create whitelists of domains that will not be blocked.

```
*.salesforce.com  CNAME rpz-passthru. ; SalesForce - sales
dropbox.com CNAME rpz-passthru ; Drop Box - engineering
```

The CNAME rpz-passthru is a reserved CNAME in BIND that tells BIND to pass on the correct response to the domain query. Note that in the above example, as well as the previous examples, there are comments after each entry explaining why the domain is on a particular list. Because the status of a domain can change over time (eg, a compromised site patches a security hole and is no longer serving up malware) having the comments in place will allow other DNS administrators to understand why the domain was on the list in the first place.

It may make sense to separate the whitelisted domains from the rest of the domains and create a unique RPZ file just for them. By doing so, DNS administrators can make a separate zone entry and set a default policy of PASSTHRU for all of the domains contained within that specific RPZ file. The response-policy entry would look something like this:

```
response-policy {
zone "rpz.whitelist" policy PASSTHRU;
};
```

And the full response-policy entry would look like this:

```
response-policy {
    zone "rpz.whitelist" policy PASSTHRU;
    zone "rpz.blacklist";
    zone "rpz.surbl.org";
    zone "rpz.spamhaus.org";
};
```

This method has another advantage; BIND processes requests according to the first match. By placing the whitelist RPZ first, the domains in that whitelist will be processed before the domains in any of the other lists. So, if there happens to be a conflict between the whitelist and one of the blacklists, the whitelist answer will be the one returned.

LOGGING

BIND has a number of facilities to log queries and responses. Of course, it is not enough to simply enable logging in BIND. Collecting BIND logs should be part of an overall strategy for dealing with and managing log files. This section will walk through the BIND logging options and offer some strategies for maximizing the security of the BIND installation using those logs, however those strategies do not mean anything unless they are accompanied by similar logging strategies from other systems on the network.

For example, suppose a recursive query from a local host is NXDOMAIN'ed because the domain is associated with the Angler Exploit Kit. It is great that the event was caught, but that single event does not give the security team the context they need to determine if there is a bigger problem on the host making the request, or was it potentially a false positive. On the other hand, if that log entry is sent to the Security Information Event Manager, along with the logs from the client (whether those logs are native to the host or antivirus) it is possible to correlate the DNS logs with the host logs to get a better picture of the incident and to chart the correct incident response.

To that end, BIND logs should automatically be sent to the syslog facility on the server and forwarded to a central location where logs from other systems on the network are also sent. In addition to making the security teams' job easier by having all logs in one place, using a centralized log collection system improves the security of the server. Security is improved by centralized log collection because it means that if an attacker does gain command-line access to the server she will not be able to cover her tracks as easily. Can she cover her tracks once she gains access by disabling syslog? Yes. What she cannot do is cover any logs generated gaining access to the server or hide the fact that she shut down syslog, which will generate a log to the remote collection server. As long as someone is vigilantly monitoring the logs, there is a better chance that the attacker will get caught faster.

Syslog logging can be enabled in the logging statement within *named.conf*:

```
logging {
channel default_syslog {severity info;};
};
```

In BIND 9 and later the logging statement is parsed last, so it does not matter where it is placed in the named.conf file. There are seven severity levels within BIND logs: critical, error, warning, notice, info, debug, and dynamic. The first five, critical through info, are standard syslog levels, which is why they can be sent to a syslog facility. The last two debug and dynamic are unique to BIND and must be written to a local file:

```
logging {
channel default_syslog {severity info;};
channel default_debug {
        severity dynamic;
        file "/var/named/logs/debug.log";
};
```

Now, there are two channels, one for log events that are info and above that will be sent to the syslog server, the second is for events at the dynamic level, these will be written locally to debug.log. Of course, it is important that debug. log has the correct permissions and can only be viewed/written to by the BIND process owner.

In addition to the actual log data, there are several other pieces of information that a centralized log management system (LMS) needs in order to process the log and possibly alert on it. The LMS needs to know the severity of the log, the time the event occurred, and category of the event. Fortunately, BIND can provide all of this information. Unfortunately, it is all turned off by default. Going back to the examples above, adding the following lines will provide that additional information:

```
logging {
channel default_syslog {
        severity info;
        print-category yes;
        print-time yes;
        print-severity yes;
        };
channel default_debug {
        severity dynamic;
        file "/var/named/logs/debug.log";
        print-category yes;
        print-time yes;
        print-severity yes;
        };
};
```

The final step is to determine which categories get logged to which facility. There are 20 categories that BIND supports, and one special category. The categories are client, config, database, delegation-only, dispatch, dnssec, general, lame-servers, network, notify, queries, resolver, rpz, rate-limit, security, unmatched, update, update-security, xfer-in, and xfer-out. Each category can be given a different logging profile depending on the number of channels available:

```
category general { default_syslog; };
category security { default_debug; default_syslog; };
category config { default_syslog; };
category resolver { default_syslog; };
```

Note that the logs can be sent to more than one channel. If the DNS administrators need to be able to access log files to troubleshoot issues, but do not need broad access to the LMS, logs can be directed to both places.

There is a 21st category known as default. The default category performs exactly how one would expect; it sends logs generated under all categories not specifically named the channel defined in the default statement. If there is no need to distinguish between different categories a default statement would work:

```
logging {
        channel default_syslog {
                severity info;
                print-category yes;
                print-time yes;
                print-severity yes;
                };
        channel default_debug {
                severity dynamic;
                file "/var/named/logs/debug.log";
                print-category yes;
                print-time yes;
                print-severity yes;
        };
        category default { default_syslog; default_debug; };
    };
```

This takes all logs, in all categories, and sends everything that has a severity of *info* and above to the syslog facility and anything that has a severity of *dynamic* and above and writes it to a local file.

The one category not impacted by default is query. Because a name server, especially a recursive name server, fields so many queries organizations often do not want to send all of those logs to a centralized LMS. Unless an organization is doing passive DNS analysis of those logs it usually does not make sense. However, it is important to be aware that not all categories of logs will be sent to the syslog server or local file using the default category.

CONCLUSIONS

BIND is a powerful tool for managing DNS infrastructure and has a great deal of capability. It also has a number of security concerns. Addressing those security concerns and then taking advantage of new features in the latest version of BIND will help organizations improve the security of their DNS infrastructure as well as the security of the entire organization.

NOTES

1. DNS Survey October 2010. Measurement Factory, 10 Oct. 10. Web. 27 Feb. 2016. <http://dns.measurement-factory.com/surveys/201010/>.
2. The chroot guide is part of the Secure BIND template that Team Cymru publishes, it is available on their web site at: https://www.cymru.com/Documents/secure-bind-template.html.

Windows DNS security

8

INFORMATION IN THIS CHAPTER

- Securing Windows DNS Files
- Dynamic DNS Control
- Queries and Transfers
- Windows Caching Servers
- Windows DNS and High Availability
- Securing Zone Files
- Logging

INTRODUCTION

By most measurements, Windows is the second most popular DNS server platform with about a third of all instances running on the Internet.[1] A small enterprise can set up a Windows DNS server with a few clicks, and a larger network can manage multiple redundant servers complete with dynamic updates and client authentication. For administrators securing a Windows DNS environment, there are a few surface areas of attack to consider: access to files on the DNS server itself, network access to the server within the firewall, network access from the public Internet, and ways the infrastructure may change under unexpected circumstances. Each of these will be discussed in detail. Note this chapter will not be a general guide to DNS on Windows, but will instead focus on the areas critical to security.

But first, a brief survey of recent security issues with Windows DNS to help understand what attacks are possible. In 2006, Microsoft patched a client-side buffer overrun vulnerability in its DNS resolver. This was labeled MS06-041 or CVE-2006-3440. If an attacker could get a client to query a specific hostname, a malicious DNS server could send a crafted response that would exploit the vulnerability and gain system-level access to the target. As Microsoft described it, "The vulnerability could be exploited by an attacker who persuaded a user to open a specially crafted file or view a specially crafted website."[2]

DNS Security. DOI: http://dx.doi.org/10.1016/B978-0-12-803306-7.00008-5

In 2007, Microsoft issued a patch labeled MS07-029 or CVE-2007-1748. It was a remotely exploitable buffer overrun vulnerability in the DNS RPC Management service. Note this was not a vulnerability involving DNS traffic itself, but rather the code that managed settings for the DNS server. It could be exploited via the RPC ports of 139 and 445.[3] Most enterprises block those ports at the firewall, but they are often open within a network.

In 2015, Microsoft announced a vulnerability in how the Windows DNS Server parses requests. It was labeled MS15-127 or CVE-2015-6125. This was a "use after free" vulnerability and was remotely exploitable by anyone who could send queries to the DNS server. According to Microsoft it could result in an attacker gaining Local System Account access to the server.[4] This is particularly worrisome to DNS administrators because any unpatched systems that handle queries from the Internet could be taken over by attackers.

SECURING WINDOWS DNS FILES

As in BIND, zone files form the core of Windows DNS settings. They store all domain records as well as delegations and DNSSEC signatures. The permissions on zone files will control who can update those records. Windows provides a graphical interface, called the DNS Manager, to help administrators configure the zone file. Microsoft also provides checklists of steps to follow in securing different versions of their DNS servers, from which many of these suggestions are derived.

Windows, like BIND, has distinct concepts of a domain and a zone. Subdomains may all be in the same zone or may be moved into separate zones as desired. An administrator normally creates a new zone when adding a new DNS server to manage a portion of the domain. There may be other cases, such as if one of the subdomains changes often and another does not, where it also makes sense to create separate zones within the same domain.

Windows has several different zone types: primary zones, secondary zones, stub zones, forward zones, and conditional forward zones. As with BIND, a primary server must have the zone file stored locally, either on the file system or in Active Directory (AD). When hosting a secondary zone, some other server will be acting as the primary zone, and the secondary server will not store the zone file locally. Instead it must have network access to the primary server to retrieve the contents of the zone. Like BIND, Windows has a notion of stub zones, not to be confused with stub resolvers. A stub zone can answer queries, but only by providing the authoritative servers for the zone. This can be useful if a network has many child zones and administrators want to limit the number of recursive queries hitting the internal root.[5] Finally, forward zones and conditional forward zones can be thought of like resolvers. They will send queries upstream to find answers on behalf of clients.

An initial step in securing a Windows DNS environment is determining the network architecture of what hosts should be able to connect to what components of the service. In the simplest case, this means differentiating between clients that will make recursive queries and clients that will query for authoritative records. In many cases this also involves separating internal-only resources like a wiki or an employee portal into their own domain. In some environments administrators may want to hide the presence of certain systems from other employees. For example, an auditing team may be working within a company, and it may be important to keep their workstation names from being queried. In all cases the DNS configuration should be planned in combination with network-level segregation and filtering. In most cases, this is just a matter of setting firewall rules to limit connectivity to the internal server. The setup should be monitored for deviations, such as queries to internal resources being sent out to the Internet.

A DNS server must know the IP address of the root in order to bootstrap all other information. In the case of a server that will answer queries for Internet domains, this information can be retrieved from IANA in the root hints file (https://www.iana.org/domains/root/files). If administering an internal-only intranet, or an air-gapped network, this will be a different file pointing to the internal root. If this is misconfigured it can lead to internal queries leaking out to the public DNS root. For example, say a company uses ".internal" for private sites on its LAN. If only the public DNS root is used, then queries will be directed to the root and fail. If both the public root and an internal root are used, the server may round-robin queries to the root in which case some of those queries will leak before the SOA record for .local is cached. Recall that the full query will be sent to the root and possibly visible to anyone monitoring that connection. If the root is set up correctly, with .local being owned by the internal server and everything else by the public root, typos could still be directed outside the network. For this reason it is important to consider the sensitivity of internal hostnames when mixing internal and external resolution on the same server. And queries should be monitored for unexpected leakage.

Zones can be managed either by editing a text file or through the DNS Manager GUI. Even if an administrator does not regularly make changes to DNS settings it is helpful to look through the menus to understand what options are available. When creating a zone, Windows will provide the option of making it AD-integrated. This means the canonical copy of the zone file will be stored in AD instead of in a file on the disk. This is only available if the server is a Domain Controller, but it enables some additional features like secure dynamic updates, which will be described in a later section.

As described earlier in the book, DNS infrastructure can be used for reverse DNS queries that map an IP address to a network name. These zones are called reverse lookup zones, and sometimes regular DNS queries are called forward lookups to differentiate between the two. Reverse zone entries can be managed similarly to forward zone entries, either through a Windows GUI or through the command line. In the zone files, reverse entries are stored as PTR records in reverse dotted-quad notation as part of the in-addr.arpa domain. For example, the reverse entry for 1.2.3.4 would be 4.3.2.1.in-addr.arpa. Reverse zone entries can be especially important when a network has publicly accessible services. For example, spam filters will often do reverse lookups on inbound email to see if the sender address is coming from an expected location.

By default, Windows assigns a handful of accounts and groups full access to zone files: Administrators, DnsAdmins, Domain Admins, Enterprise Admins, Enterprise Domain Controllers, and System. Administrators can add or remove accounts and also change the roles that accounts can perform. The different roles include Full Control, Read, Write, Create Child Objects, and Delete Child Objects. Note Writing is separate from Creating Children because an administrator may want an account to be able to add subrecords to the zone without modifying existing entries.

Note that Windows may store backups of non-AD-integrated zone files in the %systemroot %/DNS/Backup folder. These will usually have the same permissions as the regular zone file. If the zone file contains sensitive information, administrators should take care to protect these files in the same manner as the regular zone file.[6]

One common pitfall in managing a complex zone is keeping track of all accounts that have access to the zone files. Since many Windows servers that host DNS also run other services, different administrators may have access to the system. Often system admins will add every user who needs to perform any system maintenance to the Administrators group, and they will then inherit complete access to all services on the domain, including DNS. A best practice is to limit zone file access to only the administrators who absolutely need to have it. As this book has hopefully made clear, someone with full access to DNS on a network has a surprising amount of power. At a minimum, network managers should periodically audit which accounts have access to zone files to understand the breadth of access.

This problem has a further complication and trade-off with zone delegation. Say a zone has two subdomains, and an administrator wants different people to be responsible for each. The simplest approach is to delegate each to a different server, and create accounts on those servers for only the administrators who need access. This solves the immediate problem but if additional accounts are created on the two new servers, or if other users are part of the Administrators group in order to run other services on those boxes, then the problem scope has arguably increased.[7] For this reason it is important for the entire network to have good auditing processes in place to always have an accurate picture of who has access to which resources (Fig. 8.1).

How many people should have access to the zone files? This is, of course, a difficult question to answer concretely. For any large network the answer is almost certainly two or more. In the authors' experience, enterprises for which security is considered mission critical will often try to keep the number below 10. ICANN has provided some quantification in designing the root of DNSSEC. They

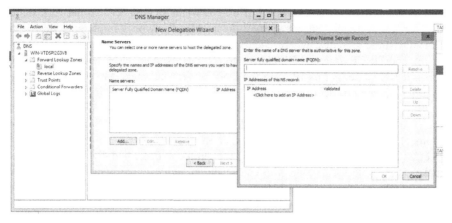

FIGURE 8.1

DNS zone delegation in Windows Server 2012.

assume a 5% "dishonesty rate" for any individual administrator, which is presumably the odds they would be willing to compromise the keys over any time period. In the DNSSEC root, this number is used to design a key combination scheme such that the odds of an actual compromise are less than one in a million.[8] Using ICANN's dishonesty rate, the odds of a compromise from any of 3 administrators is about 14%, and from any of 10 administrators is about 40% (one minus the odds of honesty raised to the power of the number of people). If this seems high, remember it is the odds of any compromise happening over any time period, and does not take into account added layers of security. With good auditing, for example, the risk will be significantly lower.

If an administrator enables DNSSEC on a Windows zone, there will be additional considerations for how to manage the keys. The different types of keys are discussed in detail in Chapter 10, but briefly there is both a Key Signing Key (KSK) and a Zone Signing Key (ZSK). The KSK is used to generate the ZSK, and the ZSK, as its name implies, is used to sign the zone file. DNSSEC RFCs recommend keeping the KSK on separate hardware, ideally completely off-line. But in most Windows environments the keys are kept on the primary server. Windows provides a GUI to both generate the keys and manage their rollover. As of Windows Server 2012 this is called the Key Master service and it can be enabled as a role in AD.

DYNAMIC DNS CONTROL

Say a network runs DHCP and names each workstation after the person to whom it is assigned (as discussed in the Multicast section later in the book this can be a bad idea, but it is just an example). If user A wants to connect to a network share on user B's computer, how can they do it? Most networks implement this with DNS Dynamic Updates, where each workstation will periodically report its hostname and DHCP-assigned IP address to the DNS server. User A can then query for user B's name, get its IP from the DNS server, and make the connection. The dynamic update protocol is described in RFC 2136, first release in 1997.

But what is to stop a malicious workstation from reporting its hostname as, for example, "mail.example.com" and intercepting all email sessions? Within the protocol itself, nothing prevents this. As RFC 2136 states: "In the absence of [RFC2137] or equivalent technology, the protocol described by this document makes it possible for anyone who can reach an authoritative name server to alter the contents of any zones on that server."[9] The RFC recommends that updates be secured with TSIG-shared keys. But this creates two new problems: how to securely distribute the keys to potentially thousands or tens of thousands of hosts on the network and how to authenticate new systems that join the domain. Windows solves both these problems by integrating the DNS client with AD. AD handles authentication with its existing accounts and then generates a key that the DNS client can use for updates.

Dynamic updates will be sent any time a workstation's IP address changes. This includes adding or removing an IP from a network interface, acquiring a DHCP lease, or when the computer starts up. This can sometimes lead to counter-intuitive behavior. For example, running "ipconfig/release" on a host with a misconfigured network connection can actually cause the client to hang while trying to send an update message to the DNS server.

The protocol for dynamic updates is described in RFC 2136 and runs entirely within DNS packets. It adds a new Opcode, 5, for an update type request. It also adds several new response codes, like RCODE 10, indicating the requested update does not belong to the target zone. One situation introduced by dynamic updates is how to handle a host that goes off-line while it is registered with the DNS server. Windows solves this by periodically "scavenging" records that have not been updated in more than a certain amount of time.

What would happen if attackers sent bogus dynamic update messages? This would allow them to spoof update packets to the server to assert that a target hostname is now running on the attacker's IP address, and it could be used as a mechanism for intercepting connections intended of the victim's system. Prior to issuing a patch in 2009, Windows servers were vulnerable to this type of attack targeting the proxy server. As described in CVE-2009-0093, an attacker could register the "wpad" hostname via dynamic updates, which would cause other hosts on the network to attempt to use the specified IP as a proxy server. This, of course, could let the attacker read or modify web traffic from other hosts on the network.[10]

Several factors complicate this attack vector in most enterprise networks. To begin with, it would require an attacker to already be running inside the victim's network and be able to spoof network traffic. It could also cause conflicts within the network devices which would likely be logged and probably noticed by an administrator. For example, if a workstation spoofed the proxy hostname on a large network, it would begin receiving significantly more traffic. This could overwhelm routers or IDS in that corner of the network. In some configurations, unexpected errors like failed NetBIOS connections may result if an attacker spoofs a file share. An attack would likely be targeted at a specific application for a short period of time, such as a way to intercept push notifications. But despite the complexities involved, it should be considered as a potential vector when administrators architect their enterprise software suite.

Fortunately, Windows includes a Secure Dynamic Update feature to protect against spoofed updates. It will include a one-time key shared between the client and the server when sending update packets. This is similar to using TSIG keys in the DNS packets to authenticate between the client and the server, but is technically a different protocol called GSS-TSIG. The keys are generated as Kerberos session keys and only used once for an update. They are sent as TKEY records. To enable the synchronization of keys, the zone file must be managed by AD instead of a flat file for Secure Updates to work. It is important to note that this simply secures the channel over which updates are transmitted to prevent spoofed updates, it does not provide any additional authentication of clients when they join the AD. For example, an AD system that allows any client on the network to join the domain is still vulnerable to spoofed dynamic updates. A best practice is to both use secure updates and strong authentication methods for the domain itself. It is also important to note that Secure Dynamic Update traffic is not encrypted in transit, so anyone who can sniff the network can see the full content of the updates. This can prove especially problematic in networks where guest network segmentation is not properly handled. It could allow unauthenticated users (including those sitting in the parking lot with a Pringles can) to sniff for DNS traffic, thereby exposing internal naming conventions.

Windows allows dynamic updates on a per-zone basis. It can be enabled in the DNS Manager as shown in Fig. 8.2.

QUERIES AND TRANSFERS

As described earlier in the book, a zone transfer is the mechanism by which a primary server sends updates to secondary servers. Requesting a zone transfer is also a classic attack vector against a DNS server, and one any adversary would attempt against a network. If it is allowed, an adversary would get a complete list of all hosts in the zone, which could help with further attacks and may contain sensitive information in and of itself. There are two interrelated goals for managing zone transfers: slave servers should receive updates as seamlessly as possible and no one except the slave servers should have access. By default Windows will only honor zone transfer requests between primary and slave servers, but it is important to check the setting (Fig. 8.3).

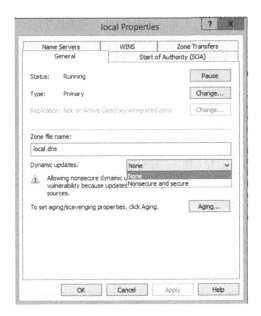

FIGURE 8.2

Enabling secure updates in Windows DNS.

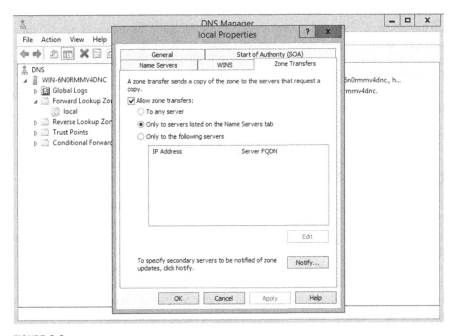

FIGURE 8.3

Limit zone transfers in Windows DNS.

In some cases administrators decide to run DNS in what is known as a split horizon configuration. This will restrict what queries can be performed based on the source of the traffic. The most common scenario is when a DNS server is acting as an authoritative source for both publicly facing domains and internal-only domains. Prior to Windows Server 2016, the main way to run this configuration was to set up two separate DNS servers. This was known to create management headaches, such as whether to attempt partial zone transfers or manually edit both files. Since version 2016, Windows Server has included a feature called DNS policies that can implement different views of the same zone. This is the recommended way to enable split horizons. Microsoft provides the following example commands to set up a record with different internal and external answers:

```
Add-DnsServerZoneScope -ZoneName <zone> -Name "internal"
Add-DnsServerResourceRecord -ZoneName <zone>  -A -Name <hostname>
-IPv4Address <External IP>
Add-DnsServerResourceRecord -ZoneName <zone>  -A -Name <hostname>
-IPv4Address <Internal IP> -ZoneScope "internal"
Add-DnsServerQueryResolutionPolicy   -Name   "SplitBrainZonePolicy"
-Action ALLOW -ServerInterface "eq,10.0.0.56" -ZoneScope "internal,1"
-ZoneName <zone>
```

Note the "10.0.0.56" IP is notional and should be replaced with the IP on the internal interface of the DNS server. After running these commands the server will respond with the "Internal IP" record for queries from the internal interface, and the "External IP" for all others.

This setup can also be used for what are called DNS proxies. This term can mean different things in different contexts, especially since any recursive resolver essentially performs the role of a proxy. But it generally refers to controlling the localization or routing of queries based on some criteria. Some nefarious examples are services that will evade geo-filtering on streaming media content. If, for example, Netflix is blocked in a certain country, the server will route those DNS queries through a resolver in an allowed country, but route all other queries normally. More legitimate uses can be other ways to enforce the separation of internal queries and external queries. Instead of using a split horizon server, one could run separate internal and external servers and use a DNS proxy to route requests depending on the interface and domain queried. This is a less common configuration, but may gain more usage with the new features in Windows Server 2016.

DNS ON WINDOWS WORKSTATIONS

Anyone securing a Windows DNS environment should also look at the workstations within the enterprise. For example, a common malware tactic is to rewrite the hosts file on an infected system. They will often add bogus entries for antivirus update sites to prevent the software from getting new signatures. They could also add static entries for banking domains that will direct users to a phishing web site. The basic goal of an administrator should be to verify that clients are coming to the correct DNS server for all queries and that answers are getting transmitted back without alteration.

Windows follows a somewhat complex resolution algorithm, mostly due to backward compatibility with older protocols. Say a user queries www.example.com. First, Windows will check the hosts file, usually stored in %system32%\etc \hosts. If that contains an answer, Windows will use it without running any network queries. Note this can also be managed through an API, so if an administrator wants to look for static entries she will have to both check the file and look for entries that have been programmatically added on that host. Next, Windows will check its cache.

Note Windows will display the contents of its DNS cache with this command:

```
ipconfig /displaydns
```

The cache can be cleared with:

```
ipconfig /flushdns
```

If the record is not cached, Windows will query its configured DNS server. Another common malware tactic is to set an infected host to use a different DNS server controlled by the attacker. This allows them to respond with spoofed entries as long as the setting remains. Many enterprises will stop those queries by blocking spurious port 53 traffic at the firewall, but users running at home could still be affected. Finally, if Windows does not get an answer from the DNS server it will attempt the query over NetBIOS.[11] This is an often overlooked aspect of the protocol. Many networks set up robust DNS infrastructure and assume it is the only thing clients will use. But if that infrastructure fails, or if attackers block it, workstations will happily act on NetBIOS responses.[12]

WINDOWS AND DDoS

As discussed earlier in the book, DDoS attacks are a common problem with DNS infrastructure. Networks can be involved either as the target of the attack or as an unwitting participant, and administrators should prepare for either scenario. On Windows there are three areas to explore: so called "out of bailiwick" responses, response rate limiting (RRL), and BCP-38 configuration. As of 2016, all three are still under active discussion in the DNS community, so recommendations may change based on new development.

If a server is configured as an authoritative name server but not a recursive resolver, how should it respond to recursive requests? More technically, how should it respond to requests for which it is nonauthoritative? One approach is to ignore them or return an error. Historically DNS has taken the approach of always trying to provide useful information, so it will often return an "upward referral response" that contains the root hints file. The logic being that the client can query the root to start finding the actual authoritative server. These responses are called "out of bailiwick" because the server is not authoritative for them. In reality, most resolvers will ignore out of bailiwick responses, since they can be considered a form of cache pollution. And while seemingly innocuous, the practice of returning root hints can be used in DNS amplification attacks, since it is a relatively large response. An attacker would take advantage of this by querying DNS servers for nonauthoritative or nonexistent domains. A best practice for administrators is to disable this behavior since it provides little benefit to clients. As of Server 2016, Windows will respond with an error by default. On earlier versions, administrators can disable the behavior by deleting the root hints file.[13]

Another addition in Windows Server 2016 is what is called RRL. The motivation is to mitigate DDoS attacks by capping how many packets a server will send to a particular IP. Instead of generating responses at line speed, a server will only send (by default) five identical responses per second to any given client. By default this is disabled, but can be turned on with the command "Set-DNSServerRRL." The rules can be further tweaked to limit how many error messages are sent per second, how many IPs should be grouped together for filtering, and how often the filters should be overridden to allow responses to "leak" out.[14] The Leak Rate is to help prevent RRL itself from being exploited as a DoS vector. For example, if an attacker knew that the IP address 1.1.1.1 used the DNS server 2.2.2.2, it could launch what appears to be a DDoS attack against 1.1.1.1 using spoofed packets sent to 2.2.2.2. If the DNS server used RRL, it would then dutifully block further queries from 1.1.1.1 (assuming the attacker used domains the target would be legitimately querying). This could turn a relatively small DDoS attack into a complete lack of access to DNS. As described by Paul Vixie and Vernon Schryver in their memo on RRL, "LEAK-RATE must be from 2 to 10 and should approximate the real victim's retry count on a legitimate query."[15]

When large-scale DDoS attacks take place against DNS infrastructure, a common refrain is that the problem would be largely fixed if everyone implemented BCP-38. In fact, its title is "Defeating Denial of Service Attacks which employ Address Spoofing." BCP-38 is essentially a set of network-level filters, such as verifying the reputed source IP on a packet is within the range of IPs connected to an interface. If, for example, an ISP sees many packets coming from a residential customer with the source IP of a government web site, it should be able to tell that those are spoofed. Since these are network-level filters there are not too many direct implications for a Windows administrator. It is simply another available tool when setting up a security plan.

WINDOWS CACHING SERVERS

So far this chapter has mostly focused on how to secure a DNS server operating in its authoritative role—giving authoritative answers for hostnames within the domain it controls. The other role of any DNS server is to provide resolution for hostnames outside its domain (eg, web sites on the Internet). Although this is in many ways the more common role for any DNS server, it has fewer settings for an administrator to worry about. This section will discuss three topics for a Windows administrator to consider: cache pollution, upstream resolution, and network configurations.

An interesting quirk of the DNS protocol is response packets may contain answers for records that were not queried. For example, if a site is hosted on a content distribution system, the DNS response may contain both a CNAME and its corresponding A record. This saves the client from requerying for the CNAME. For example:

```
$ dig @8.8.8.8 www.palantir.com
; << >> DiG 9.8.3-P1 << >> @8.8.8.8 www.palantir.com
; (1 server found)
;; global options: +cmd
;; Got answer:
;; ->>HEADER<<- opcode: QUERY, status: NOERROR, id: 45494
;; flags: qr rd ra; QUERY: 1, ANSWER: 2, AUTHORITY: 0, ADDITIONAL: 0
;; QUESTION SECTION:
;www.palantir.com.  IN A
;; ANSWER SECTION:
www.palantir.com. 299 IN CNAME e.ssl.fastly.net.
e.ssl.fastly.net. 29 IN A 23.235.46.230
```

Note the response contains an answer to the original query (www.palantir.com) which points to a subdomain on fastly.net. But it also includes the IP for that fastly.net subdomain. In this case the response is valid, but what if a malicious server returned a CNAME pointing to, for example, google.com and provided a bogus A record as well? The server must decide if it should treat the A record as a valid answer for this specific query, and also whether to cache it for future clients. In Windows this is called "cache pollution" and the general recommendation is to not allow it. It can be disabled with the screenshot, as shown in Fig. 8.4. In some cases this may cause increased latency in queries.

As mentioned earlier, Windows has a concept of Forwarding Zones, or Forward Zones, that will make requests on behalf of an authoritative zone. In theory these perform the same function as caching resolvers: they make recursive queries, cache the answers, and return results. Forward Zones are often deployed in large networks to limit the load on authoritative servers. The busy server can offload recursive queries to the Forwarding server and just receive responses. Some people argue that this is a more secure setup as well, since the authoritative server is not directly querying the Internet. Typical DNS attacks like spoofing responses would be equally effective in this setup, since the authoritative server

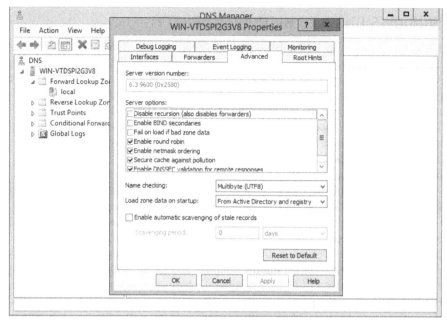

FIGURE 8.4

Configuring cache pollution.

would receive the same bogus answer from the forwarding server. Also, if the resolver libraries themselves were vulnerable to malicious response packets, both the forwarding server and authoritative server would be exploitable by the same payload. But it does limit some network-related risks, such as a misconfigured firewall that allowed the public Internet to query the resolver.

The resolver for an entire network can be configured as a forwarding zone that just queries another resolver, rather than performing recursive queries. This can be the case on a home network, if the router acts as a DNS server and forwards requests to the ISP's resolver. Some small enterprise networks will also operate this way. One can think of this as a security measure, although there is an inherent trade-off. A server operating as a forwarder can be restricted at the network level to only communicate with the upstream resolver, which will limit the ways attackers can probe that machine. But this is a small amount of protection because any outbound traffic that server sends will still ultimately be routed to the same place on the Internet. So for example, it does not mitigate the risk of data exfiltration over DNS. It ultimately comes down to whether the upstream server provides enhanced security mechanisms. If it is more resistant to cache poisoning by, for example, adding entropy to requests, or is more robust to DDoS attacks, it could create a better security posture. If an administrator chooses to have the caching resolver perform recursive queries, they will simply need to load the list of root servers, which Windows will do automatically.

WINDOWS DNS AND HIGH AVAILABILITY

DNS High Availability generally comes in two flavors: one if the zone will be relatively static but needs to always be online and one if it will be regularly changing and updates must never be lost. The common differentiator is whether the server primarily answer requests from the public Internet, or whether it manages a domain with many clients that are sending Dynamic Updates via the RFC 2136 protocol. The main security concern in high availability environments is that they introduce additional infrastructure with links that must be secured and monitored. To understand potential weak points, this section will first provide a brief background on how to set up the environment. Specific security steps are discussed at the end.

A classic example of a DNS server that will have many clients on the public Internet is one hosting the domain for a popular web site. The administrators may want to ensure the site is resilient to hardware failures, network problems, and even large-scale power outages. A common configuration is to run multiple instances of the web server in different data centers across the world. The DNS record for the site can contain multiple entries, and clients will generally try them in order until one works.[16] If, for example, the hardware in Virginia goes off-line, the web browser will simply try the next IP address and successfully connect to the server in California. More sophisticated services will prioritize the entries depending on the geography of the client, so a user in New York will always receive the Virginia IP before the California one. Also the DNS entries for very large web sites will generally not point directly at a webserver but rather to a load balancer sitting in front of a cluster of webservers. Technically this configuration applies to more than just the DNS server for a popular web site. Any time a zone will have few updates, high uptime needs, and clients from diverse networks, an administrator may want to consider this approach.

In the above scenario, system architects will often want to also replicate the DNS server itself. This can be done by adding multiple IPs to the NS record for the domain and replicating the DNS server in multiple places. If one of them is unavailable, clients will try the others (either sequentially or at random, depending on the implementation). This section will describe how to configure two redundant servers in different data centers, but the same configuration could be used for multiple servers in the same location, or even for multiple servers sharing the same IP with a switch-level failover. Windows networks generally implement this configuration by making one instance the primary DNS server and the others secondary.

The second scenario to consider is one where a Windows DNS server supports many clients within an enterprise. This could be either to provide a caching resolver for external domains, an authoritative server for internal domains, or in many cases both. The role of the server is different than the first scenario because records will often be updated more frequently, and clients will have some level of trust. In many cases clients will be publishing dynamic updates directly to the server. High availability in this case may be required to sustain access to critical internal services or to provide general Internet access to a large company.

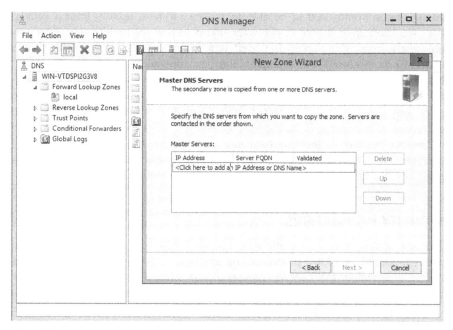

FIGURE 8.5

Adding a secondary zone.

In this scenario, administrators will often be relying on AD for storing the records so AD itself will need to be highly available. This can be achieved with AD Replication. When this is enabled Windows will store AD data on multiple servers, so if one of those systems dies or loses network connectivity, clients can connect to the other.[17]

WINDOWS SETUP INSTRUCTIONS

The primary interface for setting up either configuration is the Windows DNS Manager. In the first configuration, one would add additional answers to existing records. According to Microsoft, support for different address prioritizations based on geography will be included in Windows Server 2016. This will be part of the DNS Policies feature.[18] For the second configuration, or for adding redundant DNS servers to the first scenario, one would create a new secondary zone on the new hardware, as shown in Fig. 8.5.

RESTORATION TIME

In worst case scenarios, an administrator will need to completely rebuild a DNS server within a downtime window. For example, a 99.9% uptime guarantee means a service can be down for no more than 43 minutes in a month. This means an administrator would need to be able to restore services, usually from a backup file, in a short enough time to allow for first detecting the problem and then running the restore. The backup file itself is a commonly forgotten source of data that must be protected. For example, blog posts document cases of finding database backups that were accidentally stored in a web server folder and are accessible to everyone on the Internet.[19] Backups should generally be secured in the same way zone files are protected, with limited user access to the files and encryption if necessary. If backups are transferred off-site (often a good practice to protect against large-scale hardware failure) the network link should be encrypted with something like ssh or sftp. Using public key authentication with good key management is generally recommended as well.

SECURITY IMPLICATIONS

The first security practice to follow in high availability environments is simply to perform normal lockdown procedures on any new infrastructure. For example, if adding a secondary DNS server, one should be diligent about checking network settings on that server, securing the host file, logging requests, etc. The second consideration is how to secure backup files, as discussed above. One scenario for smaller companies that use a hosting provider to keep in mind is what could happen if the provider itself is hacked. If the servers use virtual hosting it may allow an attacker root access to every system running on that provider. In this scenario administrators should be cognizant of what information is stored in a virtual host, and what security steps the provider is following to keep out attackers.

The final consideration is how to be prepared if a hack or other attack is itself the cause of downtime. For example, in the Sony hack of 2014, it was reported that the 6000 employees of their studio lost access to computers and even landline phones. This left employees, including those responding to the attack, communicating with cell phones and outside email accounts.[20] Similarly, if a DDoS attack causes a DNS server to crash or become unavailable, and high availability infrastructure routes all traffic to a secondary server, it may cause cascading failure. A good disaster recovery plan should take these scenarios into account. For example, if a DNS server is hacked, how much downtime would be acceptable to the business if it must be taken off-line? How would contingency plans be communicated to customers and employees? These should ultimately be part of any robust security plan.

LOGGING

This section will cover two topics: how to configure Windows to generate different types of DNS logs and Windows-specific topics related to analyzing that data. Administrators often face a quandary when designing logging and analysis infrastructure. Collected data is only useful if humans can access it, understand it, and make decisions. But often times the important questions are only known after it is too late to go back and record the data. Any security professional who has gone through an incident response knows small scraps of data can be invaluable in piecing together what happened. But collecting everything is often prohibitively expensive. For example, storing even a week of full packet captures for a large network can easily cost millions of dollars per year.

Fortunately Windows makes it fairly easy to customize how much DNS data it will record. At the lowest level, which is generally the default setting, Windows will create what it calls Audit Logs. These will show changes to the zone file, like entries being added or DNSSEC keys changing, but not individual queries or responses. At the most verbose level, Windows can log every event happening inside the DNS server, such as the state of each socket. This is usually called diagnostic logging or debug logging and can be enabled with the tracelog.exe utility.

A middle ground is the setting called Analytical Logging and is recommended for security-minded administrators. This will capture queries, responses, timeouts, and failures. Analytical logging will require more disk writes than the simpler Audit logging, but for all but the most heavily used servers it should not present a serious performance overhead. Microsoft reports that servers with fewer than 50,000 queries per second should see no slowdown, and servers with 100,000 QPS will experience a 5% performance hit.[21]

Analytical logging can be viewed and managed either within the Event Viewer or DNS Manager, as shown in Fig. 8.6.

The log file is often stored by default in the path %systemroot%\System32\ Dns\Dns.log.[22] This can be configured when setting the log level options or changed in the DNS Manager. Note debug logs will be stored in a format called ETL, which is separate from the regular DNS logs. Many third-party log aggregation packages, like Splunk, will provide a "forwarder" program that will export the logs from the domain controller and ingest them into the other system. Alternatively, some administrators use syslog utilities to transfer the logs.

WINDOWS LOG ANALYSIS

One simple (and free) suite of tools administrators can use to store and search the logs is the stack called ELK. This stands for ElasticSearch, LogStash, and Kibana. They are designed to work with each other, and there are many tutorials online for getting them set up on either Windows or Linux platforms. There are also prebuilt virtual machine and docker images available to get started quickly. LogStash handles the plumbing of receiving data from different sources, so it will be the main component administrators need to configure. It can either listen for messages (similar to syslog) or run a collection agent on the DNS server to push data into its central repo. Windows Powershell can also natively support exporting event logs as JSON.[23] Once a pipeline is set up to push DNS logs into LogStash, the data will be stored and indexed in Elastic Search, and the analyst can log into

FIGURE 8.6

Configuring logging in Windows DNS.

Kibana to run queries and view aggregate statistics. For log collections of hundreds of gigabytes or more, tuning the ElasticSearch setup will become important. It needs to hold a portion of the indexes in memory for queries to be performant, so it will likely need to be sharded as the scale grows.

As described in Chapter 6, there are a variety of patterns one can look for in DNS traffic to find indicators of malicious activity. These apply equally to Linux and Windows-based networks. For example, at a basic level, administrators should look at histograms and frequency counts of inbound requests to see if they match the expected authoritative domains. They should also examine outbound requests to see if they match domains from the Alexa list, or if instead there are many requests to unusual locations. For a more complicated analysis, sysadmins could look at the length and entropy of hostnames in outbound requests to detect command and control channels. Two analyses that are especially important in Windows environments are looking at dynamic updates and looking for indicators of malware.

Historically, Windows was vulnerable to the attack described in CVE-2009-0093 which allowed clients to send bogus dynamic updates and impersonate the proxy used by other workstations. While this is now patched, it is indicative of a common flaw in how Windows networks are often administered: The DNS server usually relies on AD for authenticating users, but in large networks those services are often run by different people. For example, do the DNS administrators know what checks are performed when new accounts are added to AD? Are they notified when those policies change? By looking at aggregate records of how dynamic updates are actually happening on the network, the DNS administrators can gain a better understanding of how all parts of the network are configured. By looking at this data regularly they can spot changes or deviations. For example, say a network has a portal for third-party vendors to submit invoices, and those accounts are maintained on an AD separate from the rest of the domain. Are those accounts submitting any dynamic update requests? A well-established log analysis system should be able to answer a question like that.

Approximately 80% of malware targets Windows systems.[24] This is because either Windows is the most popular operating system or a more attractive target, depending on who is asked. But it means administrators should pay particular attention to indicators of malware when analyzing DNS logs from a Windows-heavy network. Chapter 6 described more sophisticated techniques, but at a minimum logs should be checked for known bad domains on a regular basis.

A final, under-appreciated form of analysis is measuring the completeness of data collection. That is, are all DNS queries from all workstations actually being logged? One way to look for this is to count the number of queries for an update site, such as Windows updates, and see if it matches the number of workstations on the network. One could also use net flow data to count the number of outbound port 53 sessions, and see if it matches the total number of logged queries. On smaller networks, this could be as simple as checking that logs have been received from the server every hour, and they have not dropped off dramatically in size.

CONCLUSIONS

Most of the security topics and recommendations discussed in this book can be implemented in Windows environments. Administrators can follow these basic steps to ensure they have considered all the relevant areas:

- Network documentation and appropriate segregation of clients
- Access to the servers is restricted
- Zone files have appropriate permissions

- Monitoring for cache poisoning or pollution
- Workstations are configured with correct DNS settings, and behavior is monitored
- Secure dynamic updates
- Appropriate redundancy and failover
- Backups are secured
- Logging of queries and responses
- Analytical infrastructure
- Disaster recovery plan

NOTES

1. http://w3techs.com/technologies/overview/operating_system/all
2. https://technet.microsoft.com/en-us/library/security/ms06-041.aspx
3. https://technet.microsoft.com/library/security/ms07-029
4. https://technet.microsoft.com/en-us/library/security/ms15-127.aspx
5. https://technet.microsoft.com/en-us/library/cc771898.aspx
6. https://technet.microsoft.com/en-us/library/cc755193.aspx
7. https://technet.microsoft.com/en-us/library/cc755193.aspx
8. http://www.root-dnssec.org/wp-content/uploads/2010/06/icann-dps-00.txt
9. https://www.ietf.org/rfc/rfc2136.txt
10. http://www.cve.mitre.org/cgi-bin/cvename.cgi?name = CVE-2009-0093
11. https://support.microsoft.com/en-us/kb/172218
12. http://blogs.msmvps.com/acefekay/2009/11/29/dns-wins-netbios-amp-the-client-side-resolver-browser-service-disabling-netbios-direct-hosted-smb-directsmb-if-one-dc-is-down-does-a-client-logon-to-another-dc-and-dns-forwarders-algorithm/
13. https://blogs.technet.microsoft.com/teamdhcp/2015/09/03/upward-referral-responses-from-authoritative-dns-servers/
14. https://blogs.technet.microsoft.com/teamdhcp/2015/08/28/response-rate-limiting-in-windows-dns-server/
15. http://ss.vix.su/ ~ vixie/isc-tn-2012-1.txt
16. For example: https://www.digitalocean.com/community/tutorials/how-to-configure-dns-round-robin-load-balancing-for-high-availability.
17. https://technet.microsoft.com/en-us/library/cc755994%28v = ws.10%29.aspx
18. https://blogs.technet.microsoft.com/networking/2015/05/11/geo-location-based-traffic-management-using-dns-policies/
19. https://blog.sucuri.net/2015/06/websites-hacked-via-website-backups.html
20. http://www.wsj.com/articles/behind-the-scenes-at-sony-as-hacking-crisis-unfolded-1419985719
21. https://technet.microsoft.com/en-us/library/dn800669.aspx
22. https://support.microsoft.com/en-us/kb/242046
23. https://blog.rootshell.be/2015/08/24/sending-windows-event-logs-to-logstash/
24. https://redmondmag.com/blogs/the-schwartz-report/2015/09/malware-strikes-windows-pcs.aspx

DNS outsourcing

9

INFORMATION IN THIS CHAPTER

- DNS Outsourcing
- Deciding How Much to Outsource
- Working Securely with a DNS Provider
- Monitoring DNS Infrastructure
- DNS Outsourcing and DDoS Protection

INTRODUCTION

In October of 2013 visitors to the web site of penetration testing software company Metasploit were redirected to a site owned by a group of Palestinian hacktivists known as KDMS Team. KDMS team did not need to break into the Metasploit web server or even their DNS server instead they sent a fax to the domain registrar for *metasploit.com* asking the registrar to update the A record.

In September of 2011 a number of organizations, including The Register and The Telegraph, had their authoritative name servers pointed to servers owned by a Turkish hacking group calling themselves Turkguvenligi. The attackers were able to launch SQL injection attack against the control panel of the organization's domain registrar and use that access to redirect NS records for the targeted domains to infrastructure owned by the attackers.

In December of 2014 several employees of International Corporation for Assigned Names and Numbers (ICANN) were victims of a successful spear phishing attack. ICANN maintains databases for many critical systems on the Internet, including the DNS. The attackers were able to gain access to ICANN's internal network and were able to access several critical systems, including the Centralized Zone Data System, before being discovered a week later.

In February of 2015 the hacking group calling themselves the Lizard Squad used a SQL injection vulnerability to infiltrate a domain registrar in Malaysia. Rather than simply making changes through a control panel, the Lizard Squad was able to upload a root kit and had full access to make changes to the domain they chose. In this case they targeted Lenovo and Google Vietnam. Both web sites were directed to servers owned by the Lizard Squad.

DNS Security. DOI: http://dx.doi.org/10.1016/B978-0-12-803306-7.00009-7

Domain registrars are subject to network attacks, just like any other organization. In fact, domain registrars may be higher profile targets because each domain registrar provides information on hundreds of thousands of targets not to mention an immediate ability to damage those targets.

Given all this information, the question any organization has to ask itself: should the organization outsource DNS? If so, how much of an organization's DNS infrastructure should be outsourced and how can DNS administrators as well as security teams ensure the integrity of the information managed by its DNS provider?

DNS OUTSOURCING

Let us start with an obvious statement: Unless an organization is one of the 13 that maintain a Root Name Server at least some part of that organization's DNS is going to be outsourced. Even if zone files and recursive DNS are managed in-house the domain name itself has to be registered through a domain registrar. That domain registrar is relying on the Country Code Top Level Domain (ccTLD) or Generic Top Level Domain (gTLD) registry of that domain to properly point to the right authoritative name servers. The ccTLD and gTLD rely on the 13 Root Name Servers to point users to right root name servers for the specific registry.

In other words, once a domain is registered, there is a lot about the security of the domain that is out of control of the registrant. This is why it is so important for organizations to maintain control over the parts of DNS outsourcing that they can.

That control starts with making smart choices about where the organization registers its domains. The security of the domain registrar is something that is given little thought by most organizations. In fact, the security team is often unaware when a new domain is registered until there is a potential problem. Different groups within an organization will register domains for various activities without understanding the potential risk of their actions.

Over time, an organization may accumulate dozens, or even hundreds, of domains all maintained by different people, registered at different times and through different registrars.

Within security there is something to be said about diversity. Maintaining accounts with multiple registrars might help improve security as long as those registrars are properly vetted and the security team has a list of all company-registered domains and who the registrant of each domain is. While diversification of registrars is a possible method for minimizing potential impact, it requires additional administrative overhead, which in a company that may not keep records of ownership well. Often, transitions within IT operations and ownership records fail to pass along, and procurement teams will try to consolidate registrations to attempt to get an economy of scale. This is where politicking within IT becomes important, as you have to work closely with IT finance to ensure all communications to registrars in companies names are documented and handed to the security team.

When a new domain is registered the domain registrar asks for three contacts: Billing, Administrative, and Technical. The billing contact should be an alias for the billing department, to ensure all domain renewals get processed on time. If an organization has a DNS administrator that person can be listed as the administrative contact, if not then the person who needs the domain name should be listed as the administrative contact. The technical contact should be a distribution list that includes security and information technology people on it. This will allow both IT and security to track any changes at the registrar, be aware of any maintenance and be notified if an unauthorized person attempts to make changes to the domain.

Gathering a list of all the registered domains, who registered each domain, and where those domains are registered is the first step in building a secure outsourced DNS program. This should be part of the process of developing a DNS security program, outlined in Chapter 2.

Once the required information about existing domains has been gathered, the next step is to decide which domain registrar or registrars the organization is going to use going forward. Obviously, any chosen domain registrar should meet the business requirements of the organization, but it should meet the security requirements as well. Though, given the importance domain names play in the ability of an organization to function, security should be baked into the business requirements. After all, if a domain registrar is unable to meet an organization's security requirements it could have a very negative business impact on that organization.

What are the security demands that an organization should have from its DNS provider? It really depends on the organization and their risk profile. Which is why the discussion around the security of the domain registrar is so important, it allows the DNS administrators to approach each domain registrar with a consistent set of questions. Those questions can really be divided into two types: the security of the domain registrar itself and the security features available for an organization's domain.

Examples of questions to ask a domain registrar about its security can include:

1. Does the registrar have a web portal to administer domains? If so, has the portal been tested by a third-party pen tester looking for SQL injections and other common web application vulnerabilities?
2. Does the registrar portal have Role-Based Access Control capabilities, so portal administrators within the organization can create multiple accounts and limit the access of those account owners?
3. What security measures are taken to protect the registrar's authoritative name servers?
4. What Distribution Denial of Service (DDoS) prevention capabilities does the registrar have in place to protect its infrastructure, especially its authoritative name servers?

5. Does the registrar support two-factor authentication for both portal and phone logins?

Examples of questions to ask a prospective domain registrar about the security of its domains include:

1. Does the domain registrar support DNSSEC?
2. Does the domain registrar support registry locks that prevent things like client domain transfer?
3. What types of domain or WHOIS change monitoring does the registrar offer? How are contacts alerted when a change occurs?
4. Does the domain registrar offer WHOIS privacy options?
5. Does the registrar log domain changes? If so are those changes available to the customer? Can these changes be automatically downloaded into a Security Incident and Event Manager?
6. What methods of authentication does the registrar use to confirm that a caller/emailer is the actual owner of a domain?

There are undoubtedly other questions a security team may want to ask of a domain registrar and honestly, there are a lot of domain registrars out there that will not answer any of these questions. It is up to each organization to decide if it is worth the potential loss to the organization due to a registrar security breech to not have the questions answered.

THIRD-PARTY DNS MONITORING

There are third-party services from companies like DomainTools and DNSstuff that will monitor for changes in the WHOIS record, independently of the services offered by the domain registrar. The downside to these services is that they often require WHOIS information to be public. Hence, it may require a security trade-off exposing WHOIS information for an organization's domains in exchange for third-party verification that no changes to the authoritative name servers or contacts for those domains. A compromise could be to only use those services to monitor for changes in authoritative name servers. This allows the organization to maintain its WHOIS privacy while independently monitoring for domain hijacking attacks.

DECIDING HOW MUCH TO OUTSOURCE

Another factor in selecting a registrar is how much control over their DNS infrastructure an organization wants to cede to that registrar. For smaller organizations, with a simple DNS requirements and little in-house expertise, completely outsourcing DNS management may make sense. Larger organizations with complex DNS infrastructure and a good deal of DNS expertise may want to keep most of the DNS management within the organization.

The decision regarding how much to outsource is also dependent on the capabilities of the domain registrar of choice. While this may seem like an obvious statement, too often domain registrars are chosen for one feature, for example, price, with no consideration given to the needs of the rest of the organization. Some registrars limit the size of the zone file they will support, or limit the number of A or CNAME records they allow. Some registrars will even limit the number of queries they will allow per month. These limitations need to be taken into consideration when choosing a domain registrar and when sizing the subscription type from that registrar.

Even if an organization is perfectly capable of managing DNS infrastructure it may decide that it does not want to manage the additional traffic generated by DNS queries. The organization also may not want to manage the complex infrastructure involved in creating a highly available DNS farm. This is especially true for organizations that maintain high traffic services, whether it is a high volume web site, email service, or mobile app that sees a lot of traffic. While DNS queries may be small, fielding millions of them an hour from all over the world requires a robust and redundant infrastructure and the know-how to manage it, which is a different skillset than managing a DNS server.

MANAGED DNS

To this point, the conversation around outsourcing has revolved around working with an organization's domain registrar to manage outsourcing. There is another option though: using a managed DNS provider. There are a number of managed DNS providers such as Amazon's Route 53, Dyn, EasyDNS, MarkMonitor, and Neustar that take the management of DNS beyond the traditional portal typically offered by domain registrars.[1]

While managed DNS providers are more expensive, they also offer a wide range of features that traditional registrars do not offer. Specifically in the area of security most managed DNS providers offer services like Anycast and load balancing which will improve the availability of an organization's DNS service. Many of these providers also assign accounts to specific account manager. That manager gets to know the account well, making it harder for the account manager to be fooled by social engineering attempts, so an organization's domain is less likely to be hijacked.

Managed DNS services offer more advanced DNS monitoring capabilities for their clients, than traditional registrars. For example, rather than just being notified when contact information is changed or the domain switches registrars. Managed DNS services will often monitor for changes to a domain's zone file and even alert when there is a sharp uptick in queries.

Finally, because they are more expensive, managed DNS providers tend to attract high-profile organizations whose domains are frequently targeted for attack. The experience of working with domains that attackers are targeting means that managed DNS providers know what to look for in an attack and are able to take steps to prevent those attacks, often before they can happen.

SPLIT DNS

Many organizations solve the outsourcing dilemma by opting for a split DNS model. Split DNS allows an organization to have their public, high-traffic, DNS record queries answered by their DNS registrar or managed DNS provider while the internal DNS server answers queries for hosts internal to the network. In other words, the internal DNS server acts as an authoritative DNS server for the organization's domain.

For better or worse, modern network architecture has made this relatively easy to do. Most networks of any size make use of Microsoft's Active Directory, which requires DNS to function therefore most server administrators enable Microsoft's DNS Service on the Active Directory server. In the simplest form of split DNS the zone file from the registrar's authoritative name servers is copied to the local DNS server and additional records for the internal network are added. Because the internal DNS server thinks it is authoritative for the domain name it will answer all queries authoritatively and users inside the network will never pass a query through to the real authoritative name server.

While this works, it does lead to a number of potential security problems. The first problem is that, especially in active networks, the zone files could very quickly fall out of sync, meaning employees on an organization's internal network would receive incorrect query responses from the internal DNS server for the organization's external hosts. Which leads to a second security problem: If a domain is tampered with at the registrar level, the employees, especially the security team, will have no way of knowing. While the rest of the world is complaining about web sites being misdirected, everything will look fine to the employees within the organization's network.

A better way to manage split DNS is by using split horizon DNS, as shown in Fig. 9.1. Most modern authoritative name servers can be configured to present different responses, depending on from where the traffic originates. Take a look at the configuration of this in BIND:

```
acl corp-network {

  192.168.1.0/24;

};
// Internal
view "internal" {

    match-clients {corp-network; };
    include "/etc/named.internal.zones";
    include "/etc/named.common.zones";

};
// External
view "external" {
```

```
    match-clients { any; };
    include "/etc/named.external.zones";
    include "/etc/named.common.zones";

};
```

The first step is to create an Access Control List (ACL), in this case called *corp-network*, and define the IP space for that ACL. The above example uses the 192.168.1.0/24 network, though keep in mind if a domain registrar hosts the authoritative name server, RFC 1918 addresses will not work. The next step is to simply create two different views: in the example above they are called *internal*

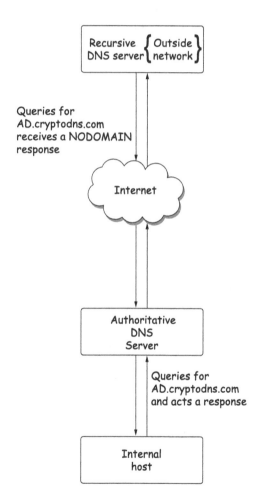

FIGURE 9.1

An overview of split horizon DNS.

and *external.* The internal view is served up responses from one zone file, while the external view is served up responses from a different zone file. Note that there are also common zone files that return the same query responses irrespective of whether that query comes from an internal or external host.

By maintaining two separate zone files on the same authoritative server, managing those zone files is simplified and it is easier to keep them in sync.

A third way of splitting a zone file is to move all internal hosts to a subdomain and assign that zone to an internally managed name server. For example, an organization may use the domain *dns-book.net* for web, mail, and other public-facing hosts, but all internal-only hosts would fall under the domain *corp.dns-book.net.* So, the fileserver would be *fileserver.corp.dns-book.net*, the printer would be *printer100.corp.dns-book.net.* The authoritative name server would have an NS record for the *corp.dns-book.net* pointing toward internal servers, something like this:

```
corp.dns-book.net.    3600  IN  NS  ns1.corp.dns-book.net.
corp.dns-book.net.    3600  IN  NS  ns2.corp.dns-book.net.
ns1.corp.dns-book.net.    1800  IN  A  192.168.1.14
ns2.corp.dns-book.net.    1800  IN  A  192.168.1.15
```

It does not matter that the A records for the two NS records point toward RFC 1918 addresses, the only people who need to access those servers are sitting within the organization's network.

Another way of splitting domain views is to append a different TLD to internal hosts. Many organizations have taken to using the TLDs .local or .internal to identify local-only hosts, which allows them to maintain a completely separate zone file for internal hosts versus external hosts. While, this is not yet a standard practice, it is one that continues to gain in popularity.

This type of split DNS setup offers several different security advantages. To start, it creates the important separation of the organization's internal hosts from their external hosts. It is also easier to maintain because the DNS administrator no longer needs to worry about syncing files, each record only gets set up in one place. This type of setup presents the same view of external hosts to both internal and external (to the organization) visitors to the external hosts. This means that if there is a problem it will most likely impact both sets of visitors and allow the security team to respond faster to the potential problem.

OUTSOURCING RECURSIVE DNS

Most organizations do not give too much consideration to outsourcing recursive DNS infrastructure. Either their Internet Service Provider (ISP) provides them with a pre-configured modem that is loaded with resolver IP information or server administrators load one of the many available public resolvers into the settings of the server. In fact, according to a 2014 study performed by the Asia Pacific Network Information Center

(APNIC) 90% of Internet users forward their DNS requests to less than 1% of the visible resolving servers (∼2000) and 23% have their queries answered by resolvers' farms owned by three entities: Google, China Net, and China 169.[2]

While there is certainly a great deal of wisdom in allowing professionals to manage the security of recursive DNS and not having to worry about securing yet another service within the network, there is a lot of value to managing recursive DNS in-house. Microsoft makes it simple to enable recursive DNS on an Active Directory server, in fact Active Directory requires DNS in order to function properly. The trade-off for a security team becomes monitoring the security of that DNS server versus potentially missing an attack because DNS queries are all sent to a server outside of the network.

On top of that, given the fact that the recursive servers managed by ISPs are very attractive targets they are constantly under attack. So, even an ISP with the best security team may fall victim to a lucky attacker (as shown several times throughout this book). A recursive DNS server managed in-house, that is not publicly accessible, and with sensible security precautions in place may be more secure than the recursive servers available from an organization's ISP. Again, it will also give the security team invaluable information about potential attacks targeting or happening inside the network.

WORKING SECURELY WITH A DNS PROVIDER

Once a DNS provider is chosen that meets all of the organization's security requirements and the organization has determined how much of their DNS infrastructure is going to be outsourced to that provider or multiple providers, the next step is to set the ground rules for secure communication. The ground rules will vary from organization to organization, but should remain consistent within each organization, irrespective of who registers the domain.

Some ideas for communicating securely with a DNS provider include:

1. Never use a personal email address to register a domain. All domain contacts must include an email address from that organization.
2. Two-factor authentication should always be enabled, but variants of two-factor authentication that are easily spoofed, such as fax, should be specifically prohibited.
3. The two-factor authentication process should be well documented within the organization and provided to those who have a need to know how it works.
4. If security questions are required for access to make changes to a domain, there should be a standard set of questions/answers (more than the minimum three that are usually required) that are well documented and provided to users when necessary.
5. If possible, portal access to the DNS provider portal should be restricted to only networks owned by the organization.

6. Any email between the organization and the DNS provider should be encrypted. Note that it may not be possible for standard notifications, such as domain expiration notices, to be encrypted.
7. Similarly, all communication using the DNS provider's web portal should be encrypted (in this case that usually means communication that uses Transport Layer Security (TLS)).
8. When possible, the DNS provider should provide logs of all portal accesses and changes made to the organization's domains during those accesses.

Having a set of rules for interacting with a DNS provider helps to ensure the security of the domains owned by the organization and it makes it easier for the security team to ensure that domain security is given the proper attention.

Of course, it is not enough to just set the guidelines internally. The organization must also work with the DNS provider to make sure it understands and respects the security restrictions the organization is enabling for communication. A clear understanding by both client and provider of the security requirements of the client as well as the security capabilities of the provider helps to ensure that fewer mistakes will be made.

A word of caution is in order here. If an organization has been around for any length of time there is a pretty good chance that there is little or no process in place for procuring and managing domains. Suddenly creating a new policy, especially a particularly strident one, as a described above could create disgruntled employees. As anyone who has been in security knows if the security restrictions are too harsh, users will find a way to subvert them. That is why security experts recommend one of two ways to implement sweeping changes. The first option is to implement the changes gradually, getting acceptance from the user community one step at a time is often easier than it is to gain acceptance for wholesale change. The second option is to meet directly with the people involved in domain registration and explain to them the threat, why implementing the proposed steps will alleviate the threat and earnestly seek their feedback. Most of the time when users are included as part of the process and are directly contributing the security plan they are much more accepting and less likely to subvert the new rules.

MONITORING DNS INFRASTRUCTURE

"Is it just me, or is it down for everyone?" Is such a common question among information technology professionals that there are whole monitoring services built around that theme (see www.downforeveryoneorjustme.com). Monitoring is an important part of building a DNS infrastructure, but it is one that is too often overlooked.

This is especially true for organizations that outsource a large part of their DNS infrastructure. Many of these organizations think that the domain registrars or DNS providers are actively monitoring their DNS infrastructure, so the organization does not need to worry about it.

Even if that is the case, third-party monitoring of DNS infrastructure can help ensure that DNS services are responding correctly and in a timely fashion. There are a number of aspects of DNS infrastructure that can be monitored: availability, response time, and unauthorized changes to infrastructure or zone files. The strange thing is that even though organizations routinely monitor other outsourced services, like web or email, they often do not think to monitor DNS infrastructure.

There are a number of options available for monitoring DNS infrastructure. If there is already a proven monitoring system in place for monitoring web and email servers it is usually possible to add in DNS capabilities to that same platform.

There are also a number of monitoring services dedicated to specifically monitoring DNS traffic. Services like ThousandEyes, Constellix, and RIPE Atlas can monitor DNS performance and availability, providing different views from around the world. These services are designed to work with larger DNS infrastructure operations but they do provide multiple views and historical performance information. They also have the advantage of being completely distinct from the organization's network, so they are not impacted by outages that are specific to the organization.

Of course, performance and availability are just two aspects of DNS availability. It is also important to monitor for changes in the DNS infrastructure. Companies like ThousandEyes and DNSCheck can monitor for changes to an organization's zone file and updates to their authorized name servers. Other companies, like DomainTools, offer bigger picture monitoring services. For example, DomainTools tracks changes to name servers and registrants. While this is primarily used to track competitors or attack groups, it can also be used to monitor for changes to an organizations own DNS infrastructure.

Some security teams prefer to use homegrown solutions to monitor different services. DNS lends itself very well to a homegrown solution as well. Many organizations simply use a number of geographically dispersed Virtual Private Servers to do the monitoring. There are a number of excellent DNS monitoring scripts available that will monitor for both DNS performance and changes in DNS records. This can be an effective solution as long there is alerting mechanism outside of email or some other method that relies on DNS for delivery (SMS or SNMP are often good options in this case).

Whatever solution is chosen, the important thing is that the DNS infrastructure is being properly monitored and alerts are being sent in a time fashion and in a way that is actionable to the DNS administrative and security teams.

DNS OUTSOURCING AND DDoS

DDoS attacks are a threat to every organization and they are not going away. It is too easy to launch an attack against a target organization and there are simply too many people with a perceived axe to grind. According to *Akamai's State of the Internet—Security Report* DDoS attacks grew 180% between the third-quarter of

2014 and the third quarter of 2015. In addition to more attacks the attacks are lasting longer, on average a DDoS attack lasts for almost 19 hours and Akamai has seen attacks as large as 222 million packets per second.[3]

The point is that, unfortunately, there is a good chance that an organization of any size will eventually come under a DDoS attack. In addition, because of its lack of built-in security features, DNS is a prime target for these DDoS attacks. While it is outside of the scope of this book to discuss DDoS prevention tactics, the fact is that many DNS providers, especially managed DNS providers, have a great deal of experience in dealing with and mitigating different types of DDoS attack.

By outsourcing significant portions of an organization's DNS infrastructure, that organization may get the added benefit of DDoS protection for their DNS servers. Beyond the standard protection that a robust DNS provider already has in place, some managed DNS providers also offer enhanced DDoS protection, for a fee. Managed DNS providers such as Akamai, Neustar, and Verisign also have DDoS protection services against other protocols as well.

DDoS ATTACKS CAN BE EXPENSIVE

Many DNS service providers charge by the query; an organization is entitled to x number of DNS queries depending on the subscription level. It is important to find out before a DDoS attack what happens if the DNS infrastructure is targeted as part of the DDoS attack. At the time of the attack, the monthly bill to the DNS provider will be the least of anyone's concerns, but as part of the after-action report it will be nice to have that information available.

Even other providers that do not offer enhanced DDoS protection can usually offer good advice, because they have had to withstand numerous DDoS attacks over the years. It is important to take advantage of the knowledge that managed DNS providers can offer and use that knowledge as an additional security asset before and during an attack.

CONCLUSIONS

Businesses seem to move in cycles. Today there seems to be a trend toward outsourcing and moving more services to someone else's computer. That makes sense because it lets an organization focus on its core competencies and allows experts to take care of other aspects of the business.

The challenge with outsourcing is that an organization often gives up too much control and too much insight into what is happening with the outsourced service. To prevent that from happening with an organization's DNS infrastructure it is necessary to outsource intelligently: come up with a set of requirements that balance the need to outsource with the need to be able to secure and monitor the service and select one or more DNS providers who can meet those needs.

Maintaining a good balance between the security needs of an organization and the needs of end users who register domains will create a more successful DNS security program. Communicating an organization's security requirements clearly to a DNS provider, or providers, will help keep that DNS security program on track. A good DNS provider is a security partner and has as much at stake in keeping an organization's domains safe as the organization itself.

NOTES

1. Full disclosure: Both sample domains used in this book, dns-book.net and cryptodns. com, are managed by Dyn. Dyn has not provided any compensation either in payment or free services, the authors simply like their service.
2. Huston, G., 2015. The Resolvers We Use. APNIC, 05 Aug. 2015. Web. 16 Jan. 2016. <http://www.potaroo.net/presentations/2015-05-08-resolvers.pdf>.
3. Akamai, 2015. Q3 2015 State of the Internet—Security Report | Cloud Security Trends. Akamai, 8 Dec. 2015. Web. 30 Jan. 2016. <https://www.stateoftheinternet.com/resources-cloud-security-2015-q3-web-security-report.html>.

DNS security extensions

10

INFORMATION IN THIS CHAPTER

- DNSSEC Background
- Cryptographic Concepts
- Protocol
- NXDOMAIN Responses
- Implementation
- Best Practices
- Criticisms of DNSSEC

INTRODUCTION

When looking at successful DNS spoofing attacks, people have often wondered why DNS cannot run over a secure protocol, similar to the way web traffic can run over SSL/TLS. Fortunately, researchers have been thinking about this problem since the early days of the Internet, and the result is the DNSSEC protocol. This chapter will describe the motivation for DNSSEC, the difficulties of adding security to a massively distributed, fault tolerant system like DNS, and the design decisions that go into the protocol. Finally it will include examples of how to configure and operate DNSSEC on a real-world network.

BACKGROUND

In November 2011, Brazilian Internet users going to popular web sites found a message saying they needed to install a program called "Google Defence" before they could continue.[1] The program was actually a piece of malware, and the attack vector was DNS cache poisoning. Someone had changed the cached DNS records at large ISPs so queries for legitimate sites would be sent to a server that returned the malware program. This attack was particularly dangerous because the perpetrators did not need to reach out to specific targets, they just poisoned a few popular domains and waited for victims to come to them.

DNS Security. DOI: http://dx.doi.org/10.1016/B978-0-12-803306-7.00010-3

From the victims' perspective, non-savvy users had no way of knowing they were being targeted. They simply browsed the web the same way they had before and received forged messages from their upstream provider. Interestingly, other layers of network security had the ability to mitigate much of this attack. For example, browsers will display a warning message before running downloaded programs, and some antivirus programs could block the downloaded file. But it shows how a single case of DNS cache poisoning can affect millions of users.

Another incident took place in January 2014 and blocked Internet access to large portions of the users in China. A DNS server began returning the same IP address for all DNS queries. This could have been the result of cache poisoning, a different malicious attack, or a mistake by infrastructure administrators.[2]

Since the 1990s researchers have been proposing ways to add security to DNS, and the resulting protocol is called DNS Security Extensions or DNSSEC. RFC 2065, written in 1997, describes the motivation: "The Domain Name System (DNS) has become a critical operational part of the Internet infrastructure yet it has no strong security mechanisms to assure data integrity or authentication."[3] Two cryptographic concepts used in securing data are encryption and authentication. Encryption scrambles a message so that only someone with the right key can read the contents. Online banking web sites will encrypt all information between the client and the server so that, for example, someone monitoring traffic on a public WiFi network cannot read the contents of those pages over the wire. Authentication allows one to verify that a message has not been tampered with. An oft-cited low-tech version of authentication is a royal seal affixed to a letter to show it came from the king. In fact, the terminology of "signatures" and "certificates" are still used in modern cryptography to allude to older practices of securing hand-written letters. DNSSEC explicitly chooses to focus only on authentication and not encryption. As stated in RFC 2065, "It is part of the design philosophy of the DNS that the data in it is public and that the DNS gives the same answers to all inquirers." As the protocol is described below, it is important to remember its focus is only on verifying DNS responses have not been tampered with, not on obfuscating the contents on a response.

CRYPTOGRAPHY OVERVIEW AND TLS

Before looking at the specific choices made in DNSSEC, this section will present a brief background on the cryptography involved and look at the most popular secure protocol on the web, SSL/TLS. There are three important tools in modern cryptography that form the basis for both TLS and DNSSEC: public key encryption, hashes, and signing. Public key encryption involves generating a public key and a private key. Messages encrypted with the public key can only be decrypted with the associated private key, and vice versa. Note that the public key itself cannot decrypt a message after it is been encrypted with the public key. RSA was the first public key algorithm to be published and is probably the most well known. The second concept is hashing which means taking a message of any size and producing a fixed-length "digest" based on that input. SHA1, a common hash algorithm, always has 160 bits of output no matter if the input is 1 character, 1000 characters, or 1 million characters. Sometimes file distribution sites on the Internet will include a hash value next to the download link, which enables someone to hash the file locally after it is been downloaded, compare it to the published digest, and verify the file has not been corrupted in transit. Finally, the concept of signing is used to demonstrate that a message came from a particular sender and was not altered in transit. This is done by encrypting a message with the private key and publishing the result. Remember that only the public key can undo the encryption of the private key, so anyone can retrieve the sender's public key, use it to decrypt the message, and know it must have been created with that specific key pair. In practice signing and hashing are generally used in tandem. For example, to send a large file and verify it has not been altered in transit, one could send the file along with a signed hash of the file. The recipient would compute the hash, then decrypt the signed hash with the sender's public key, and verify the two values matched. If they do not match the recipient will know something in the file was changed, and he or she can request that it be resent.

These tools allow users to send data over an insecure network and still maintain confidence in the authenticity of the messages. Note two important caveats in the above scenario: it does not guarantee the recipient will ever actually receive the correct data, only that he or she will be able to verify whether the information is correct; and it depends on her being able to retrieve the sender's correct public key. The second caveat presents a major weakness because a clever attacker could intercept the file, change the contents, sign the hash with their own private key, then present their own public key when the recipient tries to retrieve the sender's public key. This is called a "man in the middle" attack. SSL/TLS uses what is called Public Key Infrastructure to solve this problem. The first detail, that users may receive data that fails validation, presents a complication for DNSSEC which will be described at the end of the chapter.

The most widely used cryptographic protocol on the Internet is SSL/TLS. Technically TLS is the successor to SSL although the terms are sometimes used interchangeably. The whole protocol can be thought of as a way for a user to get the public key for a web site. Once they have that public key, a user can encrypt data, verify signed hashes, and ultimately exchange any data with the web site without an attacker being able to read or alter the contents. The infrastructure includes three components: a client, a server, and something called a Certificate Authority (CA). In practice the CA has predistributed its public key to the client before any connections between the client and the server begin. With this one predistributed key any number of subsequent public keys can be distributed securely. As of 2016, Firefox included more than 180 trusted CAs, such as Comodo, GoDaddy, Symantec, and even Wells Fargo.[4] A web site operator can go to one of those 180 CA providers, provide its public key, and the CA will return something called a certificate that includes the domain of the site, its public key, and a hash of all the contents signed by the CA's public key. The CA will (hopefully) follow steps to verify the person requesting the certificate is indeed connected to the domain, such as sending an email to webmaster@ < domain > or calling the phone number provided in whois records (note this could be a vector for DNS spoofing). Then when a client first connects to the server, the server will present the certificate issued by the CA. The client can verify the signature in the certificate using the public key of the CA that has been predistributed and verify that the key from the server has not been altered. The client then makes up a random session key, encrypts it with the server's public key, and sends the encrypted contents to the server. Note this last step enables encryption between the client and the server, which is important in TLS but not part of DNSSEC. This "TLS handshake" happens every time someone on the Internet visits an HTTPS web site.

Why cannot DNS just run on top of the TLS protocol? One obvious problem is that DNS runs over UDP by default (until query responses are larger than 512 bytes) whereas TLS runs over TCP. Proposals and implementations do exist for both always running DNS over TCP and running TLS over UDP. So in theory a stack could be set up that runs DNS over TCP and secures that connection with TLS (in fact this was proposed in an IETF draft in 2015). But these changes would present a significant departure from the standard DNS concepts that developers and administrators are used to. For example, when querying over a TCP socket how long should a resolver wait before contacting the secondary DNS server? Should it let the TCP stack handle those timeouts or implement them within the application? And will core DNS servers have enough bandwidth available to handle the extra traffic involved in a TLS handshake? Lastly since TLS requires storing state for each connection (such as the session key) will core services be more vulnerable to Distributed Denial of Service (DDoS) attacks? There are of course intelligent approaches to each problem, but would require designing a new protocol.

Another set of problems with mixing TLS and DNS are introduced because of caching. TLS generally assumes the client will connect directly to the end point server so they can negotiate a session key, whereas DNS is designed to allow intermediate servers to cache results. One possible caching implementation would allow intermediate servers to store certificates so that public keys could be distributed and authenticated, but this would require adding a Time to Live (TTL) notion to TLS. What about keeping DNS records as-is, and caching them the same way, but connecting to DNS servers over TLS? This would be similar to the DNS over TLS approach described above, and it also would not fix all cache poisoning attacks, like the example from Brazil described at the beginning of the chapter.

One persistent problem TLS has faced, which DNSSEC aims to avoid, is how to handle compromised keys. If a web site loses access to its private key, it will need to reissue a certificate and try verify that the old certificate is not used by malicious attackers. If a CA is tricked into issuing a certificate to an unauthorized person, or if the private key for the CA itself is ever compromised, this problem becomes magnified. TLS adds a notion of Revocation Lists (now often implemented as the Online Certificate Status Protocol) which can be downloaded from the web site itself or from other trusted parties. This introduces the problem of how to distribute what can sometimes be multimegabyte files at the beginning of every secure connection, and it adds a potential DoS point. DNSSEC attempts to mitigate some of these problems by creating two keys, a Key Signing Key (KSK) and a Zone Signing Key (ZSK), as will be described below.

A related problem is online signing. Since the main components of a TLS certificate are the domain and public key, they do not need to be updated very often. A CA will ideally keep its private key segregated from the Internet and only allow access when needed to sign new certificates. DNS zones often require more frequent updates. For example, every time new hostnames are added to a network, or every time additional capacity is added to load-balance a large site, it could require resigning records.

DNSSEC PROTOCOL

Conceptually, DNSSEC adds two features to DNS to enable authentication: records include a signed hash and parents provide the public keys for their child zones. Technically the child zone provides multiple public keys and the parent provides the hash of one of them, but those details will be discussed later. With a public key and signed hash, the client can verify the records for a zone have not been altered. And with each parent providing the public keys of its children, the client can build a "chain of trust" all the way back to the DNS root. The root key is usually compiled in to the resolver, so the client can trust the public keys provided for each child zone, and ultimately trust the answers to the query. This process usually runs from the bottom up, so a client does not know if the entire chain is correct until it gets far enough in the sequence to find a trusted key. The examples below will walk through the process from the bottom up. DNSSEC stores this information in new record types, specifically an RRSIG record for the signed hash, and a Delegation Signature (DS) record for the parent to communicate the public key of the child.

For example, here is the record for ripe.net:

```
$ dig @8.8.8.8 www.ripe.net + dnssec
; << >> DiG 9.8.3-P1 << >> @8.8.8.8 www.ripe.net + dnssec
; (1 server found)
;; global options: + cmd
;; Got answer:
;; - >> HEADER << - opcode: QUERY, status: NOERROR, id: 29930
;; flags: qr rd ra ad; QUERY: 1, ANSWER: 2, AUTHORITY: 0, ADDITIONAL: 1

;; OPT PSEUDOSECTION:
; EDNS: version: 0, flags: do; udp: 512
;; QUESTION SECTION:
;www.ripe.net.      IN  A

;; ANSWER SECTION:
www.ripe.net.    18076  IN  A  193.0.6.139
www.ripe.net.    18076  IN  RRSIG  A  8  3  21600  20160129112402
20151230102402 48975 ripe.net. b1p/E3oVheJxSJLk98G4eJixmN905 + NY7800S
fzTlnHdOWKMV7ZRsHmW 9ZH4RrHaeIrhKtTRC9nyUxvJbLb5yBOIOvqVkND6p/OTqAXA
hwtq4QYt oBLsmfZJxUlPNavHRrJ7KihDXCAEX6gO/qiVPV5ntKJbEBBNm3lk/Mbz WzY =
```

Note that this response contains an A record and an RRSIG record, which is a signed hash of the contents of the www.ripe.net A record answer. The additional DNSSEC record is sent in the same way as any other and has all the same fields like a query, TTL, and type. Technically the RRSIG is the signature of an "RRSet" containing all A records in the answer, so if there were multiple IPs for www.ripe.net there would still be only one RRSIG. This is done to save space in the response packet. The client can verify the signature using the server's public key, so if it already had a trusted copy of the public key the process would be over here. The rest of the description below can be thought of as just a way to securely retrieve the server's public key by building a chain of trust back to the root.

DNSSEC provides the zone's public key in a DNSKEY record, so the next step for the client is to retrieve that record and follow a process to verify it. But the keys must fit into a DNS packet so they are generally shorter than corresponding TLS keys. For example, RFC 6781 recommends using 1024-bit keys for DNSSEC, whereas TLS best practices are to use at least 2048 bits in public key pairs. This increases the chances that a key could be cracked within a reasonable time period, so DNSSEC needs to have a mechanism to regularly rotate the public keys. DNSSEC also attempts to solve one of the common problems with TLS—if a key is compromised an administrator has to go back to the issuing authority and get a new key signed. So it actually uses two keys—a ZSK and a KSK. The RRSIG is signed by the ZSK, the ZSK is signed by the KSK, and the KSK is signed by the parent's ZSK. This can be thought of as just "the public key for the zone" but using multiple keys provides several benefits in practice. If the administrator wants to issue a new key, they simply generates a new ZSK, signs it with the same KSK, and does not have to update the parent zone. The same process of issuing a new key can be used to revoke compromised keys. When a client goes through the validation process (as shown in an example below) it will query for the ZSK then the KSK, so anyone attempting to use a forged record with the compromised ZSK will not pass a check with the new KSK. Also, as described in RFC 4641, separating the KSK and ZSK means the private portion of the KSK can be stored in a more secure location, such as off the network. When adding or removing records from the zone, only the ZSK will be needed to resign the zone. In busy networks that may happen on a daily or even hourly basis. But the KSK will only need to be retrieved when a new ZSK is created, which generally happens on a weekly or monthly basis.

Below is an example of how to retrieve the different keys:

```
$ dig @8.8.8.8 ripe.net DNSKEY
;; Truncated, retrying in TCP mode.

; << >> DiG 9.8.3-P1 << >> @8.8.8.8 ripe.net DNSKEY
; (1 server found)
;; global options: +cmd
;; Got answer:
;; ->>HEADER<<- opcode: QUERY, status: NOERROR, id: 1462
;; flags: qr rd ra; QUERY: 1, ANSWER: 3, AUTHORITY: 0, ADDITIONAL: 0

;; QUESTION SECTION:
;ripe.net.      IN  DNSKEY

;; ANSWER SECTION:
ripe.net.    2326  IN  DNSKEY  256  3  8  AwEAAX8cuWXOvIh2UwlGOc+YUpy
NDN2p9qAVYNERccLjgvD1K9LH48U1 aHSMzMLP/63HDIMoEwJRQFCr96GuAjZWlX72r3
j3lxubXnQo7IV8rylhoqk2HsuziwiTfkIlE2 zOan9n8BpLT54OlqOZSfbOLMZLcjTci
Jxst4hT8GtwCZuv
ripe.net.    2326  IN  DNSKEY  257  3  8AwEAAb6Wg3SaF8e4bNx2DFdvB+A7x
k8ithqbvSKKjLglJlhmsQRNqf5i B66+1clTfgXj7J+scklahImRxq4/Kp+1xeJEC
x9X5Cqrli8z9nDugYAY fV774kLeJ+Eb6hXOXTdOKOo 86hBmGOzaiyeO1Z+uJRUyZk
lReLSH7sU7  CTbY6XBkDo8yp2aJjEv3jZImV6etbPBQtUAxdMtTBeUet6h1umT4h5Lu
24yaMRZfIApTIFlSOM6H2WwO9oyUfj4Dql28OCVtP9QLS8aIizrl2WmK  6mQSST49+
XVMnWkgUJsGzjF22WLpwLhSh4H5kuhure+JOy//hIOpF+Yz vcEkiDEpPsM=
ripe.net.    2326  IN  DNSKEY  256 3 8 AwEAAY6L5HgLu1Rfad/6ehXzxJkh6/
wBVZHEo5WlhVVZWYr9OzZojaaU  GuAph4Ot/BL2wbpYiO3zGy56Aj8/4i2hxi4F83OX
qjUDpZjQxCba9L/i   uXDPvKOqtpj1HtGuQ4dGHWQNHEQVQ3THo+xomVYA96MeQh5os
7oXgui3 Ig7W5yQJ
```

The ZSK is type 256 and is the first record in the response. The KSK is type 257 and is the second record. Note the KSK is longer than the ZSK, since it is generally active for longer and needs to withstand a larger window of brute force attacks. In this case there is a second ZSK, the final record in the response.

As discussed later, when rotating ZSKs it is important to keep both the old and the new keys accessible so cached records can still validate.

The final step in authenticating this zone is to retrieve a DS record from the parent zone. This is a hash of the KSK for the child zone, so the client can verify it matches the KSK retrieved from the child. This step and the step above can be thought of as "getting the public key from the parent" although of course multiple keys are provided by the child and only a hash of the KSK is provided by the parent. The DS record will also have its own RRSIG that is used to continue the validation chain.

```
$ dig @8.8.8.8 ripe.net DS

; << >> DiG 9.8.3-P1 << >> @8.8.8.8 ripe.net DS
; (1 server found)
;; global options: + cmd
;; Got answer:
;; - >> HEADER << - opcode: QUERY, status: NOERROR, id: 50955
;; flags: qr rd ra; QUERY: 1, ANSWER: 1, AUTHORITY: 0, ADDITIONAL: 0

;; QUESTION SECTION:
;ripe.net.       IN   DS

;; ANSWER SECTION:
ripe.net.    21599  IN   DS  4331 8 2 C8565943D2B8F9478E441E1A8E58F3820
4131A5284F53F8E39AFBD08 B323789E
```

With a public key from the zone and a signed hash of the record, one can now verify the original query for www.ripe.net did not receive a forged response. The chain to follow is:

- Compute the hash of the RRSET
- Use the ZSK to decrypt the signed hash in the response and verify they match
- Compute the hash of the DNSKEY RRSET (note this query was not shown)
- Use the KSK to decrypt the signed hash of the DNSKEYs, which will validate the ZSK
- Retrieve the DS from the parent zone and verify it matches the hash of the KSK
- Repeat the process for the DS record on parent.

This process will continue all the way up to the DNS root where the client will eventually find a key that is pretrusted. Most resolvers will include the root key already compiled in or it can be retrieved by running "dig. DNSKEY." If implementing DNSSEC on a closed network, an administrator would generate their own root key and distribute it to clients. Some enterprise networks follow a similar pattern of distributing "trust anchors" for their own domains, or other trusted domains, to their resolvers. This would allow clients to validate queries as soon as they trace back to a trust anchor instead of iterating all the way back to the DNS root. Validating the DS record on the parent zone follows the same process as above, where the client queries for an RRSIG for the DS record, then the key material, then if necessary the DS record for that zone's parent.

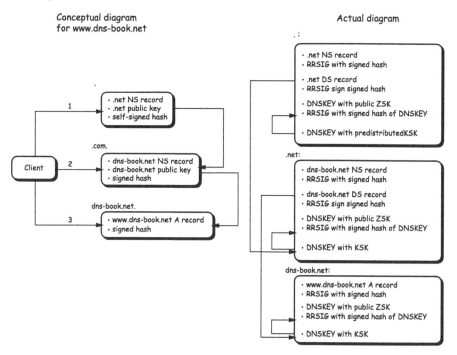

Let us now walk through a full DNSSEC verification chain. Dig provides helpful output that describes the process it is following.

```
$ dig @8.8.8.8 www.ripe.net + sigchase + trusted-key = ./root.keys
;; RRset to chase:
www.ripe.net.    2515  IN  A  193.0.6.139
;; RRSIG of the RRset to chase:
www.ripe.net.    2515  IN  RRSIG  A 5 3 21600 20160101160313 201512021
50313 35970 ripe.net. AP7BeT7 ShUou8M + 15t5FALv2ptFQ4Qa5pcrZzUB5sKxNs
PkLSBR8RgnJ waUd + AtahawE7g + Dd7wEJBcpkzT690qxI2JkWROZV6jRLsThwPBGZz
AV 9jwGOfPOouaO/jq5XXyMYGTazs3Ggqm7OKzJl/cieYtwIhmaexo9Anvj Fdg =

Launch a query to find a RRset of type DNSKEY for zone: ripe.net.

;; DNSKEYset that signs the RRset to chase:
ripe.net.    2390  IN  DNSKEY  256 3 5 AwEAAYZR8W3SReJDELYz1FRNjOesSPf/
4M3z + Wo6YOuyVY7FKodDeZ81    e1zuGkUMKRms67mGSXRoL3OrFJTwwAvW +/+ aIes
```

CI4SP + 5 + MFOduBZIa 9tCt1Ja8 + OVWHx4/UVS4yda2KkKNj2FSZDDRqY7MzEOLP34
+ rqPy06wV YHtlYO/f
ripe.net.   2390 IN DNSKEY 256 3 5 AwEAAXaEO7mYgEFCXkWAMWCssHA4m
pOSIdeqOImM4Hxj7/kSzu2 + K5dn   X72VVtn9kBFoSaSOaSoc9UHxpzNT7eQPlhCyO/
91V8bw6/wu5k/13ee0   dF32YnyAZhMoraHWpv2pjmt/CF6KjmtJyeprh + VVv8y127
zHThTdwh0t hDcwPGz3
ripe.net.   2390 IN DNSKEY 257 3 5 AwEAAalnxwsXNVENfxBjxSy5LJbTVKa
NZmlNoSdexcCEEEg3BnZrNYVb PpWT/OdW7cPHNpvjOMp9VBaMNWoM + cwdB4LEfkzfhIDb
lTyBS/KqxsOE OTzlnL + 7MgODsVFesrf3cG + Ys7XtJScqL7T9jnUfHUgLSS7VbNRLdODx
4Oelfn9WgaRZkq7Oj6wUeadwDn6zaBPw4Vc3yH6VQpj54cqBBGSULOiR X35a 8VoKBGU4C
nhSUjgOuo4iA8xCUizU/1DkloNyEYIdj8UZFdNT2IBO WSaF9wRG6FkLBfMsP6qHg7qn3lO
tzCeKLfzNrQ/gFOzZ1MuNxfmuF7QK 65SjPoDRdDE =

;; RRSIG of the DNSKEYset that signs the RRset to chase:
ripe.net.   2390 IN RRSIG DNSKEY 5 2 3600 20160101220244 201512022
10244 65306 ripe.net. NbVqWH6F5kBQp5fuzEqO/meoIrSrQMM8xe7fKGk1l5NOXuM
sEe++y5Q9 OYcSblmaIuNhjO8b5T59elGpdEScPF6dDV + 6ZMyONjPgADue2xm89cnV
pYqyvwxW4AIai4GbGZMsjvQEhea766oZFCqEMCPwzqaJ9pI1zoYNYzHX cowUbf9Kqpm
fopx29IRXZhSxC/ub20DIRr2gu3qfxmbuuiZw2tabCsop pV2uPJyUm5267FJFQtw3n
HuBMr9oOJpmLc6ushrtk2VvsRIiLUQVC8J8 + aNdj1CCqQ5ZvOAII5eKYZ5g9brWy59
Sbakz3NqXWFixjAb6 + 16N/CxC coMAKQ ==

Launch a query to find a RRset of type DS for zone: ripe.net.

;; DSset of the DNSKEYset
ripe.net.   21599 IN DS 65306 5 2 DCAB3FF242EA54F6583DCE08D7762D020
B2F32C23E720A4CCEA977C4 CCA28EF6
ripe.net.   21599 IN DS 65306 5 1 F48B9AE1104DD42C39486C0B7406031B
FC7C9CC6

;; RRSIG of the DSset of the DNSKEYset
ripe.net.   21599 IN RRSIG DS 8 2 86400 20151206062323 201511290513
23 37703 net. CSv58uFqBP1tOdEmY6ptb + brAjs7 + XOTG + oJB8CesX9jThisTEDe
kYW + eOrnGpNMburx2B31cFzuk/77lyrPLONCMIaX9Eu1II8RFVELdblk8wBx VYv2iR
GpCMKsCQgX/GZLYcpgumkHzFkGOve30KmGAtcfCCDm3DZKf3// 9Hw =

;; WE HAVE MATERIAL, WE NOW DO VALIDATION
;; VERIFYING A RRset for www.ripe.net. with DNSKEY:35970: success
;; OK We found DNSKEY (or more) to validate the RRset
;; Now, we are going to validate this DNSKEY by the DS
;; OK a DS valids a DNSKEY in the RRset
;; Now verify that this DNSKEY validates the DNSKEY RRset
;; VERIFYING DNSKEY RRset for ripe.net. with DNSKEY:65306: success
;; OK this DNSKEY (validated by the DS) validates the RRset of the
DNSKEYs, thus the DNSKEY validates the RRset

;; Now, we want to validate the DS : recursive call

Launch a query to find a RRset of type DNSKEY for zone: net.

;; DNSKEYset that signs the RRset to chase:
net.   7028 IN DNSKEY 257 3 8 AQOYBnzqWXIEj6mlgXg4LWCOHP2n8e K8X
qgHlmJ/69iuIHsalTrHDG6T cOra/pyeGKwHOnKZhTmXSuUFGh9BCNiwVDuyyb6OBGy2
Nte9Kr8NwWg4   q+zhSoOf4D+gC9dEzgOyFdwTODKEvmNPtOK4jbQDS4Yimb+uPKu
F6yie   WWrPYYCrv8C9KC8JMze2uT6NuWBfsl2fDUoV4165qMww06D7n+p7Rbdw
WkAZOfA63mXVXBZF6kpDtsYD7SUB9jhhfLQE/r85bvg3FaSs5Wi2BaqN 06SzGWI1DHu
7axthIOeHwgOOzxlhTpoYCHOldoQz+S65zWYi/fRJiyLS Bb6JZOvn
net.   7028 IN DNSKEY 256 3 8 AQOakXaXBtSEU5Ir+ZTQb9SgDAfWOsTaqt
bHN2F+2m4BCeh49ciHTw4H   uYB/i1/3HEOxaaj+quEAmloGvjWXbHOcpU4176Wao
M+3POHO6nC5jYyN X89o7Jnwwcdo2yTidRmBjpcvEEoMGr85Utj72TF3myUyF6ha86G
9hLiJ gmLF9Q==

;; RRSIG of the DNSKEYset that signs the RRset to chase:
net.   7028 IN RRSIG DNSKEY 8 1 86400 20151212173857 2015112717335
7 35886 net. MAd6ZjSgQL6hPcjwxEtFM9T/n4m9vqKpkMdPGgUO/J/Dzufh4Atd/rK2
h7bi8UN31WPuG26RXi1jeuEc44dPPDNJrd+VvS5Re9r5w3109pJm+hlW WH4hF1jOf
9yn7NuV4Q+iPEuSSVML5AODkQHJr/RQraT6fItiKlennOAx Ji0+xqo/G35AeygLcu
BvxVpzjTpym3nkWUO+RCYTm1iNiL4jG2COUWke k35LEGtFtJynC74hR9P2j2WOfmH5
cOx514aeGLHUfOqUZxbBa5+nXrm9 DdcuQAgsEZLRivqW9NlLxIuuJ4HG67qdGxqxwg
conZwbFgO5YcsL7e6x mDgWkw==

Launch a query to find a RRset of type DS for zone: net.

;; DSset of the DNSKEYset
net.   7799 IN DS 35886 8 2 7862B27F5F516EBE19680444D4CE5E7629819
31842C465F00236401D 8BD973EE

;; RRSIG of the DSset of the DNSKEYset
net.   7799 IN RRSIG DS 8 1 86400 20151212170000 20151202160000 62530 .
FuH3UU1r7QHxcEVfG9CtOTt/8N1RO2Tp6a5jCxfhRkGgHXR4fymSwNlW +VBJl7ZqYqNO
HiUY+TQpaBU+GsI7RWnAwTx3dMonmmKH96MkBUSU1oXF 1Fixju0T fxo78faCwqmBA7
VCQPn4S/ZImfkr+Z55homVK90eqECGFSf8 mHE=

;; WE HAVE MATERIAL, WE NOW DO VALIDATION
;; VERIFYING DS RRset for ripe.net. with DNSKEY:37703: success
;; OK We found DNSKEY (or more) to validate the RRset
;; Now, we are going to validate this DNSKEY by the DS
;; OK a DS valids a DNSKEY in the RRset
;; Now verify that this DNSKEY validates the DNSKEY RRset
;; VERIFYING DNSKEY RRset for net. with DNSKEY:35886: success
;; OK this DNSKEY (validated by the DS) validates the RRset of the
DNSKEYs, thus the DNSKEY validates the RRset

```
;; Now, we want to validate the DS : recursive call

Launch a query to find a RRset of type DNSKEY for zone: .

;; DNSKEYset that signs the RRset to chase:
.      3076  IN  DNSKEY  256 3 8 AwEAAbgVvZmZibtBpha3AIykUOOY4gcCXTcs
kYJUxGsdmV/awfmKcHlS rjNMioSgy4sByj + HpcbsyrZVGPp + JBXzYwwuEF/6w1k7v
KYTK6vMSqgV cgooNkfb5MaRF2y7MEpPxfStnfwu8knE24ExBOhYE1URxJ9CqB3zMS1/
vicXYXX1
.      3076  IN  DNSKEY  257 3 8 AwEAAagAIK1VZrpC6Ia7gEzahOR + 9W29euxh
JhVVLOyQbSEWOO8gcCjF  FVQUTf6v58fLjwBdOYIOEzrAcQqBGCzh/RStIoO8gONfnf
L2MTJRkxoX  bfDaUeVPQuYEhg37NZWAJQ9VnMVDxP/VHL496M/QZxkjf5/Efucp2gaD
X6RS6CXpoY68LsvPVjROZSwzz1apAzvN9d1zEheX7ICJBBtuA6G3LQpz W5hOA2hzCTM
jJPJ8LbqF6dsV6DoBQzgul0sGIcGOY17OyQdXfZ57relS Qageu + ipAdTTJ25AsRTAo
ub8ONGcLmqrAmRLKBP1dfwhYB4N7knNnulq QxA + Uk1ihzO =

;; RRSIG of the DNSKEYset that signs the RRset to chase:
.      3076  IN  RRSIG  DNSKEY 8 0 172800 20151214235959 20151130000000
19036 . E6g bSVVI9acmgAMsdx8 + OtRCkrdxd1n2r8KfGYM9ncrCi4MOGAOsh/xb QqL
fThUmRr77Wq4Xm5uvAlwAaMoKD1/1kEQOmmHDfzjmtEhc + jkd4/pW  eNF32tX4nq/r
WEer4MEqpkdbKGTt/MzzYlvAXp2OKHgFKBXj3dvQPgY9 hftu8de9XwMXCgXzFitA7wE
GdBCPRYuiiQJE8XedyVBKQagDzNqbsR3A hVJnWpQr5qhoo0JyiY71Wk6MTk68u0 + 21
d + dZaMYYX1X1906ZKTyoHfC V1EOM5CDt7a92 + /41px9Iz2gNPy6PPVSPoJUkLo94z
YTYcipNTOVaa3Y ibBxSQ ==

Launch a query to find a RRset of type DS for zone: .

;; NO ANSWERS: no more
;; WARNING There is no DS for the zone: .

;; WE HAVE MATERIAL, WE NOW DO VALIDATION
;; VERIFYING DS RRset for net. with DNSKEY:62530: success
;; OK We found DNSKEY (or more) to validate the RRset
;; Ok, find a Trusted Key in the DNSKEY RRset: 62530
;; Ok, find a Trusted Key in the DNSKEY RRset: 19036
;; VERIFYING DNSKEY RRset for . with DNSKEY:19036: success

;; Ok this DNSKEY is a Trusted Key, DNSSEC validation is ok: SUCCESS
```

NXDOMAIN RESPONSES

One important complication with DNSSEC is how to handle negative responses, indicating that a domain does not exist. Recall that DNS handles this by setting the response code to NXDOMAIN and not including answer records. Since

DNSSEC does not sign the header of DNS responses, it has nothing to authenticate without changing the structure of responses. One alternative approach would be to include explicit "domain does not exist" records in the answer section. But the problem with this approach is DNSSEC wants to enable admins to sign records off-line, so the server would somehow need to presign every domain that does not exist. Another option would be to have a single, signed NXRECORD response that the server would return for any nonexistent domain. The problem there is an attacker could store that response and then return it for valid domains, creating a DoS. The approach DNSSEC adopts is to use a NextSecure (NSEC) response, which returns the preceding and next sequential domain surrounding the queried domain. These records can be signed off-line by sorting every hostname in the zone and creating an NSEC record for each sequential pair. If a client gets an NSEC response, it knows the queried domain does not exist. The NSEC record is signed by an RRSIG like other responses.

Clever readers may notice a timing flaw with this approach. Say a domain has three subdomains: a, c, and d. It will create three NSEC records: a - > c, c - > d, and d - > a. Note that with this set of records an attacker cannot replay NSEC responses to falsely assert a valid subdomain does not exist. For example, if a client queries for a, the attacker cannot replay a record containing "a", and they cannot use the c - > d record because the client will know that record does not lexicographically cover "a". But say the domain adds the subdomain "b". Now an attacker can replay the signed a - > c record, and falsely assert b does not exist. As described in RFC 4470, this is a known issue with the protocol. The two ways to combat it are to change keys often so older records cannot be replayed after a small amount of time or to somehow limit the lexicographic space covered by each NSEC record (which will be described later).

Here's an example of an NSEC record:

```
$ dig @8.8.8.8 asdf.ripe.net +dnssec

; << >> DiG 9.8.3-P1 << >> @8.8.8.8 asdf.ripe.net +dnssec
; (1 server found)
;; global options: +cmd
;; Got answer:
;; ->>HEADER<<- opcode: QUERY, status: NXDOMAIN, id: 51647
;; flags: qr rd ra ad; QUERY: 1, ANSWER: 0, AUTHORITY: 6, ADDITIONAL: 1

;; OPT PSEUDOSECTION:
; EDNS: version: 0, flags: do; udp: 512
;; QUESTION SECTION:
;asdf.ripe.net.      IN   A

;; AUTHORITY SECTION:
ripe.net.    299  IN  SOA  pri.authdns.ripe.net. dns.ripe.net. 1449054
483 3600 600 864000 300
```

```
ripe.net.    299  IN  RRSIG  SOA 5 2 3600 20160101220244 20151202210244
35970   ripe.net.    CqALQMFG6RUszLf+U7fKHEMJEtIPrXspcMp7/zgBHxBwx1
+NO35Wk+jK  NMjWs2nuXj93NLfd1nvpmsqxLFv7yTI7MBOSnOlU/pTYOIvglxgzcv
Sr W4IHguKfzKYTVXJAXVjeThk7pAeX3vSqGUBE6jPQc66AGIeBsJbf7Sm4 Nwg=
ripe.net.    299  IN  NSEC  256cns.ripe.net. A NS SOA MX AAAA RRSIG NSEC
DNSKEY
ripe.net.    299  IN  RRSIG  NSEC 5 2 300 20160101220244 20151202210244
35970 ripe.net. P+t7qsYnkEuKB5PtDurI92KmNEBVKUTPeAKq4xNb6S/IjSpwSGFC
3V1D PUZfvzPzqS1ODfxBH2TIKQzPh2RBHkaOq7LVRsboVx6BygfBO6wTAeHi UYlSCk
bDtLH2SosJufFUocBYhxr1JtMcOFhJxoZ0iS8cGwC6806Ssful cK8=
ns1.nl-ams.as112.ripe.net. 299  IN  NSEC  aso.ripe.net. A AAAA RRSIG NSEC
ns1.nl-ams.as112.ripe.net. 299  IN  RRSIG  NSEC 5 5 300 20160101220244
20151202210244 35970 ripe.net.  V3u1qNsV6yHSzQfPIqOufCan3cZmlGH618Fi
ZOFcgB4FuWP5K5U1xEV1
gHIpD5rdwOh2uD8jDImI1qopidyjskUyvEPX3ZvuBetamAcaWcfp2GvT sY3cC4Be8WV
21vaSu4tbjTCyKaSzhMPu/xcBA3DcW3OlQVIZkGrXd3wV Ht8=
```

Interestingly this approach itself creates another problem—the server tells the client two valid hostnames that the client did not necessarily know about, which can be considered an information leak. Subdomains might contain information like the purpose of the server (eg, webserver-backup.example.com), the operating system, or even employee names or roles. A clever adversary could walk the entire directory to find that information. Best practices are to consider DNS names as information that could be made public and not to use any information that could be helpful to an attacker. Another mitigation is splitting DNS zones as discussed earlier in the book.

Other mitigations have been proposed: RFC 5155 introduces NSEC3 records that return a hash of the next domain instead of the domain itself. The examples of setting up DNSSEC on Linux below use NSEC3 records, and it is becoming a common practice on the Internet. As processing power has increased, online signing of responses has also become feasible which allows the server to make up a new, nonexistent domain and sign that response as opposed to returning an existing domain. This is generally called a "white lie" response because the server will return nonexistent domains but it does so in a way that conforms to the DNS specification. RFC 4470 describes one such approach, called "minimally covering NSEC records." There is also a proposal for NSEC5 which will add stronger cryptography to the hashed responses.

IMPLEMENTING DNSSEC ON LINUX

Enabling DNSSEC on a domain involves two steps: signing the DNS records and submitting a hash to the parent zone (often the registrar) to include in the delegation record. As described above, signing the records actually involves many different substeps, such as generating separate KSK and ZSK values, signing each

RRSet, and creating NSEC records. Fortunately there are standard tools to automate most of that process.

The zonesigner command will do the work of generating keys, signing the existing records, and adding them to your config file. It comes with the dnssec-tools package. This command will generate keys and sign all records in an existing zone file:

```
zonesigner -genkeys -usensec3 -zone example.org pri.example.org
```

To enable BIND to handle DNSSEC queries, the next step is to add "dnssec-enable yes" and "dnssec-validation yes" to the options section in named.conf. The final step is to point the relevant domain's file option at the new signed zone file. Once this is done and BIND has been restarted, it will begin answering DNSSEC queries. These steps will need to be repeated on any slave servers as well.

The last step is to add the DS record to the parent zone. Administrators who also run the parent zone can do this by adding the DS record to the parent's config. If the parent is administered by a registrar there is usually a web interface available to submit the record. The registrar generally wants a hash of the KSK as well as the key id and algorithm used.

One additional step one can take is to periodically resign the zone without changing any of the keys. This will generate new salts for NSEC3 hashes and makes it more difficult for adversaries to enumerate the zone by brute forcing the hashed values.

IMPLEMENTING DNSSEC ON WINDOWS

Configuring a zone on Windows can be done either through the command line or the GUI, but these examples will show the command line.

To enable DNSSEC on a windows server:

```
DnsCmd.exe <Servername> /Config /enablednssec 1
```

Windows uses the term "trust anchors" to refer to the predistributed root keys. For DNS servers on the public Internet this will be the root key described above. Either the DNSKEY or DS records for the root can be used, since the DS is just the hash of the KSK. These are usually stored in active directory (AD), but for non-AD servers these can be stored in a text file.

For administrators who run the parent zone, DS records can be added to the parent with this command:

```
C:\>   Import-DnsServerResourceRecordDS   -ZoneName   example.com
 -DSSetFile "c:\windows\system32\dns\example.com"
```

OPERATING A DNSSEC ZONE

With the tools described above, setting up DNSSEC on an existing zone is relatively automated. Most of the complexity in operating a zone in practice comes from managing the cryptographic keys. As described in RFC 6781 the main things to think about are how to store the private keys, how to handle key rollovers, and how long to keep the keys active.

The best way to protect DNSSEC private keys is to generate them on a standalone computer segregated from any network access and use them only on that computer. More paranoid users could even use a Hardware Security Module which will keep the keys on separate, specialized storage media. Signing the zone file will have to be done on that same computer, so the best practice is to perform all edits on that computer and only copy the signed zone file off when needed. This is a very secure setup but means it is more cumbersome to make changes and will not allow dynamic updates to the zone. Some administrators choose to keep the private key from the ZSK on the name server, which decreases the security posture but makes management easier. Standard precautions should be taken to protect the key file as much as possible, like having it only be readable by the name server user, using strong passwords, and periodically auditing access to the server.

In theory, keys only need to be changed if they become compromised. But in practice it is a good habit to change keys routinely so brute force cracking cannot be accomplished with reasonable resources. Also performing regular key rotations means the process is better understood and less prone to error if an emergency key change is needed. As described below, periodic rollover is enforced in the DNSSEC protocol by including an expiration time in every key. The main complexity in changing a key is that resolvers may have cached the old keys or old RRSIGs, so both the old and new keys will need to be supported for some period of time. There are actually two recommended procedures for changing the keys, called prepublishing and double signature. More details on both are in RFC 6781. The steps involved in prepublishing ZSKs are:

- Start with an existing signed zone
- Generate and add a new "future" zone key and resign the config with the old key. This is called "prepublishing" the new key, since nothing will be signed with that key
- After some time remove the old key, generate a new "future" key, and resign the config with the prepublished key.

Note that following these steps means there will always be two ZSKs in the zone: the currently active one and the next key that will be used in the future.

Rotating a key signing key generally follows the double-signature method. The basic steps are:

- Generate a new KSK and add it to the DNSKEY section
- Sign the modified key set with both the old KSK and the new KSK (hence the double-signature name)

- Publish the new KSK to the parent zone
- After some amount of time remove the old KSK and resign the DNSKEY section with just the new key.

Note the example DNSKEY output shown earlier included two KSKs because it was using the double-signature method.

MANAGING KEY VALIDITY TIMES

Regular DNS already has TTL fields in each record, but DNSSEC adds a signature validity period. This is set to an absolute time instead of a number of seconds, so it is important to keep clocks synchronized between DNS servers. Expiration times are often set on the order of weeks, sometimes one week or sometimes one month. A short validity period means keys will need to be rotated more frequently, but a longer period gives an attacker more time to steal or crack the keys. Since DNSSEC uses shorter public keys than TLS, brute force attacks are actually possible in time spans of months or years. One calculation from 2014 estimated keys could be cracked in 30 days using AWS hardware for about $1 million.[5] Note RFC 6781, written in 2012, says that no 1024-bit RSA key has ever been cracked in any amount of time. So while attacks are getting better, and the protocol is designed to mitigate future threats, 1024-bit keys should be safe over a period of months for the foreseeable future.

Since DNS results are cached by intermediate servers, administrators plan for a rollover period when choosing expiration times. For example, if rotating keys every 30 days, a standard practice is to set the expiration time to 37 days so there is a 7-day period when both keys are active. As described above, this is how long someone will need to wait before removing the old keys from the zone.

DNSSEC LOOK-ASIDE VALIDATION

The designers of DNSSEC faced the challenge of relying on a chain of trust that can touch many different domains in the DNS hierarchy, but different organizations may implement DNSSEC at different times. For example, as of 2016 the .ae top level domain (TLD) did not support DNSSEC, so even if subdomains implemented DNSSEC the chain of trust could not be established all the way to the root and thus DNSSEC would be ineffective. To mitigate this problem there is something called DNSSEC Look-aside Validation. This is a separate service to which administrators can submit hashes of their keys, and some clients will know to query this service if they are verifying a key through a parent zone that does not support DNSSEC. However since the vast majority of TLDs do support DNSSEC, this service is not necessary in most cases.

OTHER USES OF DNSSEC

With most of the core DNS infrastructure on the Internet now supporting DNSSEC, it presents an interesting opportunity. The infrastructure provides a way for clients to securely find authoritative servers for any part of the DNS namespace. It has many layers of caching that have been developed over more than two decades, and it is built for short-term expiration of data. So it is no surprise that people have proposed distributing TLS certificates via DNSSEC, for example. This process, originally proposed in RFC 6698, is called DNS-based Authentication of Named Entities (DANE). If widely implemented it could create competition for TLS CAs. DANE could also be used to distribute cryptographic keys for email, instant messengers, or other protocols.

DNSSEC AND DDoS AMPLIFICATION

One final debate within the DNS community is whether DNSSEC will make DDoS attacks more severe. A common DDoS tactic is to send millions of requests with spoofed source IPs to large DNS servers. The servers will dutifully respond to the spoofed IP, which is the intended victim of the attack. If an attacker can send 50 bytes in the request and get the server to respond with 500 bytes to the victim, they have "amplified" their attack by a factor of 10.

On the surface it appears DNSSEC packets can be used in these attacks, since they will contain large keys. In fact, reports of this already happening in the wild came out in February 2016. The DDoS volume in this incident peaked at 123 Gbps, and most of the traffic content was made up of DNSSEC keys.[6] The counterargument is that this is not unique to DNSSEC. On closer examination of the 2016 attack, the adversaries were sending spoofed requests for ANY, so it was not specifically targeting DNSSEC. Paul Vixie argues the blame lies elsewhere entirely: "what slows down a firewall isn't the total number of bits per second (which can be increased by using larger messages, and EDNS0 and DNSSEC will do), but rather the total number of packets per second."[7] It is difficult to give definitive guidance, other than to say that administrators should closely monitor their network for evidence of a DDoS attack.

DNSSEC CRITICISMS

Criticisms of DNSSEC usually follow two themes: it is complicated and until it is enabled everywhere it provides incomplete security. Performing a query with full validation will require three queries for each component of the hostname (the query, the DNSKEY, and the DS). For relatively simple domains like www.example.com this means nine queries instead of one. This could mean queries will take an order of magnitude longer when using DNSSEC. Also if DNS traffic suddenly increased by nine times across the world it would certainly strain the existing infrastructure. But much of this is mitigated by the caching already built into the system. Resolvers will quickly build up a list of keys for popular domains so queries for new hostnames on those domains can be authenticated without any additional queries. Performing the cryptographic algorithms will also put more CPU load on DNS servers and resolvers, but it is generally minimal. For comparison, TLS requires more complicated operations, but hardware and software improvements over the last 10 years mean it can be run with a performance impact of less than 10%.[8]

A related problem is the manual effort still required to run a DNSSEC zone with the highest standards of security. For example, keeping key material on off-line servers usually means an administrator must hand-carry a signed file from one network to another every few weeks. Complexity like this has even caused problems with the Internet backbone. In March 2016, DNSSEC for large portions of the ARIN address space went offline due to a faulty script.[9] As DNSSEC gains more widespread adoption the tools and processes will need to be streamlined so managing a secure zone is no more cumbersome than handling TLS certificates.

It is true that a query cannot be validated unless the entire chain from the hostname to the DNS root has implemented DNSSEC. It was first enabled at the DNS root in 2010, and as of 2016 most TLDs are using DNSSEC, including .com, .net, and .org. So almost all domains could enable DNSSEC and establish a trust chain that would work on the vast majority of caching resolvers. Also many large DNS providers such as Google Public DNS and Cloudflare are enabling DNSSEC by default. So most of the infrastructure is in place already.

Another variant of the criticism is that actual end users will not be protected by DNSSEC. For example, many users in corporate environments do not perform DNS queries on their own computers, but rather connect to a web proxy or an email server where the outbound queries are actually made. In other network configurations the enterprise DNS server may validate queries with DNSSEC but not securely communicate that fact when returning results to the client. In both scenarios, users could be in the position where DNSSEC validates the query between the destination and the corporate server, but data is then transmitted unauthenticated over the last hop to the client. A cryptographer would argue the entire query is therefore insecure, since an attacker inside the network could spoof responses to the client. However the risk of requests being poisoned over the public Internet is significantly higher than the risk of an attacker spoofing packets within a corporate network, so in practice these configurations would still add significant protection.

One area that needs more development is integrating DNSSEC validation into all DNS resolvers. For example, most web browsers do not yet have support built-in. Some libraries are adding new functions for DNSSEC-aware resolution, such as the val_gethostbyname function on Linux. One major complexity to consider is that DNSSEC adds a new error case to queries—the query might get an answer that fails validation. If a web browser encounters such an error, how should it display that back to the user? This could be considered the same as not getting any answer, but there may be cases where a user still wants to go to an unverified page. The most likely approach is that browsers will handle invalid DNSSEC signatures the same way they handle invalid TLS certificates. The browser could display a warning along with details of why the signature is invalid and allow the user to proceed anyway. But this functionality has yet to be built into most browsers, and most users will need to learn what the error messages mean.

CONCLUSIONS

DNSSEC is fraught with complexity and additional overhead, but its potential to authenticate all DNS traffic is a compelling vision. At this point understanding the details of record types and key rotation is important to properly set up and maintain a DNSSEC zone. As the toolset becomes more developed and key management becomes more automated, it will likely become a standard part of an administrator's zone. Creating DS records at a registrar could eventually become as routine a practice for a system administrator as downloading certificate files.

NOTES

1. https://securelist.com/blog/incidents/31628/massive-dns-poisoning-attacks-in-brazil-31/
2. http://blogs.wsj.com/digits/2014/01/21/chinas-sina-baidu-and-other-big-websites-are-hit-with-disruptions/
3. https://www.ietf.org/rfc/rfc2065.txt
4. https://wiki.mozilla.org/CA:IncludedCAs
5. http://stoneyforest.net/ ~ chris/blog/freebsd/dns/dnssec-rollover.html
6. https://www.stateoftheinternet.com/downloads/pdfs/2016-state-of-the-internet-threat-advisory-dnssec-ddos-amplification-attacks.pdf
7. http://serverfault.com/questions/708076/what-kinds-of-security-vulnerabilities-does-providing-dnssec-expose/747213#747213
8. http://www.cs.rice.edu/ ~ dwallach/pub/tls-tocs.pdf
9. http://lists.arin.net/pipermail/arin-ppml/2016-March/030726.html

Anycast and other DNS protocols

11

INFORMATION IN THIS CHAPTER:

- Anycast Motivation
- Anycast Description
- Implementing Anycast
- Anycast and DDoS
- Multicast DNS
- Tor Hidden Services

INTRODUCTION

This chapter will describe some real-world examples of complex or exotic DNS configurations. First it will look at anycast, which powers much of the DNS backbone. Large-scale networks are increasingly using anycast to distribute infrastructure around the world. Then it will look at multicast DNS (mDNS) and DNS Service Discovery (DNS-SD), which are popular on mobile devices. Finally it will look at alternative DNS protocols like Tor Hidden Services and BitTorrent's distributed hash tables (DHTs).

ANYCAST MOTIVATION

To understand the importance of anycast, one can start with some statistics about the DNS backbone. Recall that the "root" of DNS is the set of servers that will point to authoritative servers for .com, .net, and any other Top Level Domain (TLD).

Due to the maximum size of a DNS packet, the number of root servers is limited to 13. This calculation leaves room for headers and assumes the smallest possible owner names.[1] The root servers are labeled a.root-servers.net through m.root-servers.net. Every time a client resolves a domain, assuming nothing has been cached, the first query will always be to retrieve a list of the root servers (technically this is a query for "."), followed by a query to one of those root servers to resolve the TLD.

DNS Security. DOI: http://dx.doi.org/10.1016/B978-0-12-803306-7.00011-5

```
$ dig @8.8.8.8 . NS
; << >> DiG 9.8.3-P1 << >> @8.8.8.8 . NS
; (1 server found)
;; global options: +cmd
;; Got answer:
;; ->>HEADER<<- opcode: QUERY, status: NOERROR, id: 31592
;; flags: qr rd ra; QUERY: 1, ANSWER: 13, AUTHORITY: 0, ADDITIONAL: 0

;; QUESTION SECTION:
;.          IN  NS

;; ANSWER SECTION:
.      10404  IN  NS  i.root-servers.net.
.      10404  IN  NS  l.root-servers.net.
.      10404  IN  NS  f.root-servers.net.
.      10404  IN  NS  g.root-servers.net.
.      10404  IN  NS  d.root-servers.net.
.      10404  IN  NS  j.root-servers.net.
.      10404  IN  NS  a.root-servers.net.
.      10404  IN  NS  k.root-servers.net.
.      10404  IN  NS  m.root-servers.net.
.      10404  IN  NS  c.root-servers.net.
.      10404  IN  NS  e.root-servers.net.
.      10404  IN  NS  b.root-servers.net.
.      10404  IN  NS  h.root-servers.net.
```

Sometimes this query will include an "additional answers" section with A records that specify the IP for each server. This is optionally displayed by dig and may also depend on whether the recursive server forwards that information.

Estimates for the total load on root DNS servers range from hundreds of thousands of queries per second to millions per second and depend on the time of day and whether the infrastructure is under attack. In early 2016, the k-root server was handling between 40,000 and 60,000 queries per second.[2] The load tended to peak around midday in the UTC time zone and hit a trough around midnight. On the same day, l-root experienced between 30,000 and 45,000 queries per second.[3] Since the root servers are queried in a round-robin fashion, it is a reasonable approximation to multiply the load on one server by 13 and conclude that total root traffic is between 400,000 and 800,000 queries per second. In an extreme case, an attack against the root servers in November 2015 generated an estimated 5 million queries per second which was absorbed by the infrastructure.[4] Cisco estimates that Internet traffic grew by a factor of 5 between 2010 and 2015[5] and total traffic at the Amsterdam Internet Exchange, one of the major peering points, grew at a similar rate.[6] The number of DNS queries is not perfectly correlated with total Internet traffic since streaming video now dominates bandwidth, but it does give a rough approximation for future network growth. Based on this, it is reasonable to say the root DNS infrastructure will need to handle average loads of millions of queries per second, with a peak load several times that number.

How can an infrastructure handle this load and remain highly available? In designing the system for the root servers one would face at least two bottlenecks: network bandwidth and processor capacity. High end routers are generally designed to process packets at "line speed," so a gigabit router handling nothing but 512-byte UDP DNS packets should be able to transfer around 250,000 packets per second. Routers may encounter other limitations like security filters or logging, but those either would not apply to a publicly available service like DNS or could be tuned away by experienced administrators. A bigger concern would be handling larger numbers of queries over TCP because those require more packets, and routers often have some overhead for each new connection. Also as DNSSEC becomes more widespread, it will add two or three times as many queries to perform validation. One could handle this by constantly running larger routers, and in fact the B root server takes this approach.[7] Of course, upstream network capacity will have to be similarly provisioned to avoid creating bottlenecks.

The other constraint is processing capacity on the server. The root server needs to receive the DNS request, pass it through the IP stack, retrieve an answer from memory, create the response, and transmit a packet back out. A general rule of thumb is a server can handle tens of thousands of UDP packets per second without much tuning. Cloudflare recently reported on the limitations encountered when trying to scale this number as high as possible. A simple first approach is to write a loop that sends essentially empty packets using sendmsg and recvmsg, which can be used as bulk versions of the send and recv syscalls. This will send between 200,000 and 350,000 packets per second. To go beyond this limit, one must understand more about the specific network hardware and CPU being used. For example, most NIC cards have multiple send and receive queues that can be processed by different CPU cores in parallel. But this is often load-balanced depending on the source IP, destination IP, source port, and destination port. So a large amount of traffic on a single socket will bottleneck on a single CPU core. As described in their report, by spreading the traffic across multiple RX queues, multithreading the sending and receiving application, and keeping the threads accessing the same physical RAM, it is possible to send 1 million packets per second.[8] This is not taking into account any processing to create the packets, just purely sending and receiving. A simple implementation of the root nodes would require a map of TLDs to SOA records, which would require at least two memory accesses for each response. Since local memory access is particularly important for maintaining packet throughput to the CPUs, any memory lookups will be in contention with the packet queues.

The final consideration is maintaining low latency on queries. A common threshold for operations to be considered fully interactive is 100 milliseconds. This supposedly originated in telephony systems, where people will begin to change their speaking patterns if the delay is longer than 100 ms.[9] For DNS infrastructure, the ideal latency is at least half or a third of that number because there will often be multiple recursive queries, and the query will likely be followed by more network requests like downloading a webpage. The root servers publish monitoring data, and on a day in early 2016 the median latency over a 10-minute period ranged from 9 to 165 ms, with the majority being below 50 ms.[10] For comparison, Netcraft periodically publishes a list of the "most reliable hosting companies" and in November 2015, the top 10 had DNS query latency of between 94 and 278 ms.[11]

The way the DNS root is able to achieve low latency despite such high load is by distributing the traffic over many servers located across different parts of the Internet. Since each DNS query can be processed independently, it is an easily parallelizable algorithm. But recall that each root server can only have a single IP address, since they must all fit in a single DNS packet. The way a single IP address can point to multiple servers in different parts of the Internet is a technique called anycast. This allows the L root server, for example, to operate more than 100 instances all using the same IP address.

ANYCAST

As described in RFC 4786, anycast is "the practice of making a particular Service Address available in multiple, discrete, autonomous locations, such that datagrams sent are routed to one of several available locations." A few terms are important to understand. Administrators need to differentiate between an IP address that is "anycasted" and specific instances of a server using that IP. They also cannot speak of a client connecting to an IP because that will mean different things depending on the client and network state. So the term "service address" is used to refer to the IP address that will be shared and the servers which share it are called "anycast nodes" (technically a service address is a more general category than an IP address, and it can refer to any address in any routing scheme, but in this context it generally refers to the IP being shared). The anycast nodes can be described as "internally connected" because an administrator should have some way of accessing each node directly, often via a separate NIC with its own IP. Each anycast node will have a "catchment" which refers to the portion of the network that will be routed into that instance. Finally anycast nodes can be either "local" or "global" depending on whether their catchment is restricted to part of the network or open to everyone.

It is best to think of anycast from the perspective of the clients. It is a way of configuring routing so two clients connecting to the same IP address will be directed to two different destinations. So, for example, a client in Germany will connect to a server in Germany, a client in the United States will connect to a server in the United States, and clients anywhere else will connect to a server in Tokyo, even though all connect to the same IP address. Using the jargon, this would be two local-scope anycast nodes with catchments in Germany and the United States, and one global-score node in Tokyo.

IMPLEMENTING ANYCAST

It is important to note that anycast is not a protocol, it is just a set of routing rules. One could implement a trivial version of anycast on a home router by adding a rule to send all traffic from, for example, 192.168.1.100 destined to 8.8.8.8 to the loopback interface. This would mean that traffic destined for 8.8.8.8 would go to different locations depending on the source IP (either to the router's loopback interface or out to the actual IP address on the Internet). On the Internet this is implemented with multiple BGP routes to the same IP. For example, if one were to anycast the IP 1.1.1.1 with a node in Germany and the United States, both the German and American data centers would announce a 1-hop route to that IP. The core routers in Europe would prefer to route traffic to the German data center, and vice versa for the North American backbone. A simplified diagram is shown in Fig. 11.1.

The simplest way to run an anycast service on the Internet is to buy the infrastructure from someone who has already set it up. Most large hosting providers do not publish price lists publicly, but they will offer the service at negotiated

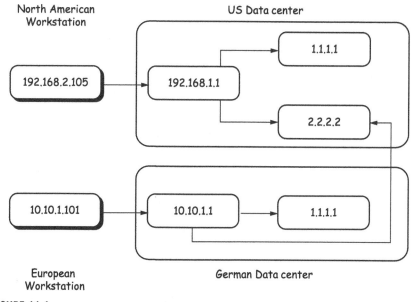

FIGURE 11.1

In this example, the IP 1.1.1.1 is anycast and 2.2.2.2 is unicast. Note clients from different locations will visit a different instance of 1.1.1.1 but always the same 2.2.2.2.

rates. Often times BGP routing tables will only store entries for each /24 netblock, so one would need to control at least a class C of IP address and anycast the entire range. Then routes to those IPs would need to be advertised or otherwise added to BGP tables around the Internet.[12] On a private network, one would simply need to configure the routing tables on edge routers to implement the same thing. For example, one could use the same IP for the root DNS server in an enterprise with locations in New York and Berlin, and add a route on the core router in each site to send that IP to a local destination. The usual practice when setting up anycast is to use two interfaces on the server: one for the shared IP address and one specific to that host. That way one can always connect to a specific server to perform maintenance.

Anycast is becoming a popular choice for distributing services, but it has many limitations both in theory and in practice. One is that it does not provide any load-balancing guarantees. From our example, the German server will probably be busier than the American server when it is morning in the United States and the middle of the night in Germany, and anycast makes no attempt to balance those. For a service like the DNS root where both users and infrastructure are widely distributed, this just means that not all nodes will have the same level of usage at the same time.

Anycast can also create routing headaches. For example, on an internal network a host may be equally close to two different anycast nodes. Using a routing algorithm where distance is the primary factor, such as OSPF, the client may constantly flip between destinations. For DNS this usually is not a problem since it primarily uses single UDP packets and is a stateless protocol. The public Internet uses BGP for internetwork routing which tends to choose stable routes. But for a stateful application like a web site, or even for any TCP session that involved multiple packets, there is always a chance that routes will flap mid-session. The closer topologically the instances are, and the longer the sessions run, the more likely these issues are to arise. Also in all cases the routing state needs to be closely coupled with the status of the application. For example, a route should not be advertised before the application is available, and it should be withdrawn whenever the service is off-line.

Another potential problem is the "cascading failures" scenario, where a large volume of traffic going to a single node will overwhelm it, then all that traffic will be routed to the next closest node and repeat the problem. One configuration to help avoid this is to use many local nodes and a few global nodes, which can be thought of as two tiers of service. If a local node fails the clients will be directed to a more powerful global node instead of failing over to another local node. The F root server uses this configuration, with two global nodes in San Francisco and Palo Alto, and more than 30 local nodes around the world. They tend to deploy the local nodes at Internet exchange points and mark the routes as nonexportable in BGP.[13]

For extremely high availability, a related best practice is to avoid doing software upgrades at the same time across all nodes, and in fact to vary the version and software packages themselves at different points in the network. This is to prevent bugs from taking down the entire system. Sometimes bugs can be extremely subtle and will only manifest based on the large volume of real-world Internet traffic. This practice can be seen at large scale across the DNS root, where different providers run BIND, NSD, and Knot DNS. Of course, running different types and versions of software is much more administratively complex; this can result in human errors that are worse than the cascading software failures. Therefore it should only be attempted on critical infrastructure with a large administrative operation.

One final hurdle an administrator may encounter is that many routers employ reverse path forwarding (RPF) checks to verify that they are not forwarding traffic with a spoofed source IP. They do this by checking if the interface on which they receive a packet matches the current routing table. Specifically, the interface on which a packet is received must match the interface on which it would be sent if going back to that source IP. There are scenarios where anycast will break this assumption, since the network view from the source IP may not be identical to the view from the intermediate router. For administrators facilitating anycast traffic, the topic of RPF within multihomed networks is discussed in RFC 3704. There is not much an end user can do if an upstream router blocks anycast traffic from part of their network, other than trying to negotiate with that provider. This is another argument for leasing infrastructure that has already been set up and tested.

Anycast creates several challenges for security analysis, mostly around detecting route hijacking. For example, without anycast, one may try connecting to a service from different regions to verify they all get routed to the same place. Or, one may try tracerouting from different locations to see if the connection includes unexpected hops. On an anycast network, one would expect to see wildly different routes depending on the origin or even the current state of the network. For example, if a user in Country A connects to an anycast service that has a node in Country A, but is actually routed to an end point in Country B, is that an example of route hijacking or is it simply a time when the network in Country A was experiencing congestion? These analyses can still be accomplished by comparing many different hosts that are topologically close together, but it is more difficult than the pre-anycast scenario. DNS helps with this problem by providing an optional NSID field that can return an id number for each server. Administrators can use this to determine which server they are being routed to. Dig will provide this info with the + nsid option.

ANYCAST AND DDoS

Networking aficionados will often cite anycast as a solution to Distributed Denial of Service (DDoS) attacks. But interestingly it will sometimes be for contradictory reasons. Some will say it is effective because it distributes the traffic over a wide range of servers and thus diminishes the load on any particular link. If an attacker needs 100 Mbps to cripple a single server, they will need 10 Gbps to cripple an anycast system that is evenly distributed over 100 different nodes. Others argue that anycast is effective because it concentrates DDoS traffic on a small number of nodes, thus preserving the rest of the network. For example, say a botnet consists of thousands of compromised hosts, the majority of which are located at universities in the United States. If it launched a DDoS attack against an anycast IP with instances in the United States and Europe, the traffic may overwhelm the US instance but will not disable the European one.

The truth is almost certainly that both aspects help in different ways. As Cricket Liu said in the quote that opened this chapter, "[u]nless attackers can source enough traffic from North America, Europe, and Asia simultaneously to swamp your infrastructure, they won't succeed."[14] Network attacks are often asymmetrical in nature, since the attackers choose the timing and method, and defenders have to prepare for any scenario. As is often repeated, an attacker can try a thousand vectors and only needs to find one that works. But this is one way to flip the scenario around—when targeting an anycast network, any link the adversaries do not properly saturate will allow the entire network to continue functioning. In 2013, a 75 Gbps DDoS attack against Spamhaus was stopped by a large anycast network run by Cloudflare. In a blog post, they mention that distributing the traffic to different data centers let them run filters more effectively.[15] This shows the other benefit of anycast—splitting that traffic across 23 different locations made it a more manageable 3.3 Gbps, where it is possible to run more sophisticated behavioral blacklists. This can form a virtuous cycle: with traffic distributed across more network links filtering becomes easier; with better filtering the network links stay up and running; and with more network links functional the traffic will continue to be widely distributed.

MULTICAST DNS

Can network services skip making DNS queries to a central server and find each other automatically? This is the motivation for mDNS which is currently active in many consumer devices. For example, if a smart phone connects to a home network, it can use mDNS to find a TV that is also on the network without the user needing to install a DNS server. A popular implementation of mDNS is Apple's Bonjour protocol which runs on most of their devices.

Conceptually, mDNS sends queries to every host on the local network, and the appropriate end point responds with an answer. For example, a device may be named "smart-tv.local" so any devices wishing to connect to the TV will make an mDNS query for that name, and the TV will respond with its assigned IP. The suffix ".local" is reserved for mDNS, and hostnames of that form are called "link-only" because they can only be used within the local network. RFC 6762 specifies that DNS clients must attempt to resolve such hostnames via mDNS. Similarly, reverse DNS queries for multicast IPs or other link-only IPs should be handled via mDNS.

Multicast was first specified in RFC 1112, published in 1989. It reserves the IP range 224.0.0.0 to 239.255.255.255 exclusively for multicast applications, although mDNS always uses the specific IP 224.0.0.251 (or the IPv6 equivalent FF02::FB). So requests sent to that IP will be routed to all clients on the network, and the device with the specified hostname will respond. With mDNS, port 5353 is used instead of port 53. Responses are generally routed back over multicast so all clients can see them, but in some cases they are sent via unicast to only the requestor. The choice in response behavior will depend on the implementation.

There are two exceptions to the conceptual model. In reality, it is an opt-in protocol and not a pure broadcast protocol. Devices communicate via the Internet Group Management Protocol (IGMP) to tell routers they want to join a multicast session, and the router will then forward packets to those devices. So if IGMP does not work for some reason, mDNS will also fail. Also nothing in the protocol guarantees that the named device will respond to a query or that it will respond with a correct answer. This leads to most of the security implications of mDNS.

As with unicast DNS, the main security threats against mDNS are spoofing and data leakage. In the simplest case, a malicious actor on the local network may respond to a query with a spoofed answer. Depending on the network configuration, this may be easier or harder than spoofing regular DNS responses. Often times unicast requests to a caching resolver will not be visible to other hosts on the local network, so in those cases spoofing multicast responses is significantly easier. In other scenarios, though, an attacker will not be close enough to the intended victim to send a forged response before the legitimate device responds.

By design, multicast queries are visible to everyone on the network. So if there is any sensitivity in the names and frequency of local DNS queries to other hosts on the network, mDNS simply should not be used. It is difficult to imagine scenarios where local queries could reveal protected information to other local hosts. After all, most users of a network are aware of the basic services available. But if there are file servers set up for special projects, or outside auditors coming into a company without everyone knowing, mDNS queries could represent an internal information leak.

More realistic scenarios are that devices may be silently broadcasting information that users do not realize. For example, many devices use a default hostname that contains the user's real name (eg, john-smith-phone.local). When these are connected to the proverbial coffee shop WiFi network, the names will be broadcast to everyone present. In some cases the mDNS packets will contain SRV records to show what services are running on those devices, revealing the same information that would be found with a port scan.[16] Periodic broadcasting of mDNS records is built into the Bonjour protocol, which runs on most Apple devices. This is to enable discovery of new services that join the network without each client needing to constantly requery.[17]

A common misconfiguration is for mDNS to be accessible from the outside Internet. This usually happens when unicast queries to port 5353 are allowed through an external firewall, and mDNS services respond without verifying that the origin is link-local. This breaks with the specification in RFC 6762, but some mDNS software will behave this way either through bugs or configuration errors. One researcher found more than 100,000 examples of mDNS services that were open to the world when scanning portions of the Internet.[18] This would leak hostnames present on the local network, as described above, to any outside actor. The researcher found MAC addresses, hardware model numbers, and even NAS configuration details with this technique. It could also be used as a vector for a DDoS reflection attack. If, for example, a multicast query for a common service would produce responses from multiple systems on each local network, a small query could be amplified many times over. A CERT advisory for this issue listed several major router manufacturers that would allow this behavior by default.[19] The best practice is to block port 5353, or any other mDNS traffic, at the firewall unless it is used for a specific purpose. Administrators should also monitor for any mDNS traffic leaving their network.

A final attack surface in mDNS is DoS against the services themselves. This is often a less critical area to protect than external DDoS protection, since attackers generally need access to the local network to attempt these attacks. As of 2016, the authors were not aware of any successful attacks. But it is often overlooked, and the fact that all clients usually cache mDNS responses means an attack can affect many different systems simultaneously. Also, because the protocol has only recently gained widespread adoption, some devices are vulnerable to parsing errors when handling the traffic. For example, a vulnerability in some Cisco routers reported in 2014 could allow remote attackers to cause a memory leak and DoS by sending malformed mDNS packets.[20]

DNS SERVICE DISCOVERY

DNS-SD is often used in combination with mDNS. In fact the RFCs that describe them were released in the same month and are sequentially numbered (RFCs 6762 and 6763, respectively). It can be thought of as an extension to mDNS, where instead of querying the local network for a specific host the client queries for a service like "http servers" or "music libraries." It is all accomplished with PTR, SRV, and in some cases TXT records. The services are named via the convention <instance>.<service>.<domain>. A client looking for music devices would query for "_music._tcp.local," and hosts with that service would respond with PTR records with their own service name. Note this response will be a service name (like jane's music._music._tcp.local) and not a hostname for the computer itself. Also note the "_music" and "_tcp" name spaces are conventions that have been established ahead of time. The client will then query for

SRV records for each PTR result in order to connect to the actual service. One of the most popular DNS-SD software packages is Bonjour, developed by Apple.

Technically DNS-SD can run on top of unicast DNS even though it is more commonly deployed with mDNS. Administrators should be aware of how DNS-SD is being used on their networks, and what host information is discoverable. Otherwise the security best practices are similar to mDNS. It should generally only be accessible on the local network, and administrators should monitor the traffic for abnormal usage. In enterprises environments where employees bring their own devices, users and administrators should watch out for inadvertent leaking of names and other potentially sensitive information. For example, if a network has scrubbed employee names from the device hostnames, they may still appear in the names of music libraries or photo albums. If these are advertised over DNS-SD, they will still be visible to anyone on the network.

Some make the argument that DNS-SD, and discoverable services in general, make systems more vulnerable because attackers know where to target their efforts. For example, attackers can look for any discoverable file share and try brute forcing common usernames and passwords. The counterargument is that those services would eventually be discovered, and they need to be properly secured instead of hidden. This is an example of the classic "security through obscurity" debate.

DNS-SD provides the option of including application-specific information in TXT records. While this has always been part of the DNS protocol, it appears to be a more common feature for discoverable services since they may need to provide connection or version information. The RFC provides several examples:

- "passreq"—password required for this service
- "PlugIns = "—the server supports plugins, but none are presently installed
- "PlugIns = JPEG,MPEG2,MPEG4"[21]

This is likely a different type of information than administrators are used to see in DNS traffic, so it again underscores the importance of monitoring mDNS and DNS-SD traffic.

As of 2016, a search of the CVE database did not reveal vulnerabilities utilizing DNS-SD, but it opens up an interesting attack surface. Developers often assume DNS will either correctly direct clients to their service or it will not, and those are the only cases that need testing. Including application-specific data in DNS packets greatly increases the possible permutations to consider. Malicious clients may not respect the data included in the responses, and attackers may spoof responses to unsuspecting users. This can lead to subtle attack vectors. SSL, for example, was vulnerable to downgrade attacks, where attackers could trick clients and servers into using a lower grade version of encryption by spoofing the initial setup packets. Similar vectors should be considered when designing DNS-SD services and networks that run them. RFC 6763 recommends using DNSSEC to protect against spoofing attacks, but as of 2016 most DNS-SD implementations, including Apple's Bonjour, did not include that support. A best practice for administrators in the meantime is to periodically review on-the-wire DNS packets with their expected contents to monitor for spoofing.

One final consideration with DNS-SD is whether Dynamic Updates are allowed and whether they are secured. This is similar to the considerations around regular DNS entries, but it expands the breadth of records that could be viewed or compromised if targeted by an attacker. The RFC recommends using TSIG if the service will allow updates.

TOR HIDDEN SERVICES

This chapter will close with a discussion of several alternatives to DNS and the trade-offs they face. The first example is Tor, which is a large-scale onion routing network that allows users to communicate over the Internet without revealing their source IP address. It has a feature known as a Hidden Service which allows a user to connect to an "onion address" and be routed (anonymously) to an IP address running that service. This happens without the server knowing the IP address of the client, and vice versa. In fact, no one in the routing chain will know that those two IP addresses are communicating, nor will they know the content of the session. An example use case often cited is a pro-democracy web site running in an oppressive country.

The resolution of onion addresses to network locations can be thought of as a different form of DNS, but it has two important limitations. The first is captured in what is called Zooko's triangle. It states that any addressing system can accomplish at most two out of three desirable features: human-meaningful names, decentralization, and security. DNS, and more specifically DNS with DNSSEC fully implemented, has meaningful names (eg, "cars.com" as opposed to a long list of digits) and security at the expense of a centralized root. Tor Hidden Services choose decentralization and security but not meaningful names. So onion addresses are 16-character pseudo-random strings instead of human-readable words. Interestingly Zooko's triangle is not a theoretical limitation, as systems have been designed that feature all three characteristics. It is more a description of common trade-offs in distributed addressing.[22]

Tor implements Hidden Service lookups with a DHT. Like a regular hash table, a DHT stores each entry in a bucket based on its key, but the buckets may be located on several different servers in the network. The key for a Tor Hidden Service is its onion address which is derived from its public key. Tor uses 80 bits to store the address in its DHT, meaning duplicates can occur if enough keys are generated (one would expect a duplicate roughly every 2^{40} or 1 trillion keys). This results in a hash collision within the DHT, and the information for the new address simply overwrites the old one. Interestingly this is a known issue that is explicitly mentioned by the designers of Tor. They describe the impact as: "all an attacker might be able to do is create two different public keys that match the same .onion name. He would not be able to impersonate already existing hidden services."[23] From a name resolution perspective, the ability to overwrite existing entries is certainly a weakness in the protocol.

BITTORRENT/P2P DNS

The idea of a truly decentralized version of DNS has been appealing to many different people over the last couple decades. But as of 2016 none has emerged as a serious contender. In 1995 a group called AlterNIC created an alternate DNS root to compete with Network Solutions that had been granted sole rights to register domains. This led to a controversy with some arguing it would allow for a more democratic Internet and others arguing it would become unnecessarily complicated for networks to interconnect.[24] Other alternate roots like eDNS and OpenRSC were also active in the 1990s. After The Pirate Bay web site was taken off-line in 2010, one of its founders started an initiative to build a DNS system not controlled by ICANN. There was speculation that it would be based on the BitTorrent DHT, which would impose similar challenges to those faced by Tor Hidden Services.[25]

While the technology may emerge to run a robust, decentralized system of name resolution, this book has hopefully illustrated that successfully running such a system at internet scale will require many other components. Caching and latency will need to be studied and optimized. Subtle interactions between different layers of the system may reveal unexpected security vulnerabilities, such as DNS rebinding. And perhaps most importantly, administrators will need to understand the strengths and weaknesses of the system to properly mitigate security risks.

CONCLUSIONS

While the core of the DNS protocol has stayed largely the same since it was first designed almost 30 years ago, it has spawned many complications and extensions. Anycast is a routing technique used to maintain low latency and high reliability across the heavily used DNS root. mDNS and DNS-SD are extensions to the protocol that allow devices to automatically configure themselves on local networks. Finally DNS-like services are being built into peer-to-peer services and anonymized networks like Tor. As digital services continue to grow, secure name resolution will remain a vital part of running any complex systems.

NOTES

1. https://lists.isc.org/pipermail/bind-users/2011-November/085653.html
2. http://k.root-servers.org/statistics/ROOT/weekly/
3. https://www.dns.icann.org/lroot/stats/

4. http://arstechnica.com/security/2015/12/attack-flooded-internet-root-servers-with-5-million-queries-a-second/
5. http://www.cisco.com/c/en/us/solutions/collateral/service-provider/visual-networking-index-vni/VNI_Hyperconnectivity_WP.html
6. https://en.wikipedia.org/wiki/Amsterdam_Internet_Exchange
7. http://www.netnod.se/dns/iroot/faq
8. https://blog.cloudflare.com/how-to-receive-a-million-packets/
9. http://www.stuartcheshire.org/papers/latencyquest.html
10. https://atlas.ripe.net/dnsmon/
11. http://news.netcraft.com/archives/2015/12/03/most-reliable-hosting-company-sites-in-november-2015.html
12. http://serverfault.com/a/648340
13. http://www.aftld.org/bk/html/meetings/docs/anycast%20root%20servers.pdf
14. http://www.infoworld.com/article/2612835/security/the-ultimate-guide-to-preventing-dns-based-ddos-attacks.html
15. https://blog.cloudflare.com/the-ddos-that-knocked-spamhaus-offline-and-ho/
16. https://www.trustwave.com/Resources/SpiderLabs-Blog/mDNS---Telling-the-world-about-you-%28and-your-device%29/
17. https://developer.apple.com/library/ios/documentation/Cocoa/Conceptual/NetServices/Articles/about.html
18. https://github.com/chadillac/mdns_recon
19. http://www.kb.cert.org/vuls/id/550620
20. http://tools.cisco.com/security/center/content/CiscoSecurityAdvisory/cisco-sa-20140924-mdns
21. https://tools.ietf.org/html/rfc6763
22. https://en.wikipedia.org/wiki/Zooko's_triangle
23. https://trac.torproject.org/projects/tor/wiki/doc/HiddenServiceNames
24. https://en.wikipedia.org/wiki/AlterNIC
25. http://arstechnica.com/tech-policy/2010/11/fed-up-with-icann-pirate-bay-cofounder-floats-p2p-dns-system/

Index

Printed in the United States
By Bookmasters